C000247320

SEE HOW
THEY RUN

SEE HOW THEY RUN

GEOFF HOON

UNICORN

First published by Unicorn
an imprint of the Unicorn Publishing Group LLP, 2021
5 Newburgh Street
London W1F 7RG

www.unicornpublishing.org

Every effort has been made to trace copyright holders and to obtain their
permission for the use of copyrighted material. The publisher apologises
for any errors or omissions and would be grateful to be notified of any
corrections that should be incorporated in future reprints or editions of
this book.

10 9 8 7 6 5 4 3 2 1

ISBN 978-1-913491-82-6

Cover design Unicorn Publishing Group
Typeset by Vivian@Bookscribe

All photographs from the author's collection unless stated otherwise.

Printed in Malta by Gutenberg Press Ltd

For Elaine, Chris, Julia and Nathalie

CONTENTS

PROLOGUE
Carry That Weight

As I listened on the radio in the ministerial car to the account of the second passenger aircraft flying into the South Tower of New York's World Trade Center, I knew in my own mind that, not only had the world suddenly and dramatically changed, but that before very long British forces would be involved in a determined attempt to deal with a wide range of threats to our peace and stability.

Most people were profoundly shocked, as they watched the endless replays on television, by the events of Tuesday, 11 September 2001. For most people these attacks came out of a clear blue sky and seemed like new and terrifying threats – but I knew that Al Qaeda terrorists had previously attacked the World Trade Center, and that they were based in Afghanistan. I also knew from long experience of the United States that no US administration would wait long before launching an all-out attack to deal with the perpetrators. It followed that Britain would want to stand by its closest ally by offering whatever support was needed.

All this was in my mind as we drove at speed back towards the Ministry of Defence. Even before that evening's meetings with the Chiefs of Staff and with the Prime Minister, I knew in my own mind that we would be preparing British forces to fight alongside those of the United States in the far off and hostile environment of Afghanistan.

I still have my original diary for Tuesday, 11 September 2001. It was planned to be a long day, given an early start to attend the first Defence and Systems Equipment International exhibition to be held at what was then the new ExCel exhibition centre in London's Docklands. Previously the defence exhibition had been a more modest affair, with attendance by invitation only, rotating between the defence centres of Portsmouth and Aldershot. Now the plan was to hold a major exhibition close to the centre of London to attract visitors from around the world, promoting all aspects of British defence equipment.

As Defence Secretary I had been invited to open the event, making a speech backing British industry, emphasising the strong support I personally gave to British industry and British exports. The exhibition seemed to be on a huge scale, with every part of the new centre filled with the latest military equipment, together with companies involved in all aspects of the defence supply chain. Even outside the exhibition halls there were modern warships moored alongside, and aircraft and helicopters parked on nearby open spaces.

After the formal opening I spent many hours touring the stands, speaking to as many representatives of British industry as I could as they explained their products and their efforts to sell them overseas. Such a tour requires stamina and energy for a minister, attempting to remain enthusiastic and interested as the details of equipment are explained – sometimes in excruciating detail well beyond the comprehension of someone who was advised to drop physics at the age of fourteen and who found chemistry something of a mystery. I was therefore slightly relieved when my Private Secretary indicated that I was seriously overrunning and I needed to make time for a sandwich before heading back into London and the Ministry of Defence.

I got to my ministerial car to find my driver, Dave, standing by the vehicle, which was unusual. He was listening to live radio reports from New York. He told me that there had been a dreadful accident; that a plane had crashed into one of the twin towers of the World Trade Centre. A few minutes later, as we were setting off back to the MOD, the news came through on the radio that a second aircraft had flown into the second tower. It became clear that this was no accident.

As we drove as fast as we could back to the MOD, meetings were being arranged with those military leaders that were actually in London. Back at base, I had a series of relatively ad hoc discussions as we also started to learn about the attack on the Pentagon. Many of the military people in the MOD had at some stage in their careers been on exchanges in the US, had friends there, and knew of people working in the Pentagon. The normal rules on international telephone calls were ignored as people tried to get in touch with their friends to find out what was happening.

I was also well aware that I had family and friends living and working in lower Manhattan. The younger cousins of the New Jersey Hoons all tended initially to start their careers in New York City, before the pressures of family life lead them back home to New Jersey for the regular daily commute into New York City. I knew that at least two of them, both lawyers like me, worked in offices in Manhattan. It took some time for me to establish that all of my family members were safe. Countless other people were in a similar position, with friends and family working in New York. Politicians sometimes talk rather glibly about the special relationship between the UK and the US; it is actually built on these very personal foundations.

By far the most poignant photograph that I saw about 9/11 was an otherwise mundane picture of a New Jersey railway station car park early on the morning of 12th September. It appeared in the local New Jersey newspaper, the *Star Ledger*. It had a much greater effect on me than all of the far more dramatic pictures of the twin towers that dominated the news for days and weeks thereafter. The photograph simply showed a number of cars distributed apparently randomly around a station car park. The railway line running through eastern New Jersey serves a series of small commuter towns, and terminates at a station immediately under the World Trade Center. I have travelled on those trains on countless occasions, as it is by far the easiest way of getting on to the island of Manhattan from New Jersey. Each one of those cars in the station car park had belonged to someone who had left their home on the morning of 9/11, setting off for work as usual at the World Trade Centre. Those people never returned home.

I am not sure that people in Britain and Europe have ever quite grasped or understood the shock suffered by the American people on 9/11. It was not just that more people died in the Twin Towers than at Pearl Harbor – and that they were moreover mostly civilians going about their ordinary everyday lives; it was the arrival on their doorstep in New York, Washington and Pennsylvania of international terrorism, which was for most Americans something that only happened elsewhere in other countries far removed from the continental United States. And when it did happen in places like Egypt, many Americans even stayed away from Europe, not really understanding the geography of the world beyond their

East Coast. I received a letter at Christmas 2001 from one of my former colleagues, a Law Professor at the Law School in Louisville, Kentucky, some 800 miles west of New York, well on the way to the Mid-West. He wrote to explain that he and his wife had only recently decided that it was probably safe for them to resume their usual life of travel and holidays following 9/11; that was the reaction of a highly intelligent, well-travelled couple. It is not difficult to imagine the fearful response of most Americans who are much less used to international travel.

Given that response, shared right across America, it is perhaps not so surprising that the US administration should have embarked on a comprehensive review of all of the potential threats to the United States and its people, right around the world. The administration had been completely blindsided by the attacks of 9/11. They were not going to be taken by surprise again.

The series of terrorist attacks on US soil on 9/11 lead to a detailed review by the United States administration of the global threats the country faced. Alongside the review was a steely determination to deal with those threats as and when they could. High on the list of threats to the United States was the regime of Saddam Hussein in Iraq. It was unfinished business for many members of the administration – and in the years since the first Gulf War, Iraq seemed to have grown stronger as Saddam Hussein dealt brutally with his internal opponents. No-one in the US wanted to be caught out again by what was a known threat. The administration knew that such a failure would be politically fatal in a country that sees itself as the leader of the western world.

That is the only real connection between the events of 9/11 and the invasion of Iraq. Given the failure to resolve the question at the end of the first Gulf War, Saddam Hussein's regime in Iraq was seen as a continuing threat to the Gulf region, where the United States had extensive interests. Attempts were later made to link Saddam Hussein's regime in Iraq with Al Qaeda. They were never persuasive. The only real connection was the threat to the American way of life which occurred on September 11th 2001, and the political imperative of avoiding any kind of a repetition.

As the Americans reviewed the threats to their people, it was inevitable and necessary for the MOD to do the same. This eventually resulted in what was described as a 'new chapter' to the 1998 Strategic Defence

Review, but which was in reality a significant amendment to the work that had been carried out previously; this time taking stark account of terrorist and other non-conventional threats to Britain's security. It was published as a White Paper in 2003, entitled prosaically 'Delivering Security in a Changing World'.

Overall, the MOD sought to provide still more emergency and expeditionary military capability. In particular I was keen to add to the support available to Britain's special forces, who were always likely to be the first into any field. There was an internal MOD battle over how this could be achieved. Newspapers often call far too readily for 'more special forces'. In reality the more that are recruited the less special they become, as standards will inevitably fall with larger numbers. At the same time there was internal MOD pressure to save money by reducing the size of the Parachute Regiment. This was fiercely resisted by General Mike Jackson, who despite his elevation to the highest levels of the army chain of command, remained proud of his red beret and his considerable background in the Parachute Regiment. The solution that I agreed, to square this circle was to establish a special forces support group, largely drawn from the Parachute Regiment, but also drawing in soldiers from the Royal Marines and the RAF Regiment.

The White Paper and the modifications made to military structures were undoubtedly a necessary contribution to the evolution of the military response to the emerging threats of the twenty-first century. Some would challenge, however, whether a military response can ever be effective against terrorists armed with kitchen knives attacking people on the streets of London, or computer hackers taking down vital security systems, or fanatics introducing chemical or biological weapons into an underground station. The list of such unconventional threats, if not endless, is certainly longer than the capabilities available to any single government to use in defence. What I had not given a moment's thought to at the time was the effect that leaving the European Union might have on Britain's ability to cooperate successfully with our neighbours in sharing intelligence, information and the means to deal with these threats.

THE SCHOOLBOY
The Old School

At my fiftieth birthday party, a close friend asked my Dad about when I was born, and whether he had given any thought at the time to the job that one day I might have. He replied without much hesitation that he had expected me to be a railwayman.

Given that I was born in Derby in December 1953, at the time a railway town, only eight years after the end of the Second World War, his view was not that surprising. My parents, Ernest and June, had met after the war when they were both working for what was then British Railways. My maternal grandfather had also been a railwayman; I once said that I was 'conceived on the railway'; a rhetorical flourish that would have infuriated my eminently respectable mother.

At the time of that birthday party in December 2003, I was Britain's Defence Secretary. British forces were engaged in southern Iraq following the most controversial military deployment in recent British history. I had by then been in the post for more than four years and was involved in all aspects of the invasion of Iraq; diplomatic, political and military.

Apart from working on the railways, my Dad's only other occupation had been his six years' service in the Royal Air Force during the Second World War. I grew up knowing that he had volunteered. His job on the railway was a reserved occupation, vital to the war effort at home. It could have exempted him from military service abroad. He could have spent the entire war at home in Derby and in relative safety, perhaps at the same time furthering his career. Nevertheless, at eighteen, soon after his birthday, as soon as he was legally able to join up, he like millions of others, volunteered to fight Hitler's Germany.

No-one today questions the morality of Britain's involvement in the Second World War. Hitler's ambitions for European, if not global domination, had to be stopped. The Second World War is rightly seen as a war of national survival, where the very existence of a free and democratic Britain was under threat. Yet it is sometimes overlooked that the trigger for the actual declaration of war was the German invasion of Poland; and that very little happened for the first six months of what is known as the 'phoney war'. During that period there certainly hadn't been any immediate and direct threat to the integrity of the United Kingdom. Given recent (sometimes angry) debates about the scale of East European immigration into the UK, I have often wondered whether, if Poland was again invaded – not inconceivable, given the growing assertiveness of Putin's Russia – there would be the same supportive reaction by Britain and its people.

The same could not of course be said about Iraq, where Britain joined an international coalition to maintain, as it was seen at the time, the rule of international law. That kind of overseas intervention, involving a large-scale commitment of British forces, whilst initially tolerated by the British public, soon proved unpopular as the death toll mounted. As with Afghanistan, it was not the initial and successful military operations that caused the loss of support, it was the long drawn out peace-keeping and nation rebuilding task which appeared to stretch on forever, leading to more and more British casualties.

After basic training Ernest Hoon was sent to India as a mechanic in RAF ground crew. On the way his troop ship called in at Simonstown, then a British base in South Africa. Years later I visited the same base as Defence Secretary, by then home to the South African Navy. As I arrived in the usual fleet of ministerial and security vehicles, I thought about him arriving there on a troop ship with thousands of others, probably on their very first trip abroad, but anxious to set foot on dry land after a long and uncomfortable sea journey from Britain.

I often wondered how my Dad, not then out of his teens, dealt with the travel shock of going from the familiarity of his home and family life in Derby to the poverty of Colonial India. Like many of his generation, he rarely talked about the war. I grew up knowing that he hadn't much liked India, and that he didn't have much time for the Japanese. It was many years before any Japanese electrical goods could be found in the Hoon household.

He was stationed in what is today the very far east of India; in that finger of the country that reaches beyond modern Bangladesh. In those days, of course, it was all British India and he was there to help prevent the Japanese from continuing their military campaign to control Asia. The RAF was there to support British forces on the ground in Burma, launching attacks against the advancing Japanese army. At least one of the RAF bases, at Imphal, has become part of Britain's military legend, as the defending forces held out from March until July 1944 against an overwhelming Japanese attack, and in the process began to turn the tide, pushing back the invading forces into Burma.

As a child I got the occasional glimpse from my Dad of what life was like for Leading Aircraftman Hoon as he repaired and maintained the equipment needed by the RAF in its campaign. He was appalled by the poverty of India, but like many of his generation tended to blame the Indians for their situation. His strongest condemnation was reserved for the Japanese. Towards the end of the war, as he waited to participate in the planned invasion of Japan, he saw some of those who had been held prisoner in the Japanese camps.

I grew up in a semi-detached house on a new estate in Long Eaton, exactly between Derby and Nottingham in the East Midlands; there were many families with young children like ours. In the days before widespread car ownership, the local boys played football across the street, the gate posts acting as goal posts. We only very occasionally had to stop playing to let a car or van go by. There were two young brothers across the road from me who often joined in. Their mother, a large and jolly woman, would often treat us to orange squash afterwards. Their father, known to us only as Mr Elmer, rarely spoke or paid much attention apparently to anyone; seeming to live in a world of his own. One day some of the boys were making fun of him, imitating his awkward walking movements as he went down the street. Fortunately, I was not involved, because as it was happening, my Dad came roaring out of our front door, shouting at the boys and grabbing me off my feet and carrying me inside. I had never seen him so angry. As I was put down I was told very clearly that if I was ever involved in making fun of Mr Elmer I would not be sitting down comfortably for a very long time to come. My Dad never hit me as a child, but I understood clearly that he would do so if he ever caught me joining in the ridicule of Mr Elmer. As he calmed down he explained that Mr Elmer had been a prisoner of the Japanese and that his condition was the result of the way he had been treated in the forced labour camps of the Burma Railway.

Many years later, after Mr Elmer's early death, the Sunday Express magazine ran a remarkable story about him. After the war he had trained as a teacher. He taught gardening at Wilsthorpe School, then Long Eaton's local Secondary Modern, apparently teaching by example rather than by using too many words. One day a new young head teacher decided that all members of staff would be required to take a turn in leading the school assembly. When it came to Mr Elmer's turn, the older members of staff tried to persuade the new head that Mr Elmer should be excused. The new head thought otherwise and Mr Elmer had to stand on the stage in front of the entire school. For some moments there was an embarrassing and uncomfortable silence as Mr Elmer stared out at his increasingly restless audience. Then, very slowly and quietly, he began to describe his wartime experiences, reducing the assembly to a complete and respectful silence; something the other teachers had never seen. He explained that he had become a gardener because in the hut where he slept after a long day working on the Burma railway there was a gap in the wooden wall through which he could see out into the jungle. Nearby there was an orchid which each day he would watch as it grew. He told the assembly that every other man in his hut died, and that going back at the end of each day to check on the progress of the orchid was the only thing that kept him alive. After his death, as a memorial to Mr Elmer, the school purchased orchids for their greenhouse.

This story was published around the time of the debate in 2000 about compensation payments to Far Eastern prisoners of war. It followed a successful and popular campaign by the Royal British Legion. No one doubted the suffering that had been experienced in POW and internment camps operated by the Japanese during the war. The campaign stirred painful memories and sometimes angry debates — not least about who should actually pay for the compensation. A number of newspapers argued forcibly that it was for the Japanese to pay. The Japanese Government pointed out formally, but very politely, that they had already paid compensation as part of the Peace Treaty agreed in the early 1950s. This came as a surprise to most people, because at the time there had been little or no debate about compensation. That was a very different time: people simply wanted to put the war behind them as they built the peace and worked to repair war-damaged Britain. I asked my Dad about the compensation payments. His response surprised me but was perhaps typical of the generation that actually fought in the war. Despite his previous anger at the Japanese, he said that he thought it was time to move on and consign those events to history.

He also surprised me one day by saying that he was glad that in the war he had not had to do what I was having to do as Defence Secretary. I was taken aback by his words. I had always taken it for granted that six years volunteer military service in India, with all of the risks that involved, never knowing when or whether he would get back home, was something infinitely more remarkable and demanding than what I was doing. I said something like that in reply, but he made clear that I had the responsibility for the lives of those who served and that should never be undertaken lightly.

Unusually for someone from his background, the long journey to India had not been my Dad's first trip abroad. In June 1925, at the age of just two, he was taken by his mother to the United States to visit his elder brother and family who had emigrated to New Jersey in 1921. His elder brother, William Hoon, was twenty-four years his senior with the result that there was a generational slippage on either side of the Atlantic. My Dad's nephew and nieces were his age and my first cousins were my Dad's age. He kept a photograph of the ship on which they sailed, the Cedric, from the White Star Line out of Liverpool. He had no memory of this two-week Atlantic crossing or of his six months in the United States. During a period of mass emigration, the fact that they were only visitors to the United States had caused confusion on their arrival. They were supposed to leave the ship at Manhattan where my uncle was waiting for them. They stayed aboard however with the rest of the passengers, who were mostly immigrants heading for a new life in the United States, who had to be processed through Ellis Island. My Dad and his mother were eventually found by my uncle in the long queue for immigration.

Thus began my family's long love affair with the United States. I grew up knowing that I had a large and growing family in New Jersey. In the days before cheap airfares there was no chance of being able to visit, but I always had a letter at Christmas from my Uncle and there were photographs and details of cousins and second cousins. In the sometimes harsh debates about the motivation of immigrants, I have always thought of my Uncle and Aunt leaving Derby in 1921 with their one year old daughter to travel initially to the wilds of rural Wisconsin, before settling in New Jersey, where they worked and brought up their family through the Great Depression. There was no social security or any other rewards for emigration. They paid their own fares, driven by that basic human desire to better themselves and their family – the classic American Dream. The confidence and commitment required to turn your back on your immediate family and all that is familiar, for a foreign and perhaps hostile place, suggests that immigrants are not the dregs of a society – but are perhaps the very best people, with an innate confidence and character to succeed. The United States was built by such people, and somewhere in the genetic makeup of their population is that drive and determination that has made it such a great country.

My Dad had left school at the age of fourteen to work in the sheds at the railway works in Derby. I simply could not imagine, as a fourteen year old, how I would have dealt with the adult world of work and the long hours and physical effort involved. He had little choice, as his father had died the day before his seventh birthday and he was brought up through the recession of the late twenties and early thirties by my grandmother who ran a sweetshop. She was a formidable woman, living to be 88, so I knew her in my childhood. The single-mindedness that she showed in looking after my Dad and taking a small child on a long sea journey to the United States was still there in her eighties. She kept house for my uncle after the early death of my aunt, always wearing a widow's black dress, which she had done for more than thirty years. One year she asked my parents what I might like as a Christmas present. I was by then, in the early sixties, listening avidly to the Beatles and the Rolling Stones. She obviously didn't care much for them so when I unwrapped the 45-shaped present I found that I had been given a copy of a much blander record; *Morningtown Ride* by the Seekers, which she apparently liked, and which I still have.

I was always aware growing up that money was tight at home. I once had a second-hand Meccano construction set for Christmas and overheard my parents discussing how much Dad had got for the camera he had sold to buy my present. At the same time, we were far from being poor. My parents and the Derbyshire Building Society owned our house, a two and a half bedroomed semi-detached on a new 1950s housing estate in Long

Eaton. We moved there from the suburbs of Derby because Dad could use his railway pass to travel into work for free from the nearby station a short walk away, rather than pay bus fares.

Instead of having a car, the railway passes allowed us to travel on the trains as a family eight times a year without payment. In addition, we could get other fares at a quarter of the full price. I was therefore one of the few children in my class at junior school who had been to London, only 125 miles away to the south, but another world for most of the children I knew. I have a childhood memory of going past Parliament sitting on the upper deck of a London bus, thinking about all of the grand and important people who worked there. My later experiences of actually working there did sometimes make me doubt the reliability of that childhood impression.

There was even a special travel agency that organised holidays abroad for railway families, taking advantage of the special rail fares on offer. When I was twelve we travelled by train through France and Switzerland for a holiday in the Italian Lakes. I woke up in the middle of the night as the train stopped in Strasbourg station. Years later I always stayed in a hotel just across the station square. I often wondered as I returned late at night to my hotel after a good dinner in one of Strasbourg's restaurants whether somewhere on a train in the station there was a twelve-year-old looking out of the carriage window wondering where exactly he was.

Both my parents belonged to those generations where people from their background were expected to leave school at the national school leaving age; fourteen for my Dad, fifteen for my mother. Both had passed their eleven plus; both were clearly clever and able people who would in different and more modern times have benefitted from further education. I benefitted instead.

The eleven plus was abolished in Derbyshire the year before I was due to take it, in 1965. Nevertheless, for a handful of pupils at Brooklands Junior School in Long Eaton it was still an option. I was entered for the exam – and, after passing, I was given a Derbyshire local authority scholarship to attend Nottingham High School, a fee-paying independent school which in those days had at least fifty per cent scholarship boys from Nottinghamshire and Derbyshire. Although I had no idea at the time, I was following in the footsteps of one of the great men of modern British politics. Ken Clarke also came originally from one of the Nottinghamshire/Derbyshire border towns. We were both taught in the sixth form by the same history teacher, David Peters, and we both went to Cambridge, qualified at the Bar and went to Parliament as MPs and later as Ministers.

Nottingham High School took some getting used to for a small-town boy whose father was a railwayman. Although I had a scholarship which covered the fees and the travel into Nottingham, the uniform was a big and continuing cost for my parents. The uniform requirement was very detailed and specific with the school crest on the blazer pocket and different coloured ties depending on which school house you belonged to. In those days it could only be purchased from two shops in Nottingham. I was taken by my parents to Nottingham and kitted out in the school blazer, and a long list of other items that had been sent to my parents when I was given a place at the school. In later years I realised that middle-class parents had no difficulty in buying their son's uniform second-hand, but for my proud working class parents, hand-me-downs were not a possibility. I remember having to put on the uniform especially so that the neighbours could see what it was like over the garden fence.

The other big adjustment involved travelling to school. Nottingham High School was 10 miles away; requiring a bus journey there and back, adding several hours to what was already a long school day. For my first few years there was also Saturday morning school which meant getting up early six days a week. Compensation was supposedly a free afternoon on Thursdays; but anyone any good at sport missed out on that because of training sessions. And for those in school sports teams, Saturday afternoon meant matches, often involving quite long bus journeys to other private schools across the Midlands and Yorkshire. I was often doing six-day weeks; something that continued even after the ending of Saturday morning school, as matches still took place at the weekend.

Sport probably saved me from a miserable time in those early years. I struggled academically in what was a hothouse for clever boys; I lacked the confidence to speak out and to participate in class. One of my first reports said that the teacher didn't really know much about me as I never said very much. This was a surprise to my parents who claimed at the time that they didn't know how to keep me quiet at home. The big change for me came when, after several years at the school, I was promoted from the third to the second stream. I had not expected this to happen, not least because at the time most of my homework was being done on the bus going home. I realised that if I was to survive at this apparently higher level I would actually have to do some serious academic work. I soon discovered that the only real difference between the two streams was that the higher stream boys did their homework properly. As I followed their example I got decent O-level results, which allowed me to join the History Sixth Form.

There was, however, a problem at home. No one in my wider family had ever stayed on after the school leaving age of sixteen. There were real doubts about my staying on, and I can recall overhearing my parents discussing the costs and loss of income involved. Young people out at work but still living at home were expected to contribute to their 'board'; a concept I subsequently tried and failed to get across to my own children. Fortunately for me in the parental debate, my Dad decided that I should be able to stay on – I have always assumed because he would have loved to have had the same opportunity as a young man to read and to study. He always loved reading, and some of my earliest memories were of going with him to the local library, which he would visit sometimes more than once in a week to make sure that he always had something new to read. He would spend hours at home in the evening reading; one of many traits he passed on to me.

Ken Clarke has written that the History Sixth at Nottingham High School was not unlike Alan Bennett's *History Boys*. It was seen by David Peters as a collection of the brightest boys, all aspiring to places at Oxford or Cambridge. Initially I definitely didn't fit into that mould, coming from the lower academic streams. I had the clear impression that I was only taken on under sufferance. He told my parents at one of the regular parents' evenings that he really didn't see me as Oxbridge material. Yet I loved history, and the limited number of subjects at A-level really suited me as I could study what I most enjoyed for the first time. Two school friends had ambitious parents who wanted them to apply to Oxbridge. I had already got a place at Leeds – chosen mainly because the Rolling Stones and the Who had played there at the Student Union. I was persuaded by my friends to apply to Cambridge. Neither of them got in, yet applying after my A-levels, I was offered an unconditional place on the strength of my results.

That was in September 1972. I still had to take the Cambridge entrance exam, so I didn't manage to leave school until just before my nineteenth birthday in December. I then had to wait until the following October before going to university. The Long Eaton Labour Exchange – not yet a JobCentre – found me a job at one of the many furniture factories in the town. Long Eaton remains a centre for high quality upholstery, but in those days thousands of highly skilled men and women worked in the furniture industry compared to the few hundreds today. I worked every day for almost a year as a labourer in a factory that made frames for high quality furniture. I kept the floors clean, I carried furniture and furniture parts and loaded lorries for deliveries. I started at the beginning of December, getting up at 6.30am to get a bus in the dark in time to clock in before 8am. I often worked late, coming home well after dark and sometimes physically very tired.

The compensations for someone who had just left school were considerable. With overtime, and even after paying my parents board, I had real money to spend for the first time in my life. I could buy LPs and afford to go to concerts. I saw some of the classic bands of the period – Pink Floyd, Roxy Music and the Rolling Stones, as well as Paul McCartney and David Bowie. My record collection expanded beyond the basic Beatles' and Stones' albums that I had previously been given for Christmas or birthdays.

I also learned some valuable lessons. There were times when the work was so repetitive and so tedious that the only way of getting to the end of the day was to calculate minute by minute how much I had been earning. I always knew, however, that I was fortunate in only being there for a matter of months before going off to university, paid for by the taxes of the same people that I had been working with.

THE STUDENT
My Prospects Were Good

After the shock of going from a railway family from a small town to a fee-paying independent school in what seemed at the time to be a big city at the age of eleven, I should have found the adjustment to the world of Cambridge University relatively straightforward. Nottingham High School sent several boys every year to both Oxford and Cambridge. Most of them were like me, scholarship boys who had benefitted from the small classes and dedicated academic teaching. Nottingham High School was where, as a schoolboy, I went to work every day. I had to live in Cambridge.

At school, however long the hours, I always knew that I would be going home in the evenings and eventually at weekends. Playing away matches at boarding schools always made me thankful that at Saturday tea time I would be going home to the familiarity and comfort of my family. After away matches we would join the opposition players for a boarding school tea. The boys seemed to be identically dressed in brown jackets as they faced yet another miserable weekend away from home.

My real life was in a small town where most of the people that I knew came from a very similar background. Looking back, it is obvious that there were children from better off families at Nottingham High School; but living ten miles away meant that although I had friends at school, they only occasionally impacted on my life at home.

Coming from a small town where the council houses looked little different from the house where I lived, I had at the time little sense of the social and financial differences that are such a part of British society. Looking back, I realise that sounds naïve – that the people from the nearby council estate probably struggled financially even more than my parents. But growing up, my maternal grandmother lived in a council house in Derby, as initially did my mother's sister and family. I never noticed that they were significantly worse off than we were. Indeed, my mother regularly remarked that the rent my grandmother had paid for her council house in the course of living there for more than fifty years could have bought it several times over. This was what it was like for me growing up in the sixties – a strong sense of equality, with full employment and the belief that there was a new age of opportunity for everyone.

Curiously, Cambridge changed all of that for me, as I mixed and became friends with people on a daily basis who were from very different backgrounds, both socially and economically. The story was inevitably always more complex than the headlines. One of the first people I met at Jesus College was Phil Vaughan. We both stayed overnight in College before our interviews and went to the pub together afterwards. He was at Harrow School, apparently a world away from small town Long Eaton. Yet as I got to know him as we studied law together, I discovered not a posh public schoolboy but a modest, warm and generous man who later became the godfather to Nathalie, our youngest child. When as a student I needed somewhere to stay in London, his parents were always the first to offer me a bed for a night and sometimes for longer. I had no sense on a personal and friendly level that he belonged in a different world to me.

Another lifelong friend made in those early days at Cambridge was Jon Manley. I met him on my very first afternoon at Jesus College. I had unpacked my suitcase in the very modern and comfortable room that I had been given; three or four times the size of my shoebox bedroom at home. I had a small transistor radio and at 5 o'clock I listened to the football results, mainly to check on Derby County's score that day. The result was important, because Brian Clough was still the manager and the team was still near the top of the old First Division. I knew that I was supposed to eat dinner in the College Main Hall at 6.30 but I was nervous about the start of what was going to be a very new life. Listening to the football results was infinitely easier than venturing out of my room. Eventually I did go down the staircase and across the quad, where I met Jon Manley, whose first words were to ask whether I knew the football results. I was able to tell him the score of every game, almost as if I was James Alexander Gordon reading out the results on the radio. I realised that there was at least one person in the College who was like me. We cemented our friendship that night with copious quantities of alcohol and both played for the College football team for the next three years.

Although Jesus was a mixed and socially inclusive college, it still had a majority of public schoolboys. I envied their confidence and was aware of their financial security. I got there in October 1973 with all of the benefits of what was then a very generous system of financial support for university students. All of my fees at one of the world's best universities were paid for. In addition, I received a grant for my living expenses, which if budgeted carefully was enough to keep me during term time. My parents made no contribution. If I needed more money there were always holiday jobs available. I had worked at a local furniture factory between leaving school in the December after the Oxbridge entrance exams and the following October and always managed to get some sort of work when I needed it during the holidays – from delivering the Christmas post to dismantling pit props at a nearby colliery.

Nevertheless, there was a world of difference between those of us who got by on grants and those students whose parents were able to finance a style of student life that seemed to be part of another world. The Cambridge clubs and societies dedicated to drinking always provided generous hospitality at their regular receptions. The annual cost of joining the Natives, the most prestigious of the Jesus social clubs, was significantly more than my grant for the whole year. Yet I went to their parties, enjoyed the company, and gradually grew into someone very different from the slightly nervous nineteen year-old that had started out at Cambridge.

Confidence was the key. Above all else English public schools seem to produce young men and women who, whatever their personal circumstances, have the self-confidence to continue to drive themselves forward. At the end of my first year studying law I had found the subject and the exams very difficult. Yet my law student friends came out of those same exams apparently full of confidence. As we stood around afterwards exchanging our answers, it seemed obvious to me that I was in big trouble. My answers seemed to bear no relationship to theirs. In the course of my weekly telephone call home I even warned my mother that I might have a problem with the law course and continuing at Cambridge. As it turned out several of those friends had managed very distinguished thirds in the exams, yet seemed entirely untroubled by the experience. I need not have worried academically, but I struggled to understand how they could remain so confident even in the face of what seemed to me to be obvious failure.

That learned or innate confidence was obvious at the regular meetings of the Junior Common Room. Those sometimes rowdy events took place in a room which doubled as a bar. The early seventies were still a time of student activism, although most students were in fact probably more interested in sport and music than politics. I had never been able to speak in public. At school in the fifth form I had had an English teacher, David Matthews, who decided that the whole class would prepare a talk on any subject of their choosing; but they would have to stand and deliver it from the front of the classroom. I had to write down every single word of my talk, even though I knew the subject really well, and stuttered through it with obvious and to me painful nervousness. When I was a Cabinet Minister many years later, we once bumped into David Matthews; he had obviously followed my political career with the interest of former teacher, but understandably he could not quite believe that I was the same person that had stumbled through his exercise in public speaking.

As far as I was concerned, those JCR meetings were initially just as difficult. I simply sat and listened. Then, at one meeting, I realised that I knew what needed to be said. But I simply could not bring myself to get up and say anything. At some point in the debate someone said exactly what I had thought. It was a young man called Andrew Kennon, who I later got to know again as a clerk in the House of Commons. I was angry with myself for my timidity and thereafter forced myself to say something. It felt excruciating at first, not helped by the fact that I still had a fairly broad Derbyshire accent with very flat vowels. My lack of confidence was not helped by my fellow students, and sometimes even my friends, making braying donkey noises as I spoke. Looking back I suppose that this probably spurred me on as gradually I learned to exercise some control over my nerves. I never overcame them – just learned to be able to put them in their place. In later years I was convinced that those nerves helped me enormously as I double and triple checked everything that I planned to say. In contrast, those with much greater confidence often seemed to speak first and think later.

There is no doubt that Cambridge did eventually give me the confidence to express myself in public and more precisely in private. Cambridge supervisions, or tutorials, involve very small groups working through relevant issues in detail. My first law supervisions were with Peter Glazebrook, the Director of Legal Studies at Jesus College. He forced me to think and analyse issues from their fundamentals, even if initially I had found the subject hard to study. The first few fortnightly supervisions proved to be a real problem. No-one had ever explained to me what a supervision was; I assumed that it was with a teacher who would tell me what I needed to know, as at school. When Peter Glazebrook began by asking me questions, rather than telling me things, I was lost. The next time, having studiously read the relevant chapter in the textbook, I was thrown again because this time he gave us a list of problems to solve legally and asked us more questions; and not for the hour that I was expecting. He would often devote two to two-and-a-half hours to just two students who were expected to think long and hard before replying. In later years teaching law at Leeds University I regretted that the rigid timetable, and no doubt university finances, would not allow me to reproduce the remarkable intellectual experience I had enjoyed at Cambridge. Peter Glazebrook taught me how to think and work through the details of a problem, not giving up until I had found an answer that I could understand and defend.

More than anything, Cambridge showed me an intellectual and social world way beyond the small town where I had grown up. I had friends who lived in and around London. I was invited to visit their homes and saw the very different way in which they lived. And, as a result, I sometimes felt as if I belonged in neither world. My friends at home made fun of Cambridge and all that it stood for – and at Cambridge it took some time before I really felt that I fitted in. Once again sport helped; I played football most days, either in matches for the College or the kind of casual games that started with a few people kicking a ball around as others joined in. Jesus was fortunate in having its own playing fields right next to the College buildings – unusually for a city centre college in Cambridge.

It also helped that by then I had met the girl I was eventually to marry. Elaine came from the same small town, growing up less than a mile away. She had also been offered the same local authority scholarship as I had at the age of eleven, but in a home where money was even tighter than mine, her parents had allowed her to go into the new comprehensive system. Instead of selection at eleven, the selection then took place at thirteen, when the brightest students were creamed off to go to what was still known by everyone in the town as Long Eaton Grammar School. Despite formally being part of the comprehensive system, it still retained the ethos of a grammar school and its students were every bit as bright as the ones I mixed with at Nottingham High School. Indeed, they had the advantage of growing up in a mixed sex environment, giving Elaine a common sense grounding that I have always envied. On her regular visits to Cambridge she always saw through the pomposity that I by then had been taken in by. It took quite a long time for her to decide to marry me – and even after forty years she still has her doubts about whether it was the right decision.

THE LAWYER
Out of College

There were no lawyers in our family; there were no family friends in the legal professions. Indeed, I doubt that I had even met a lawyer before choosing the subject to study at university. Given a completely free choice I would probably have studied history or English, the subjects that I had most enjoyed at school. But I was nervous about what would follow; I would still have to make a further choice about what to do next at the end of my university course. Law seemed to have the advantage that if I liked it there could be a career to follow; and even if I didn't like it, I would still have a useful degree.

I doubted this decision in the course of my first year at Cambridge. Law seemed beyond dull; outside of thought-provoking supervisions with Peter Glazebrook, the Director of Studies at Jesus College, it required what seemed to be a tedious exercise in remembering the details of obscure cases decided by appeal court judges that seemed to have no obvious connection to the real world. Roman law was a compulsory first year course at the time and this only added to the unreality. We seemed to spend most of our time learning about the law of slaves. My discomfort was added to by having a South African tutor. I am sure that I am doing him a disservice, but the combination of a white South African from the apartheid era teaching the law relating to slavery was too much for my strong political sensitivities. The fact that Roman law supervisions were at 9 am every other Wednesday morning definitely did not help.

Peter Glazebrook, was fortunately, an infinitely kind and patient man. I am sure that he had heard complaints like mine a million times. Nevertheless, he listened carefully to my concerns and helpfully suggested that I should see what law was like in the real world. There was a scheme that allowed students to work in a lawyer's office during the summer vacation. Inevitably most of the places were in London, but fortunately there was one in Nottingham for four weeks with a rather grand-sounding firm called Rotheras. My biggest concern was that I was only to be paid expenses at a time when I badly needed money to go travelling around Europe with friends.

Nevertheless, the four weeks went well. I was handed over to Dick Hall, the partner who ran the firm's criminal law practice, and spent the several weeks helping to prepare his cases, following him around the Magistrates Court and sitting behind counsel in the Crown Court. Dick Hall was not an obvious teacher. He once threw back something that I had written, saying only 'drafting', which took me some time to understand. Nevertheless we got on, helped by the fact that he was also from Derby, and was also a keen Derby County supporter. He had been a Royal Marine after the war and had then gone on to Oxford as a mature student. I often thought of him in later years because I once made the mistake of referring to his time in 'the marines'. I was put firmly in my place; 'the marines are American. I was in the *Royal Marines*'; something I never forgot when dealing with the service that has never quite accepted that it is actually part of the Royal Navy.

I repeated the experience at Rotheras the following summer, and realised that I had found what I wanted to do. I wanted to represent people, to understand and sort out their problems; to get the best possible result for them. At one stage Dick Hall went on holiday, apparently leaving me to run the department. I am sure that there was plenty of discreet supervision – but I was left to interview clients and witnesses as well as prepare briefs for barristers at court. I was particularly pleased with a long and academic brief that I had written on behalf of a defendant who claimed that he had found some scrap metal in the arboretum in the centre of Nottingham. I had persuaded myself with the benefit of rigorous academic principle that he was not actually guilty. Unfortunately for me, the barrister at court completely ignored my long, detailed and tightly argued brief and persuaded the defendant to plead guilty, getting him six months in prison for his pains. When I hesitantly raised the content of my brief afterwards, the barrister told me not to worry; the defendant 'wanted to be inside for Christmas'.

Things went so well with Rotheras that it was made clear to me that if I wanted I could join the firm after Cambridge, as an articled clerk, with a view one day to succeeding Dick Hall as partner. I was, at the time, delighted.

My Dad was even more pleased. He had grown up in the Depression when jobs were hard to come by. Going back to Cambridge with this offer in hand meant that my future seemed to be securely mapped out. As that final year went on, however, I began to have doubts. Cambridge had opened up new horizons and I began to think of exploring opportunities beyond the East Midlands.

My contemporaries were all talking about the big city law firms that they would be joining, with big city prospects and salaries. I knew that commercial law, representing large corporations, was not for me, but gradually the prospect of being a solicitor in Nottingham, appearing every day in the Magistrates' Court, became less appealing. My public speaking was improving and I came to the conclusion that I wanted to go to the Bar. Looking back, exactly why I reached this view was far from clear, as I had had only limited contact with barristers, and what little I did find out about the profession was only likely to put me off; there was no pay for the first six months of training, little prospect of pay in the second six months – and most of the training places were in London, where I knew I could not afford to live. Once again, I was fortunate. One of my Cambridge supervisors, David Hayton, had faced the same financial problems as a young lawyer and suggested that I should spend some time teaching law at a university, saving some money before deciding whether I really wanted to go to the Bar.

It was excellent, if at the time surprising, advice and so shortly after graduating in the spring of 1976, I took the train to Leeds with the last of my Dad's free railway passes, and found myself at the age of twenty-two with a one-year contract to teach law to undergraduates who were only a few years younger than me. I seemed to be very much younger than all of the other members of the Leeds Law Faculty, but they generously overlooked my shortcomings and always invited me to join in with their events.

One of the lecturers, Dr Claudine Levy, had been one of the first teachers of European Law in the UK. As part of the course she organised a student visit to the European institutions in Brussels and Luxembourg. Since it took place during the Easter vacation, it was not that popular with other faculty members who might have been expected to help out. It was however perfect for a young university lecturer who loved to travel. As a result I found myself on an official trip to the continent, which allowed me to visit the European Parliament, still sitting in Luxembourg, and attend briefings at NATO. Of course, I had no idea at the time how relevant those visits would be to my later life.

My understanding of the workings of the European Parliament was distinctly limited prior to this visit. It was before the first direct elections, when national parliaments appointed delegations to represent each country. Despite their national origins, the Euro-MPs sat in European political groups from left to right in a hemi-cycle. The Leader of the Labour delegation at the time was John Prescott. One particular exchange stuck in my mind. I listened to a passionate Italian Communist decrying the Common Agricultural Policy, clearly very angry, gesticulating and waving his arms around. The effect of his speech was somewhat undermined by the calm English interpretation which I heard through my headphones; 'I don't think that this is a very good idea'.

At NATO, we were briefed on the politics of deterrence at a time when the Soviet Union appeared to possess overwhelming force in the number of tanks and troops that it could put into the West German field if it ever decided to invade the West. NATO's plan at the time was to try and hold the line for as long as possible in order to allow negotiations. If that failed then NATO would be forced to use its nuclear weapons in a first strike. This shocked some of the students, who like most people at the time assumed that it would be the Soviet bad guys who would initiate the first nuclear attack. I remembered this briefing many years later, after the collapse of the Soviet Union, when it was the Russians who refused to sign up to 'no first use' because of their fear of the overwhelming force apparently possessed by the United States and other NATO countries.

I made my first visit to the United States in 1978 at the age of 24. I stayed with the Hoon family in New Jersey, travelling most days into New York with my cousin Barbara Hoon, who had just graduated from Juilliard School at Lincoln Centre, and who was at the start of a successful career in modern dance that would eventually see her work in choreographer Twyla Tharp's company and in several Broadway shows. She went into New York to take classes or attend auditions. I would wander the streets of New York, exploring places that I had mostly seen in the movies. In the course of four weeks I went to galleries and museums as well as some of the furthest reaches of Manhattan.

New York during the day was one city – at night it was another. This was the New York of *Taxi Driver*, Studio 54, graffiti'd subway trains, mugging and murder. Fortunately, my cousin knew her way around. But the Big Apple was not in those days a place for unsuspecting English tourists. This holiday visit made me want to see more of the United States, and fortunately I did not have to wait very long.

In a very similar way to my academic visit to Brussels, when the opportunity came to spend a year teaching law in the United States there were no other takers from the Leeds faculty. In late July 1979 I flew to the University of Louisville in Kentucky to be their Visiting Professor of Law. Again, despite the fact that I was younger than many of the students, I was generously received by the Louisville Faculty. I was given Common Law subjects to teach, on the basis that an English lawyer would be able to apply historic principles to Kentucky and US federal law. It was slightly surreal being given the title of Visiting Professor. I was twenty-five with a law degree and after only a couple of years of university teaching I was, being called 'Professor' when the professors who had taught me were very learned men and women and, in truth, generally what I thought of as being very old.

My legal teaching career in Kentucky did not start well. I was given a course on the law of Agency to teach; not something that I had ever studied or taught at that depth in England. The American approach to law teaching was based on casebooks, with the extracted highlights of each case printed out for the students to study and understand. The professor's job was to ask relevant questions designed to bring out the principles involved. Unfortunately, despite a great deal of intellectual effort this particular professor found that he did not understand the very first case in the casebook. I was afraid that my US academic legal career was about to come to an early conclusion. I simply could not understand why this Kentucky case from 1798 had been decided in the way summarised. Eventually I plucked up the courage to admit my ignorance and consulted a colleague. He found my difficulty funny, which didn't help my self-confidence. 'What you don't understand,' he said, 'was that Kentucky still had slaves in 1798 and since they were considered property they couldn't be agents for another person.' He dined out on my difficulty for weeks to come.

I was in the United States for fifteen months, teaching and travelling. My tax-free salary allowed me to buy a brand new Ford Mustang, and during the long vacations to visit my New Jersey family and see America. Elaine was at the time teaching in Lancashire so she was able to visit for each of her holidays. I joined the National Parks Service which allowed us to stay at the limited number of lodges that were allowed to operate in the otherwise pristine national parks. Americans are often criticised for not travelling abroad and often not even having passports. My time in the US allowed me to understand why; in a country that is three thousand miles across, the astonishing variety of scenery could take a lifetime to visit. We drove across America four times, visiting both sides of the Grand Canyon, staying in Yellowstone and Yosemite. In little over a year we drove 35,000 miles and visited thirty-five states. Over the next almost forty years we had many similar holidays, showing our children what we had seen and exploring even the more remote states of Alaska and Hawaii, eventually travelling to Montana to visit our fiftieth and final state.

In the course of our time in the United States we both realised that we would soon be married. We talked about staying in the United States, since there was the possibility of another one-year teaching contract at another US law school. It was a difficult decision, as we both loved the American way of life. Yet something held us back. We both had family and lifelong friends at home, and although Atlantic travel by then was both cheap and commonplace, neither of us wanted to become expatriates. Furthermore, following Derby County from four and a half thousand miles away would be a challenge! Although we never actually discussed having children, I think that we both probably wanted them to grow up in a similar manner to the way we had done.

As a result, I found myself flying back into Heathrow on a wet and miserable Monday morning in September 1980. We had not long since left the warm American West with its sense of space and seemingly infinite horizons. England was cold and cramped in contrast. I was regretting our decision to return before we even left the airport.

Back at the Law Faculty in Leeds at the apparently advanced age of twenty-six, I was worrying that life was passing me by; that I was not getting on with my original ambition of going to the Bar. I had passed the academic qualifications required, studying part time in my early days at Leeds. In addition, it was necessary to 'keep terms', which involved travelling to London four times a year to an Inn of Court to eat at least three dinners each term. For the great majority of Bar students based in London the dinners were only a short tube ride away. Living in Leeds it involved a long weekend visit, as Gray's Inn at the time did not do Sunday lunchtime dining. I was fortunate in having friends who would find me a bed for a night or two as I ate my way to the Bar. I was able to tell friends and family who asked about my Bar qualification that 'I had not eaten enough to be a Barrister'. Just before leaving for the US, I was called to the Bar by Gray's Inn, hiring the requisite white tie suit which unfortunately came without the necessary studs. I might be the only student to be called to the Bar with a shirt held together by paper clips.

The next problem was pupillage; the compulsory one-year training experience required of all would-be barristers. For most young lawyers this requires being taken on by a set of barristers in chambers and being able to support yourself financially for at least a year before earning any money. For the first six months it is actually against the rules to earn money from the law. In the second six months, the prospects of earnings are generally thought to be slight and even after that, in many chambers, the early days are difficult. Barristers are sole practitioners, and like actors are only as good as their last case or part. Although they club together in chambers, sharing overheads such as the cost of a clerk and a law library, it can take some time before an individual barrister is earning and receiving enough money to survive. Although Chambers and the Inns of Court make much of the various scholarships available, given the financial constraints it is hardly surprising that it is a profession still dominated by the affluent middle and upper classes.

I was fortunate in that members of the Leeds Bar taught from time to time at the Law Faculty. I was told that I could have a place in chambers in Leeds. Elaine was still teaching in Lancashire but was able to travel over to Leeds every weekend. Sadly she had been told that her father was suffering from inoperable cancer. We brought our wedding forward by a few months to ensure that he could be there to give his daughter away. Since I was setting off on a new career, we also decided to go back home to the East Midlands so that she could be closer to her parents through this difficult time.

There were three sets of Barristers' Chambers in Nottingham. The most successful at the time was known as the Ropewalk, where I was first interviewed. I was offered a place but subject to the proviso that I did not become involved in politics. The interviewing Head of Chambers, Keith Matthewman, later a locally well-known Crown Court Judge, had once thought about being an MP. My CV mentioned my time as College JCR President and he decided that I had political ambition. I was not impressed, because at the time I had no such desire, and in any event I did not see why they should be telling me what I could do in my own time. I therefore accepted an offer from the College Street Chambers, at the time less prestigious, but as it turned out it was a much better place to start. With the considerable help of the Leeds Head of Faculty, Professor Brian Hogan, I was able to organise the first six months of my pupillage to coincide with the post-Easter university period, when there was very little teaching and exams could be marked in the evenings in my own time.

I spent that first six months with the Head of Chambers, David Wilcox, himself later a Judge in what is now the Technology and Construction Court. At the time he was very much a Common Law practitioner, although anxious like most barristers of a certain age to become some sort of a judge. Although barristers can earn a good living, they are self-employed, and like many in that precarious position give little thought to pensions. The attraction of a judicial appointment of whatever kind is therefore a very attractive government pension, without having to make the kind of lifetime contributions that most people have to make to provide financial security in their retirement. Many years later this was the cause of a big row between Tony Blair and Gordon Brown. Tony Blair had been lobbied by his friends from the Bar that judicial pensions had to be significantly improved to attract the best talent into the judiciary. This went against the grain of all of Gordon Brown's instincts, as already very well paid people were to get even more – and from the taxpayer.

I had a strange and at times difficult relationship with David Wilcox as my pupil master. He obviously liked having a former law lecturer as a pupil, and for example encouraged me to write up a case in the Criminal Law Review where he had sought to change the established law by challenging the composition of a jury on racial grounds. For the first six months he encouraged my development as a barrister, but from the moment I was free to take cases his attitude completely changed. I was rather older than the usual pupil barrister who would generally start straight from completing the bar exams. In addition I was local, and still spoke with a Derbyshire accent. This combination proved attractive to local solicitors who began to brief me even in my second six months of pupillage. I was obviously pleased, as was the Clerk to Chambers, who liked having someone that he could promote amongst his contacts in the local legal world. For a few weeks I was in court regularly, thinking to myself that I was already over the hard part of starting a practice. Then suddenly the work stopped coming. I asked the Clerk what had gone wrong. After a certain amount of squirming he admitted that the Head of Chambers had instructed him not to give me any more work; that I apparently needed more time to prepare before actually going into court. By then I was with another member of Chambers as a pupil, and he made sure that the instruction was overridden. His explanation was that in the tight competitive world of legal practice, the Head saw me as a threat. Given that I had only been in practice for a few weeks compared to someone who had been at the bar for decades, I found it difficult to accept.

Despite this setback, my practice grew and I was soon on the list of Barristers briefed by the Nottinghamshire prosecution service, ensuring regular work on both sides of the criminal divide. Although most of my cases were in Nottingham, the eastern side of the Midland and Oxford circuit stretched over to Lincoln and Grimsby and I would also appear in Derby and Leicester. I began to enjoy the life and the company of barristers in the robing room before cases. They were quick-witted and entertaining. Many had outside interests where their talents were on full display. Graham Richards, from my chambers, commentated for Radio Derby on all of Derby County's matches, home and away. I had watched Derby with my Dad all through their great years in the sixties and seventies under Brian Clough and Dave Mackay, when they won the League title twice and reached the semi-finals of the European Cup. By the time I got back from America they were sliding down the divisions. I went to a number of games with Graham, who often took me with him as he travelled around to do his commentaries.

At that time as well there were a few Barristers that I knew involved in politics. They were almost all Conservatives; the one exception being Willy

Bach, now Baron Bach of Lutterworth. He was at one time in chambers in Nottingham before moving to his natural home in Leicester. That was the start of another long friendship. We used to joke that at the time we were the only local Barristers that were also members of the Labour Party compared to when Tony Blair became leader when they all seemed to want to join.

INTO POLITICS
Change the World

In my late teens I thought about being an MP in the same way I had previously thought about being an engine driver or a professional footballer: exciting to dream about, but it could never happen to me. It was one thing to fantasise in private; real life was about getting a job, getting married and paying the mortgage. Politics, like music and sport, certainly fascinated me – but I never seriously imagined that I could actually be a politician, any more than I could have been a musician or a professional footballer.

I first started as a relatively small boy thinking about political questions during the debate about arms sales to apartheid South Africa in the early 1960s. Starting from first principles, I simply could not accept that human beings could be denied the right to vote or even sit on the same seat as another person simply because of the colour of their skin. I am not even sure at the time that it was a particularly political view. I thought it was wrong because I believed that it was fundamentally unfair.

The next stage in my development followed on from that; people should always be treated equally irrespective of their skin colour, nationality or background; they should equally all have the same opportunities. That simple thought process probably lead me to define myself as being on the left – although I accept that many one nation Conservatives could have similar views. Growing up in the sixties the choice seemed clear cut – you were either on the left and therefore Labour, or on the right and a Conservative.

My instinctive support for the Labour Party was however not popular at home. I came from a family of working-class conservatives who knew their place, were deferential to those in charge and had a strong sense of what they thought of as being right and wrong. And by that they usually meant that Labour was wrong and the Conservatives were right. Their view was entirely individualistic; people got on by their own hard working efforts, not through collective endeavour and certainly not by challenging society's social divides. That was perhaps the underlying reason why there was a family debate about my staying on at school; further education and university were not for the likes of us.

In reality there was not much time in my teens for political activity given the demands of school, of sport and the painful process of growing up through adolescence. There were the occasional debates in the sixth form at school but I was far too nervous to participate. I could argue with friends in private about almost anything – but never in public. After leaving school and getting a job at a local furniture factory, I did decide that I had to do something practical in politics rather than just talking about it with my friends. Although only in a temporary job bridging the gap from December 1972, when I left school, until September 1973, when I was due to start as a student at Cambridge, I joined FTAT, the trade union for furniture workers. The local leading lights in what was an important trade union in the area were also involved in the Labour Party. Even then I was only on the periphery, delivering leaflets and taking numbers at polling stations on election days.

That very practical background was probably why I never took to university politics. I never joined the Cambridge Union, probably as much as anything on financial grounds, as I didn't see much benefit in the subscription, which was largely paid by students in their first days at Cambridge who thereafter had very little further involvement – but also because participating in their debates required a degree of confidence that I knew I did not have. The Labour Party did not seem to feature much in university politics at the time, with left-wing students apparently arguing the merits of various ideologies that seemed far removed from the kind of life that I was used to. Charles Clarke, later a Cabinet colleague, was President of the Cambridge Student Union and Mike Gapes, later the MP for Ilford, a considerable figure on the left of Cambridge student politics; although I never met either of them at the time. The future politician I had most to do with was Andrew Mitchell, also from Jesus College and still a good friend. He was exactly what I expected a future politician to be like – articulate and intelligent with the advantage of a father who was already an MP. Cambridge produces its fair share of future politicians; Andrew and Charles and Mike had all of the required abilities, and certainly seemed to be heading in that predictable direction. I doubt that anyone at the time would have said the same about me.

I suspect that I found life at the university level intimidating; more than anything I was comfortable in the College environment – where I thought that I knew most people through sport or evenings in the bar. In my third year I became JCR President, the only vaguely political position I had wanted. My very first task in that job after getting back to Cambridge at the start of my final academic year in October 1975 was to help organise a search for a missing Jesus student. He had set off from home but was not back at Jesus College. Many students volunteered to help and were given copies of a picture extracted from the big College student photograph taken when we all originally arrived. I was surprised that I did not recognise the face in the photograph. I had stupidly thought that I knew everyone from sport, or the College Bar or generally being around the place. It turned out that he was a quiet mathematician from a small town, where his success in getting to Cambridge was so remarkable that he had featured prominently in the local paper. He had found life at Cambridge very difficult; instead of being the leading light, he was simply one of very many clever students. He found both the work and social life hard to get used to. He simply could not face more Cambridge or the admission of defeat that going back home would involve. Tragically his body was found in the Fens.

It was only after arriving in Leeds in 1976 that I really became involved in politics and the Labour Party. I got in touch with the local Labour Party, saying that I was teaching at the University and wanted to join my local branch. I was almost immediately contacted by Ken Woolmer, also a university lecturer but as well the Deputy Leader of the West Yorkshire County Council, and soon to be selected as Labour's parliamentary candidate for Batley and Morley, then a safe Labour seat not far from Leeds. He was a rising star of the Labour Party and after his election to Parliament in 1979 was soon closing economic debates for the opposition from the Front Bench. His political career was however a severe lesson in the dangerous unpredictability of politics. After winning what was at the time a safe Labour seat, boundary changes split it in two, with the result that in the 1983 General Election disaster for the Labour Party, he lost by a few hundred votes. He lost again by a similar margin in 1987, and although he was later appointed to the House of Lords, what had promised to be a brilliant political career at the very highest level in British and Labour politics went in a very different direction.

I soon became heavily involved in the Labour Party in the University constituency of North-West Leeds; at the time a reasonably safe Tory seat, as its boundaries then stretched out into the leafy suburbs of the City. I felt that I fitted in immediately. Given my previous dislocation, the Labour Party was for me an agreeable mixture of university people and locals who had lived all of their lives in the area. The leading lights in the Headingley branch where I lived were Jim and Gertie Roche, who had been left wing trade union activists until the 1956 Hungary uprising when, disillusioned with communism, they became involved in the Labour Party. Jim had worked as a tailor for Burtons, the High Street menswear chain that had its origins in Leeds. I spent many evenings at their home listening to his take on the organisation of politics; he like my Dad was a largely self-educated man who in a different era would have thrived at university. He later made my first barrister's suit, complete with striped trousers and a plain black jacket.

Although by then I was giving lectures at the University and would speak at meetings, I still thought of myself as a backroom organiser rather than a frontline politician. I delivered leaflets, knocked on doors and was appointed agent in North-West Leeds ahead of the 1979 General Election campaign. That position led to my being asked to organise the 1979 European election for the Leeds European seat. There was not a lot of competition for the job. Most Labour Party members were at the time at best lukewarm about Europe; many on the left were strongly opposed, seeing it as a capitalist club that because of its rules on state aid would prevent the coming of a socialist society.

Labour's candidate was Derek Enright; born in Leeds, he was by the late seventies living in Pontefract, where he was the Deputy Head of a large comprehensive school. He was everything that I admired in a Labour candidate. A fluent and persuasive speaker, he had impeccable working-class credentials and was bright enough to have won a scholarship to Oxford. I spent many Sunday lunchtimes with his large and lively family, often waiting whilst he came back from his Sunday morning ritual of taking his mother to church, washed down with a couple of pints at the local Catholic Club. In June 1979, he won the Leeds European election comfortably, becoming one of Britain's first directly elected members of the European Parliament, where he established a formidable reputation on development issues. He was consistently pro-European, which in the early 1980s was completely out of favour with Labour Party activists. As a result he was deselected, shortly before the 1984 European election. Having given up a high-flying teaching career, he was forced to go back and spend time as a supply teacher before winning a parliamentary by-election in Hemsworth in West Yorkshire in 1991. Sadly his time in the House of Commons was short-lived.

I went to visit him at St Thomas' hospital not very long before his death from cancer. As we looked out at the near perfect view of Parliament from his hospital window across the river, it was obvious that his strong Catholic faith meant that dying held no fear for him. In those days and for many years, Tam Dalyell MP wrote parliamentary obituaries for the Independent newspaper. In the course of our conversation Derek told me that Tam had been to see him. 'I must be in really big trouble now,' he said, with a broad smile. I joined in the laughter but was actually closer to tears. He died a few days later.

Leeds in the late seventies was a strongly Labour city. It had two Cabinet Ministers as local MPs – Denis Healey in the West and Merlyn Rees in the South. The City Council and City Labour Party were run ruthlessly but efficiently by George Mudie, later a parliamentary colleague whose considerable talents were perhaps overlooked in the later landslide of Labour MPs. Although there were growing tensions between left and right, common sense and a desire to do the best for local people won out over ideology. And despite its obvious difficulties, I still felt that about Jim Callaghan's government.

In 1978, however, I attended the Labour Party Conference at Blackpool as the delegate from North-West Leeds. It gave me my first slightly shocked insight into where the Labour Party was heading. Delegates were sat in alphabetical order which put me close to London delegates. They spent most of their time booing and heckling Labour Ministers. Ideology was taking over. Although I enjoyed that conference more than any that

I had to attend in later years as a minister, it was still a shock to see the growing gap between the theories of the delegates and the practice of government by Labour ministers.

As the individual constituency election results came through in May 1979, showing that Margaret Thatcher's Conservatives had won the General Election, I was profoundly unhappy about politics and the future of the country. There was obviously a significant element of naïve idealism, but I realised as the results came in that big changes were coming – and that those changes would be difficult for most people. Sir Keith Joseph, one of Margaret Thatcher's closest advisors, was also a Leeds MP and the local paper regularly reported on his free market, small government thinking. I knew what the country was in for when the Tories won in 1979.

I have often asked myself, with the considerable benefit of hindsight, whether I would still have felt the same way about the significant changes that Margaret Thatcher brought about. After all, Tony Blair built on many of those reforms. Looking back Margaret Thatcher was right to tackle some of the structural problems of the British economy; her real problem was also ideology and not knowing when to stop. Privatisation of certain industries introduced competition that much improved the service to consumers, where previously they had often been taken for granted. But there is no real competition for example in the water industry. Ideology at the expense of common sense drove her forward and it was ideology in the form of the Poll Tax that was ultimately her undoing.

I was fortunate, however, I did not have to stay around and watch this unfold. I was off to the United States – possibly for an entirely new life – but certainly for at least a year. And before the development of the internet it was almost impossible to keep up with events back home or sometimes even in other parts of the United States. The local media was very local. The Louisville newspaper, the *Courier Journal*, like very many similar local papers across America did cover local, state and international events. Inevitably however it concentrated on its immediate area. To read the *New York Times* or *Washington Post* on the day of publication involved driving the several miles out to the airport late in the afternoon, by which time that morning's paper would be available. I did this regularly on a Sunday afternoon, primarily because somewhere tucked away in tiny print on the sports pages of the New York Times were the English football results. I needed to know what was happening to Derby County. For those not so anxious, the New York Times would arrive by post in Louisville two days after publication on Tuesday morning. Louisville is only 800 miles west of New York. Such information constraints were clearly part of another era.

Arriving back in Britain in September 1980, I had any number of important arrangements to sort out; a wedding to Elaine, buying our first house, leaving Leeds University, and arranging pupillage in Nottingham to start my career at the Bar. It left little time for politics. It was only once we had moved back home to the Derbyshire village of Breaston, next door to where we had both grown up in Long Eaton, that I again got involved. Or at least I tried to – but the local Labour party branch in the two neighbouring villages of Breaston and Draycott had collapsed, and had not functioned in many years. I got it going again and for a time, given a good mixture of people from both villages, it seemed to thrive. At local election time, the nature of village politics became clear; one end of the village had the larger houses and a polling station where there were queues of Conservatives waiting to vote. The council estate, in stark contrast, had its own polling station with a handful of people occasionally drifting in. It is a very long time since the village of Breaston elected a Labour councillor.

By then I had begun to think about one day trying to become a Member of Parliament. With experience, I had learned to control my nerves when speaking in public. I had realised that I was probably as capable as many of the Labour candidates that I had met. I also really enjoyed campaigning; knocking on doors talking to people and trying to persuade them to vote Labour. That glimpse given when the door opens, of life inside someone's home, provides a fascinating insight into their lives. What I doubted was whether I was confident enough to see my name on a ballot paper, on a poster in a window, and actually asking people to vote for me.

Trying to get to Holland or France

As my practice at the Bar grew, we decided in August 1983 that we could afford a holiday abroad; two weeks in Greece, a week touring classical sites followed by a week on the island of Poros. At around that time the Labour Party was unenthusiastically looking for candidates for the European elections to be held in June 1984. On the way to the airport I posted my letter to the local Erewash constituency party secretary, Mary Bielby, saying that I would like to be considered as a candidate for the Derbyshire European seat. I had vaguely mentioned to Elaine that I wanted to have a go to see what the selection process would be like, so that if ever I did decide to try seriously for Parliament I would know what to expect. I had spoken to no-one else about this and had no expectation whatsoever of being successful; as far as I was concerned this was a try out and no more than that. I doubt that Elaine took me seriously; I am sure that she never thought I would be successful.

In the days before proportional representation for European elections in the UK, there were eighty-one individual European seats. The drawing of boundaries across the country had obviously not been easy. In 1979 the Derbyshire seat had included the then Conservative seat of South-East Derbyshire, and given the national General Election result only a few weeks before, had not surprisingly been won by the Conservatives. Yet after only one election, by 1984 the European boundaries had been changed, with South Derbyshire replaced by a Nottinghamshire constituency; Ashfield. This caused considerable annoyance in the Ashfield Labour party, in what was a strong Labour seat, as party members did not want to be transferred from Labour Nottinghamshire into what they saw as Tory Derbyshire. In what in later years was to prove ironic to me, the Ashfield Council, under pressure from Labour activists, challenged the boundary change; although fortunately for me as events turned out, it lost.

The eight parliamentary seats that made up the Derbyshire European Constituency had little in common; they were not even all in Derbyshire. Derby itself had two at the time fairly marginal seats; one held for Labour by Margaret Beckett, the other narrowly lost by Philip Whitehead in 1983. The leafy county seat of West Derbyshire, although notionally marginal after Patrick McLoughlin narrowly won a by-election for the Conservatives ahead of the Liberals in 1986, was in reality a rock-solid Tory seat. High Peak became marginal in good times for Labour, but was mostly Conservative. Bolsover was of course at the time solidly Labour although its MP, Dennis Skinner, made it absolutely clear that he would not lift a finger to help the Labour European campaign. In 1979 each parliamentary constituency party had nominated a different candidate and it was widely expected that the same would happen again. Philip Whitehead, a popular and pro-European former MP, would have been the front runner and likely winner if he had not wanted to try to win back his parliamentary constituency in Derby North. Later he did become a Euro-MP. In his absence the local party hierarchy in Derby supported a candidate from the North-East who seemed to have no obvious local connections.

As I had hoped I was nominated by my local party in Erewash and then to my surprise by West Derbyshire. I was largely unknown to most of the Derbyshire Labour party, which proved to be a considerable advantage. Probably for the last time in Labour parliamentary selections, the decision on which candidate to choose was actually taken immediately after the speeches and questions to each of the candidates. The meeting took place one Saturday afternoon at the Derbyshire Council Offices in Matlock.

My expectations as to the likely result could be seen by the fact that I had arranged to collect my American cousin that same evening from Heathrow, at least a hundred and fifty miles away. Against the odds I won, probably because I was local and probably because I was clear that Labour's policy of withdrawal from Europe had been a cause of the electoral disaster of 1983. Labour was seen by the electorate as being out of touch with practical reality; I said that we had to make the best of it and work within the system. By the time that I had made it back home from Matlock, Elaine had already been told the result in a phone call from Radio Derby. To say that she was annoyed would be a considerable understatement. She had married a university lecturer who had given up one secure job for an unknown future at the Bar. He had then got on with that job thanks to her financial support as a teacher, only then to want to give that up for the uncertainties of politics. When later the Head of Chambers tried to throw me out she seemed to have all of her worst fears realised.

I mollified her by pointing out that Derbyshire was a Conservative seat; and that unless there was a significant change it would remain that way. The sitting MEP, Tom Spencer, was well to the left of the Tory Party. From my perspective, he seemed to have much going for him – married with four children, he lived in a lovely house in the constituency, and as a sitting MEP was well versed in all of the current European issues. I did not expect to beat him.

Yet the Labour Party was changing under Neil Kinnock. He needed Labour to do well in the 1984 European elections to show that he was successfully turning the Party around, and was capable of taking on the Tories at the next General Election. New campaigning ideas were being tried out – including a battle bus, which arrived in the Derby suburb of Allenton early one Saturday morning. I knew exactly where to meet up with it because my grandmother had lived in a council house very close by for all of her married life. The Agent for the Labour Party in Derby, John Beadle, had seen many candidates and many campaigns. Without any explanation he gave me a microphone and told me to go and talk to the local shoppers from the platform at the top of the bus. There may well be people to this day who tell their children about running for cover into the local Co-op because a madman was yelling at them from the back of a double decker bus about the iniquities of the Common Agricultural Policy.

The campaign in Derbyshire and Ashfield was particularly difficult for the Labour Party because it took place against the backcloth of the bitter 1984 miners' strike which divided communities on either side of the Nottinghamshire/Derbyshire border. On one side in Ashfield there were working miners who at the time were members of the Labour Party and members of the breakaway UDM, and who (initially, at any rate) continued to attend Labour meetings. The Ashfield MP, Frank Haynes, himself a former miner, was only able to hold his party and constituency together by making clear that he was elected to represent the whole of his constituency, irrespective of their union membership. I hugely admired his courage and resilience in the face of some seriously unpleasant, aggressive and threatening behaviour.

Just across the county border in Bolsover, Dennis Skinner kept to his word by doing absolutely nothing to help the Labour European campaign. He said that Labour should be doing all that it could to support the striking miners; a policy that would have cost Labour the Ashfield parliamentary seat and would certainly have ensured that the European election would go the same way. Dennis Skinner appeared to be entirely happy about that – publicly condemning me at a meeting in Derby as some pro-European barrister. He was entirely accurate, of course; but he left me and his audience in no doubt that he was entirely content for me not to win.

Because the Derbyshire and Ashfield constituency was right in the middle of the miners' strike, it attracted a fair amount of media interest. I did my first TV interviews; one by the then Central Television presenter Anna Soubry. She was later to join my former chambers in Nottingham as a barrister, and still later become an MP and then a minister in the MOD. Another interviewer, from the BBC, could see that I was slightly nervous about the prospect of a TV interview,

'Don't worry,' he said, 'I will only be asking you about the European elections, about voter apathy and probably the Common Agricultural Policy.' He duly did ask all of those questions and then, in exactly the same friendly tone of voice said,

'And what exactly do you think of the miners' strike?' That of course was the only part of the interview that was used as I waffled away, desperate to avoid saying anything that could offend either side.

Despite all of my best efforts, therefore, with the tailwind provided by Neil Kinnock's reforms I was elected – but not by much. My majority spread across eight parliamentary constituencies was 6,400; averaging out as a single constituency majority of well under 1,000; by any measure a marginal seat. Again, Elaine was not best pleased. To her considerable credit she put up with it, as she has always done in the face of events in her married life that were not entirely of her choosing.

My career as a Euro-MP could not have got off to a worse start. I had had three weeks away from the Bar during the campaign, and therefore for three weeks I had earned nothing. On the Monday after the result I had booked myself back into court, in a trial that I was conducting for the prosecution. On the Tuesday after the result I discovered that I was supposed to attend a meeting of the newly elected Labour Euro-MPs.

I sent a message to this effect to the Judge conducting the trial. He was clearly not impressed by my request, but kindly obliged by throwing out the prosecution case. I began to see the difficulty of trying to do both jobs. Later that same week I failed to attend a meeting of the European Socialist Group in Florence; again because I was due in court, but also because I had looked up the airfare. It seemed so enormous that I couldn't possibly justify an outlay of that kind. I had at that stage not learned about the very generous nature of European parliamentary travel expenses.

Politically I was already also in trouble. At that first meeting of the newly elected Labour Euro-MPs, having consulted Derek Enright, by then deselected and out of the European Parliament, I voted for every unsuccessful pro-European candidate for positions in the European Labour Group. I was and remain delighted that I did – but in truth the thirty-two Labour Euro-MPs, despite Neil Kinnock's reforming tendency, had all been selected in the wake of Labour's policy of withdrawal from the EU. The overwhelming majority were at the time strongly anti-European. They included the left-winger Les Huckfield, only there because in the run up to the 1983 General Election he had been beaten in the Sedgefield selection by Tony Blair. Another, Richard Balfe, actually visited Derby during the campaign, ostensibly to campaign against the iniquities of the Common Agricultural Policy – but in reality to check on the candidate's political tendencies. As an anti-European left-winger, he didn't like what he found, with the result that I was not invited to various caucus meetings arranged by the left to ensure that they won the votes at that first meeting. He was quite right not to invite me, although it has always entertained me to have followed his career since then – initially on the left of the Labour Party, through the Liberals, to where he sits now as a Conservative member of the House of Lords. I suppose I would say that my views have not changed much over that time; he could perhaps say the same – he remains opposed to the EU in an anti-European party.

It took me quite some time to get used to politics in practice; as opposed to reading and thinking about it. I really did not like what it involved for a very long time. I was probably the only Labour Euro-MP with no previous practical political experience. Most of the Labour Euro-MPs had been councillors, mostly from the big cities where they had fought their battles against the Labour Party's establishment.

There were some exceptions; most notably Barbara Castle, a great figure from the Labour Governments of the 1960s and 70s, who in 1979 gave up her Blackburn parliamentary seat in favour of her then young researcher, Jack Straw, for a new career in the European Parliament. Over time I grew to like as well as admire her political skills and abilities. She came to stay with us on a number of occasions. The first time, knowing that she was not an early riser, our then two very small children were given strict instructions about staying well away from the important guest's bedroom. That morning they seemed to have disappeared entirely, only to be discovered in bed with Barbara as she read them a story. She once said to me that her greatest regret in life had nothing whatsoever to do with politics – it was that the Second World War had got in the way of her having a family of her own.

The newly elected Labour Euro-MPs were overwhelmingly anti-European, with initially only around nine or ten out of the group of thirty-two actually believing in the idea of the European Union. Certainly to begin with, the Antis ran the Labour show. They held all of the positions in the Labour Group and tried to use their positions and views to influence the wider Socialist Group in the European Parliament, of which we were all part. They were inevitably unsuccessful as, with the exception of a handful of nationalists on the far right, every other Euro-MP believed in the value of the European project. Even the reformed Euro-Communists from Italy were more accepting of the European Parliament than most of my Labour colleagues.

I write 'colleagues' but in truth I had very little in common with most of them. It was partly about politics, but as much as anything it was about our ages. I was thirty and apart from Carole Tongue and David Martin, who were around the same age, I found that I had little in common with most of them. I thought for many months that I had taken a completely wrong turn; that my idealism about politics had been misplaced, and that I would have been doing more to help people as a barrister than as a Euro-MP. What in a sense saved me and rekindled my nascent political career was getting to know many of the talented and able people who actually made the European Parliament work as European civil servants. They were much more my age and they believed passionately in what they were doing.

The European Parliament had its own civil servants, as did each of the political groups, as well as the large number of interpreters needed to keep the European show on the road. By then most lived in Brussels, although a few with families still travelled from Luxembourg where previously the Parliamentary staff had been based. I was hugely impressed by their talents, politically and linguistically; it was almost as if a new breed of people was evolving with children in the European School required to take lessons in several different languages. I was one of the first Labour Euro-MPs to employ an assistant in Brussels; Marie-Francoise Wilkinson was French and married to a British civil servant in the European Commission. At dinner at their home, their multilingual children would start a sentence in one language and finish it in another, without apparently noticing the switch.

Britain has never bought into this shared idealism about Europe. Winning the Second World War saved us from the catastrophes experienced on the continent in its immediate aftermath. The Common Agricultural Policy is less of a political issue nowadays, as the wine lakes have been drained and the butter mountains melted. Yet encouraging surplus agricultural production in countries with a relatively recent memory of people starving at the end of the war is in that context perfectly understandable. Nor have we understood the motivation to create institutions to prevent a third European war. I visited the Bochum district of German Euro-MP Dieter Rogalla, who campaigned to remove internal European borders. He described to me his experience of being forcibly recruited in his teens into the Hitler Youth and then as the war was ending walking with his parents and family from the east of Germany to freedom in the west.

Fortunately, winning the war meant that Britain was spared such catastrophes, but too many as a result have missed the bigger European picture. My Dad was hardly a political philosopher, but he commented on a visit to the European Parliament that it was better doing what I was doing than what he and his generation had had to do. It is perhaps no coincidence that the British political generation who had had actual experience of war were the ones who were most enthusiastic about Europe and about building its political institutions; the likes of Ted Heath and Denis Healey saw the war in Europe at first hand, and were determined that it should never happen again. There were far too many people who had had no direct experience of the Second World War but who nevertheless voted to leave the EU in the 2016 Referendum on the basis that we didn't need Europe 'because we won the war'.

Not long after the European election, Neil Kinnock made a visit to Derby, aimed I am sure at helping Philip Whitehead in his efforts to win back the Derby North seat. A rally had been planned at the Assembly Rooms in Derby – a medium sized concert hall – which was to be filled with local party members eager to hear Neil speak. Philip was to do the warm up, but at the last minute I was also invited to speak. I wrote out a couple of sentences thanking everyone for their support and delivered them ahead of Neil speaking. As I finished and went back to my seat, Neil who was sitting alongside me said 'Is that it?' He then made a great speech without a single note, rousing the audience in a way that only he could. I knew that a press release had been issued in which it had been announced what he was due to say. Sitting near him as he tried to get his speech near to the words in the press release was like watching a pilot trying to land a plane on an aircraft carrier. Every time he seemed to be getting near the ship kept moving away. He did eventually say something along the lines of what he was supposed to and seemed to have completed his speech to great cheers from the audience. He then continued with another great speech, probably in celebration of the first one, and even after that a third speech, by which time the audience seemed emotionally exhausted. They were probably physically exhausted as well as it was by then getting late. I later reflected on my underwhelming efforts to deliver what had been a few scripted lines compared to his mastery of the dying art of speech making. He had delivered three great speeches. I had delivered three sentences. Sadly, the modern political world demands sentences not speeches, and at times not even whole sentences.

Keep your Comrade Warm

I almost missed one of the most significant political experiences of my life. Following the European elections of 1989, the new Chair of the European Parliament's Legal Committee was Franz-Ludwig von Stauffenberg, the third son of the July 1944 bomb plotter who had attempted to assassinate Adolf Hitler. Claus von Stauffenberg had been shot by firing squad in Berlin, and the new committee chair decided that he wanted to hold a meeting there to allow his colleagues to visit the site of his father's execution.

I had been to Berlin only a few weeks before, crossing into East Berlin for a day, keen to look around and to see whether the rumours of unrest and possible political change were true. I went in and out through Checkpoint Charlie but saw no signs of any of the rumoured demonstrations or any signs of dissent. What I did see, although I didn't know it at the time, were the final days of communist East Germany. On the way in it was necessary to purchase East German marks, at a nominal exchange rate of one to one with the West German equivalent. It was very soon apparent however that there was almost nothing to buy. Lunch cost a few marks. The bar on Unter den Linden, a lovely pre-war boulevard in the centre of the city, had run out of beer, and the shops, such as they were, had a limited supply of daily essentials. There was certainly nothing for tourists to purchase. At the end of the day the main beneficiary of the system was the taxi driver who drove me back to Checkpoint Charlie before the crossing gate closed for the night. He got more than half of the money that I had changed at the start of the day, since the East German notes were worthless in the West.

When only a few weeks later I was supposed to go yet again to Berlin, I was not that enthusiastic – not least because the usual two day Legal

Affairs Committee meeting had been extended to three, and back in Breaston, Elaine was having a hard time with two small children, and a third was on the way. I decided to skip the diplomatic extras and go for just the working parts of the meeting. I therefore arrived in Berlin at the old Reichstag building, where the meeting was taking place, on a Thursday evening just as the other members were heading off to a drinks reception. I could easily have gone with them but at that time the Reichstag stood almost alone in what was then the no man's land of Berlin on either side of the wall. The East German authorities had cleared their side of the wall to provide a shooting gallery for their border guards in case anyone tried to escape. In a curious mirror image the western side was similarly empty, with the main focus of West Berlin still centred around the Kurfurstendamm, or K-damm as it was generally called; well away from the wall. From the meeting rooms in the Reichstag it was possible to look out of the windows across the wall into East Berlin, watching their imposing border guards on patrol.

So instead of diplomatic drinks I decided to walk along the western side of the wall from the Reichstag to Checkpoint Charlie, thinking that perhaps I would try and cross to the East again. Unfortunately, I had set off for Berlin in a bit of a rush, and did not have my British passport to hand. MEPs travelled in the EU on a specially issued *laissez-passez* which provided a limited degree of diplomatic protection. When I presented this document to the very tall, very stern East German border guard he was clearly not impressed. My presence obviously caused him considerable problems, so I was kept hanging around for almost an hour as he sought superior clarification. The message eventually came back that I was not to be allowed in. Although no-one said so, this was because at the time East Germany did not recognise the European Union. Ten months later that same border guard was an EU citizen; at around 8.30 pm on Thursday 9 November 1989, I was perhaps the last person in history to be refused admission to East Germany.

What neither the border guard nor I knew, was that the Central Committee of the GDR had bowed to the pressure of East German citizens leaving their country through Czechoslovakia by agreeing to open the Berlin exit points. As this became more widely known, crowds began to gather on the East Berlin side. The barriers were lifted at around

11.30 pm and thousands of young East Germans streamed across to the West; for most of them this would have been for the first time. Less well reported was the smaller number of rather older West Berliners who went to Checkpoint Charlie, partly to see what was happening but partly as well, I was told, in the hope that they might once again see family members trapped in East Germany for a generation by the wall.

It was a lively night all along the K–damm. The young East Berliners had no money, but West Berliners bought them drinks and allowed them to sleep on the streets and in doorways. Whilst this was a remarkable celebration of political freedom, what most seemed to interest the young East Berliners in my experience were the shop windows of the smart shopping district of West Berlin's K–damm. They walked along from shop to shop, apparently oblivious to historic political change, simply revelling in looking at the choice and diversity of western consumer goods.

The meeting of the European Parliament's Legal Committee resumed in the Reichstag on the Friday morning. We were supposed to be continuing with our agenda dealing with various legal issues affecting the European Union. Yet we were all well aware that something hugely significant was taking place only a few yards away. By then young Berliners from both sides were climbing on the wall. The East German border guards were still there and still apparently on patrol, but presumably by then under orders not to shoot.

Back in Britain I wrote an article about my experiences for the *Derby Evening Telegraph*. The editor was pleased to have a local angle on an international story but wanted a political conclusion to my account – 'What does it mean?' he asked. That weekend I was not at all sure – neither was any other politician or commentator. I said that I thought that it meant that Germany would one day again be united. 'When?', the editor asked. I thought that I was taking a risk by saying 'In ten years', because no-one at the time really believed that it could happen. Ten months later, Germany was a united country within the European Union.

In the weeks and months that followed I was a regular visitor to Berlin as the committees and political groups of the European Parliament sought to join in the celebrations surrounding the collapse of communism. I was pictured with a large lump hammer, securing my own small part of the wall as it was demolished. Years later those bits of brick and concrete are still in a box somewhere under the stairs at home. Elaine once suggested that we might mount them in some way for posterity. I was not so sure. Will our children or future generations really understand why an entire country and its families were divided down the middle by ideology and that it took almost fifty years to restore national normality?

CHINA
The Farther One Travels

In addition to its various committees and political groups, the European Parliament is also organised into delegations dealing with relations with different parts of the world. After my election I put my name down for the China Delegation and, following the way in which jobs are distributed between the political groups and nationalities, according to a complex Belgian formula, I found myself in the chair.

It was not the most demanding or high-profile role – but it did mean that I went to China in May 1985, right at the start of the economic reform process. Given the incredible transformation of China since then, it is difficult to describe exactly what Beijing was like at the time. Almost the only cars on the streets were the black Russian-built Zils, indicating that the passengers were high ranking Chinese officials. Everyone else was on bikes, all fitted with the same Chinese-made bells, which were rung by the riders continually. There was only one hotel, which was not thought good enough for distinguished foreign visitors, so we stayed in a government 'Guesthouse' in the grounds of the Summer Palace. It was obviously owned and operated by the state and we were warned to be careful what we said in our rooms. There was only one shop that we could go to; the Friendship Store, close to the British Embassy, where it was possible to buy Chinese souvenirs at what were no doubt hugely inflated prices.

The only sign of the massive economic change that was about to begin was in the form of large barrows containing a variety of agricultural products on the streets of Beijing. The first state reform had been to allow farmers to sell their surplus agricultural production privately. Previously all production had to be sold to the state at state regulated prices. This limited the amount the farmers produced as there was simply no incentive for them to work harder and produce more. That all changed when the surplus could be sold at market prices out on the streets.

Many other aspects of that visit were memorable. We were taken to the Forbidden City which, apart from the members of the European Delegation and their guides, was completely deserted. We were amongst the first westerners to be taken to a newly opened section of the Great Wall of China, close to Beijing. The early signs of mass tourism were already there as I was able to buy a T-shirt with an image of the Great Wall and something written in Chinese. I did wonder whether it said something like 'This western idiot just paid a silly price for this cheap T-shirt'.

We also walked across Tiananmen Square several years before it was filled with the protesters of the 1989 Democracy Movement and the tanks and troops of the Communist government. We were on our way to the Great Hall of the People where every year for a short period the meetings of the National People's Congress took place. Our meetings with some of its members also took place there. We certainly discussed democracy which seemed to be on the Chinese agenda – at least at the local level. We were assured that locally people had a free choice of candidates and that the government was looking to develop and extend this process. I assume given Chinese timescales that they still are.

Local democracy clearly did not apply on our visit to Urumqi, the capital of Xinjiang province in the far west of China. We were flown there on a Chinese Air Force jet, a journey of almost four hours. Without any time change the sun did not set until midnight, and we got up in the pitch dark. Nevertheless, it was an impressive visit and we were shown some remarkable sights; the Himalayas from the Chinese side, the Alpine Heavenly Lake and the nearby desert.

There are estimated to be more than 11 million Uyghurs in China, mostly in Xinjiang. The Uyghur population are Muslim and Turkish-speaking and historically many were nomadic, following the herds in a regular Summer/Winter journey which took them towards the border with modern Turkey. We were told that many still spent the summer months in the hills and I was given yak's milk to drink in a wonderfully decorated yurt. The Chinese showed us the ugly concrete blocks that they had built to house the nomads in the winter. The culture clash was all too obvious. There were displays of horse riding and claims that polo evolved from the local sport which involved riders wrestling for control of the carcass of a sheep which was inevitably torn apart in the process. We were entertained at a feast where an entire sheep had been slowly roasted. I spent the first part of the meal worrying that as leader of the delegation I would be expected to eat the eyes, which were still firmly in place. Instead the Chinese tried hard to get us all drunk on Moatai, the sorghum spirit which was then still being served on state occasions.

The entire experience was colonial. The Han Chinese officials from Beijing required interpreters to be able to communicate with local Uyghurs. They seemed much put out when a Conservative Euro-MP, Bob Battersby, was able to talk directly to the locals in Turkish. That kind of contact was clearly not part of the Chinese plan and his conversation was brought abruptly to an end. The Han Chinese were obviously in control; but they were in control of a population with which they had absolutely nothing in common; language, religion, food or way of life. At least then, compared to more recent times, the Chinese appeared to tolerate these differences. Given what I saw then, however, it is not at all surprising that the Chinese seem now to be attempting what is probably the largest re-education programme in history – and perhaps an attempt to eliminate an entire culture and way of life.

UNITED STATES
Across the Atlantic

I had enjoyed chairing the meetings of the China delegation – and even more so the chance to see something of what was still a strange and foreign country as it began to implement the economic reforms that would turn it into the manufacturing and economic powerhouse that it has become. Although it was a great way to see new parts of the world, many of the delegation visits could be criticised as being little more than an exercise in political tourism. In truth all parliaments and assemblies engage in these exchanges, and if for no other reason it does promote better understanding.

There was, however, one European Parliament delegation which had a reputation for getting real things done. The European Parliament's meetings with their counterparts from the US Congress had discussed sensitive trade questions and had helped unlock some complex visa issues. It was at the time a much more demanding job as the delegation met twice a year, once in Europe and once in the United States. The Chair was also expected to host any visiting American dignitaries.

When it became clear that, following the European elections of 1989, the chair of the US Delegation would most likely be a British Labour member, there was keen competition for the job. With my US background, family, working there and travelling all over America, I was an obvious candidate. I was, however, still seen as a pro-European in a group which even after the June 1989 European elections continued to be dominated by anti-Europeans. Their candidate was the hard left Michael Hindley, the Euro-MP for Lancashire East, who had once asked me why I was taking an interest in Solidarity in Poland when it was protesting against what he described as the legitimate Communist government. However, the Labour Group of Euro-MPs was changing. Some of those who had initially wanted to be seen as on the hard left were softening their views – and as a result I won the election for the job by one vote.

The Americans pulled out a lot of stops for our visits. On our first exchange this very nearly caused domestic disaster as we had decided to combine a visit to Washington with a trip to see family in New Jersey. Although we left Nathalie, our youngest, with her Grandmother, we travelled with two small children who had to be looked after whilst their parents attended a very elaborate State Department dinner at which I was due to speak. We stayed at the Willard Hotel in the centre of Washington D.C. and in the hour or so before the dinner, the children had to be settled and I had to finish preparing my speech. This involved an exceptionally competent nanny provided by the hotel and a brilliant English secretary who helped me transform a speech written originally in German into something that I could understand and hope to deliver to a sophisticated American audience. It was a close-run thing, as the children were obviously unhappy about being abandoned with someone other than their parents or Grandmother, and the speech took a long time to translate from German English into American English.

In addition to Tom Lantos, a senior Congressman from California who chaired the US side, Dick Gephardt had also been invited to speak. He was a powerful Washington player – the House Majority Leader and very soon to be a candidate for the Democratic nomination for President. He was everything that I expected a successful US politician to be – able, articulate and impeccably turned out. As I listened to his beautifully crafted but largely empty speech, I kept thinking of the Robert Redford film *The Candidate*. Disappointingly, he disappeared after his speech and I exchanged only a few words with him.

The next year there was a similar dinner at the State Department when another powerful Congressional figure was invited. Dick Cheney, soon to be US Defence Secretary, was at the time Chair of the House Republican Conference. He gave an entertaining and witty speech, staying on afterwards to talk at length about US/European relations. I did wonder whether in later years he made the connection between the young British MEP that he was sat next to and his later incarnation as British Defence Secretary.

Traditionally, after the Washington meetings the delegations would visit the congressional district of one of the members of Congress. In return we entertained both delegations in Derbyshire during the Americans visit to Europe. Wherever we went, either in the US or Europe, we were always given the very best of what was on offer. I took some serious domestic flak when in Los Angeles we were taken to see Michael Crawford in *Phantom of the Opera*. This was another occasion when the multi-national background of the European Parliament civil servants proved to be a problem. We were taken around Paramount Studios followed by a barbecue reception in the studio lot. I had to respond to a welcoming speech by Tom Bradley, then the Mayor of Los Angeles. I was given a long and serious speech to deliver on the role and functions of the European Parliament. We were in California in bright sunshine surrounded by dismantled film sets, eating burgers and drinking beer. I gave up on the prepared speech and told a few jokes. The European civil servant who had probably worked long and hard on what in a different context might have been an excellent speech was quite put out. On another occasion we were entertained in New Hampshire by one of my favourite singers, Tom Rush. All of these events were paid for by sponsorship from US companies. It showed the very close connection between US politics and US business, irrespective of party affiliation.

THE CANDIDATE FOR ASHFIELD
Run for your life

It was typical of the generosity of the Ashfield Labour Party that it was made clear that right from my election as their Euro-MP in 1984, I was welcome to attend any of their meetings. Given constant travelling and seven other parliamentary constituencies to visit, I probably managed to attend three or four times a year and was always very well received. One particular Friday in September 1989 I had got back home from the continent reasonably early and set off up the M1 past the two motorway junctions to where the Ashfield party meeting was held.

As far as I was concerned it seemed a perfectly ordinary meeting – as ever dominated by Frank Haynes' parliamentary report when he both entertained and informed party members about what was happening at Westminster. At the end of his speech however, without any warning and without any particular change in tone, Frank suddenly announced that he would stand down as the MP for Ashfield at the next election; an election not actually expected for several years.

At the end of the meeting, as people stood around in groups discussing Frank's bombshell, several members asked if I would be interested in standing. I had not long been re-elected to the European Parliament, and although it would be dishonest to suggest that it hadn't crossed my mind, I was not entirely sure that I wanted to make the switch at that stage. I knew that Elaine would worry about my workload, not least because by then our third child was well on the way.

It was, of course, too good an opportunity to pass up. Even if I wasn't selected I decided yet again that it would be more good experience for the future. Apparently around 140 people put their names forward to be Ashfield's next MP. Some were local including a number of very good councillors, as well as large numbers of outsiders, including former MPs and former ministers. Although the Labour majority in Ashfield in 1987 was down to just over 4,000, that result had been significantly affected by the miners' strike. There was no doubt that it was seen by everyone as a traditionally safe Labour seat.

There were by then new Labour Party rules for selections, which allowed every party member to vote. Today's arrangements involve extensive canvassing and significant expenditure by the candidates with the production of glossy campaigning materials making it much harder for ordinary party members to stand without backing from a Trade Union, or out of their own pockets. While superficially more democratic, the modern process massively favours those who are already involved in politics in some way, either as political advisors or full-time trade union officials. Only those people typically have the means and can afford the time off which winning a nomination nowadays requires. Potential candidates are entitled to receive a full list of members in a constituency and will try to meet as many of them as possible, often by visiting them at home. This represents a huge time commitment given that some constituencies might have more than a thousand members.

In stark contrast to the current arrangements, I did not ask a single Labour Party member to vote for me outside of the ward hustings meetings which were arranged to consider the various candidates. I had an obvious advantage in already representing the constituency in the European Parliament, which meant that my name was already familiar to most members. Local councillors had a similar advantage in their own area, but local rivalries and jealousies meant that councillors from one town or village would not get support from somewhere else in the constituency. One of the very best local councillors was David Ayres, the Leader of Ashfield District Council, who struggled to get support outside of his own ward. Oxford educated and politically very astute, he would have made an excellent MP. It was without any trace of bitterness that he subsequently became one of my strongest supporters. The District Council and the local Labour Party were never as effective after his tragically early death from cancer.

At the same time I was not a complete outsider and could not therefore be accused of carpetbagging. I was invited to speak at all but one of the nine wards; one potential candidate ensured that I was not invited to her ward.

One possible weakness was that I knew that I was not going to live in Ashfield. Elaine had steadfastly supported my political career but I was never going to ask her to move with two, soon to be three, small children to a completely new place far from her widowed mother, just so that I could be away doing a job in London. Set out like that it makes no sense; but I knew that I was bound to be asked the question 'Will you move into the constituency?' I knew that some in a similar position had said that they would, without ever intending to do so. I knew that wouldn't work for me and would if I chose that course, be a continuing niggle in my relations with local party members. I decided to tell the truth and put the best gloss I could on the situation. I explained that in asking the question – always posed by men significantly – that they were really asking Elaine and the children to move to Ashfield, since if I was to do the job properly I would be in London for most of the week. As part of my answer I also undertook to open a full-time constituency office on a main street, so that constituents could simply drop in when they wanted. This seemed to satisfy most people, although at one meeting someone acting for another candidate attempted to shout me down on the question. The chair, a long-standing, well-respected female councillor calmed him down and concluded by saying that no-one should even think about making Elaine move to Ashfield away from her family. I cheered inwardly but loudly.

I ended up with eight ward nominations. It was well short of the numbers of nominations amassed by some of the other candidates; one local trade unionist had more than twenty. The big difference however was that I had been nominated by branches that had active members, with many of them actually attending the meetings. Most trade union branches were moribund without many actual members living in and therefore eligible to vote in Ashfield.

That was of course particularly true of the National Union of Mineworkers, which historically had by far the biggest say in who would be the MP for Ashfield. At the time of the miners' strike in 1984/5, most of their membership in Nottinghamshire had left for the breakaway Union of Democratic Mineworkers. Those that remained or subsequently joined the NUM had been politicised by the strike and had uncompromising views about the need for the Labour Party to back the union. Although the strike had been over for many years the residual bitterness still divided families and communities. As the first stage of the selection process was drawing to a close I received a surprising summons; to attend an executive committee meeting of the Nottinghamshire NUM. I dutifully turned up at their headquarters on a Saturday morning, and after a certain amount of beating around the political bush I learned the real reason for my invitation: I was being asked to stand down as a candidate in favour of Gordon Skinner, one of Dennis Skinner's brothers and an equally forthright campaigner for the striking miners. In truth it was hard to keep a straight face. Gordon Skinner was probably the one candidate who could guarantee that a safe Labour seat like Ashfield would be lost. There was simply no way in which the UDM families of Ashfield would vote for 'one of Scargill's men'. I politely explained that I had been nominated by most of the wards and that I could not simply pass on their support for me to Gordon Skinner and left. It was one of the more surreal political meetings that I have ever attended.

Despite my string of ward nominations, I nevertheless came close to blowing the whole process, and indeed had it not been for the new selection process I probably would have done. In addition to me, five people had been shortlisted for the seat – three local councillors, the local trade unionist with all the nominations, and Bryan Davies a former MP and close friend of the Leader of the Labour Party, Neil Kinnock. At some stage Frank Haynes had told me that he would be supporting me. I learned later that he had said the same to at least one of the local councillors. In the event he and his extensive network of family and friends all supported Bryan Davies, who Neil Kinnock was keen to see back in the House of Commons. The local political rumour mill had it that Frank had been promised a peerage if Bryan was selected and Labour won the subsequent General Election. Bryan was a formidable public speaker with much of the power and passion of his friend Neil Kinnock. His oratory was in marked contrast to my more measured speeches. To make matters worse for me, the final selection meeting took place soon after Nathalie, our third child, was born. We had three children under six, with two of them resisting all of our efforts to persuade them to sleep. At the final selection meeting I went carefully through an amended version of my standard selection speech. I am sure under the old rules, when the vote would have been taken at the end of the meeting by the people present, I would have lost. The new rules, however, allowed all party members to vote, whether or not they had actually attended a meeting. Many went to their ward meetings and cast their vote on what they had heard there. When the result was announced a week or so later I had won comfortably on the second ballot. The actual announcement was a bit of an anti-climax, as still fewer party members bothered to attend the formalities. I invited those that were there for a drink. One of them, Alan Simms, an indefatigable campaigner, music lover and friend to this day, described the selection meeting as being a bit like Brian Clough speaking against Sir Alf Ramsey. Despite my supporting Derby, he left me in no doubt that I was not the inspiring Brian Clough candidate.

I was, however, the Labour candidate in what most people thought of as a safe Labour parliamentary seat. As far as I was concerned the General Election could not come quickly enough.

Waiting for the Tides of Time

Almost everyone expected Labour to win the 1992 General Election. I spent the entire campaign in Ashfield, driving each day from our family home up two and three junctions of the M1. The mood was good. The Ashfield people seemed to have put behind them at least some of the bitterness of the miners' strike. They simply wanted to see a Labour government and the polls seemed to suggest that would happen, with Neil Kinnock as the next Prime Minister.

The only slight friction in Labour's campaign in Ashfield came in the final few days when Labour's Regional Office, based in Nottingham, asked for people to go to Sheffield to attend a massive rally where Neil Kinnock was to speak. Like most candidates, I was self-centredly only interested in my own result. I didn't want my campaigners sitting on a bus going to Sheffield when they could be knocking on doors in Ashfield. I couldn't actually see the point in taking out thousands of Labour activists to make up an audience for a few minutes of news coverage on the main news. At the same time, I have never accepted the argument that the rally was a significant turning point in the campaign and that somehow people were put off by Neil Kinnock's so-called TV triumphalism. For one thing the rally was only on the news for a few minutes; the idea that so many people made up their minds not to vote Labour on the strength of the coverage is hard to accept.

I had however already had at least one conversation that had sowed some doubt in my mind as to whether Labour was going to win. I knocked on the door of a council house in Sutton-in-Ashfield which was answered by an elderly lady, who was fairly obviously a pensioner. I asked her whether she would be voting Labour. She said very politely she thought probably not. I went into my routine about how Labour would provide a significant increase in the state pension which would undoubtedly make her better off. This was one of only two precise financial promises Labour was making in the election campaign. This was the era of Shadow Chancellor John Smith's tightly-costed tax policies. In previous elections Labour had made extravagant policy commitments with no real idea about where the money was coming from, making the party an easy target for the Tory propagandists warning of 'tax bombshells' to pay for its expensive promises.

It was obvious that this particular pensioner was not in any way well off. She lived in a council house on the state pension at a time when the Conservative Government was encouraging councils to raise rents to more like market levels, without any corresponding increase in pensions. I explained again how much better off she would be with a Labour Government. I have never forgotten her answer. 'Can the country afford it?' she said. An elderly lady struggling financially on the state pension was prepared to cast her vote on the basis of what was best for the country – and not what was best for her personally.

The parliamentary constituency of Ashfield was based around three towns; Sutton-in-Ashfield, Kirkby-in-Ashfield and Eastwood and as in many mining areas there were a number of small villages nearby which had also once had collieries. By 1992, most of the coal mines in the constituency had closed, but there were still significant numbers of miners living there used to transferring from one mine to another as coal-mining in the Midlands moved steadily to the east following the deep coal seam that goes out towards the North Sea. What was different about the closures of the 1980s and 90s is that they represented an end to mining, with ever fewer collieries available for transfers.

The other main industry was textiles, which employed mostly women making up a variety of clothing from underwear, tights and stockings to a range of woollens. At least one factory supplied its entire output to Marks and Spencer, but when it was hit by competition from retailers sourcing their clothing from overseas, M and S was in turn forced to look for cheaper supplies beyond Britain. Within a few years the only textile jobs in Ashfield were either highly specialised or were on the design side, both requiring significant training and skills, which the great majority of the local workforce simply did not have.

I received regular representations from the textiles' trade union which had been a significant political force locally. They wanted the government to intervene to save the industry. One day in the course of a meeting in my office, I asked them to tell me where the clothes they were wearing had been manufactured. Not a single one of the large delegation was wearing clothes made in the UK. That was the reason for the collapse in textiles; it had nothing to do with government, and everything to do with British consumers invariably buying what was the cheapest offer.

For my first two years in the House of Commons I was still an MEP, and whilst inevitably my main emphasis was on Parliament, I still travelled most weeks to the meetings of the European Parliament. This often involved a late three line whip in the House of Commons followed by an early morning flight to Brussels. I realised that I was not the only MP burning the candle at both ends when one morning as I was crossing Lambeth Bridge on the way to the airport I saw Peter Kilfoyle, the MP for Liverpool Walton and Fraser Kemp, then a senior official in the Labour Party. I was just on my way to work – it appeared that they were just on their way home, leaning on each other for mutual support.

Margaret Beckett, by then Deputy Leader of the Labour Party, came to my assistance by ensuring that I was a member of the Finance Bill Committee. I was in good company with Alan Milburn, John Hutton and Steve Byers on the backbenches on the Labour side of the committee. Alistair Darling, as a Shadow Treasury Minister, led for the Opposition from the front bench. Although it involved some very late nights, and on at least one occasion working right through the night, it was a concentrated lesson in how British legislation was made and in particular the complications of tax law, with Finance Bills running to hundreds of pages. Whenever I hear politicians claim that they will be closing tax loopholes saving billions of pounds, I think back to those sessions where complex and detailed legislation was required to deal with sometimes the most straightforward of tax changes. When we got onto the taxation of overseas earnings I was convinced that only the Minister, Stephen Dorrell and Alistair Darling had any idea what was actually being debated.

I also learned something about parliamentary presentation. Sir John Cope as Paymaster General was also a member of the committee. He would read out his brief without hesitation or interruption. He rarely needed to take interventions because his monotone delivery was such that his audience soon became incapable of thinking of a question. If he did take an intervention, he simply read the same material from his brief again.

As backbenchers we complained about the tedium, but later, as Chief Whip, I wanted ministers to get through government business with as little delay as possible. Sir John Cope was therefore the perfect minister. He got the legislative job done. In contrast, after May 1993 when Ken Clarke became Chancellor of the Exchequer and lead for the government on the floor of the House in economic debates, he would take every intervention, delighting in the debate and engaging in all the arguments. Whilst a brilliant parliamentary performer, he must have been the bane of the Chief Whip's life, wondering whether the government would ever get to the end of its business.

Ashfield in April 1992, when I was first elected to the House of Commons, was a very traditional white working class constituency. It had relatively full employment, with well-paid jobs for men in local collieries, whilst women worked in textiles. Both textiles and coal-mining jobs were about to disappear, severely damaging the structure of local society. In 1992 there were strong and well organised trade unions, the Labour Party had an active membership and people voted; the turnout in 1992 for example was over 80 per cent. My majority in 1997 was well over 22,000. By the time that I left Parliament, the turnout was down to 60 per cent with my successor holding the seat by just 192 votes. Ashfield was one of Labour's so called 'Red Wall' seats that fell to the Conservatives in the December 2019 election; largely as a result of disaffected Labour voters turning Tory.

These figures are probably typical of supposedly safe Labour seats across the country, but they are the consequence of fundamental and far-reaching changes in Britain's economy and society. In 1992, it was possible to leave school in Ashfield without any qualifications and still get a very well-paid job in coal-mining. The family income could be significantly boosted by a partner's earnings at one of the many textile companies. By the time that the last colliery in Ashfield closed in 2000, thousands of unskilled well-paid jobs had completely disappeared. Every time a coal mine closed, around 800 mining jobs were lost; never to be replaced. Although there were jobs advertised at the local Job Centres, they required skills and qualifications which far too many local men, in particular, just did not have.

Whilst no-one could ever categorise me as a Marxist, it is clear that those economic changes have had profound political effects and these are still working through our democracy. When people sometimes glibly talk about 'the working class' they are actually referring to at least two groups of quite separate workers. Unskilled manual labour previously formed a significant part of those employed in relatively well paid jobs in coal-mines, steel works and shipbuilding. Those jobs have all but disappeared, and with them large parts of the trade union movement. The National Union of Mineworkers was often described as the vanguard of the trade union movement. Its website today is mostly about memorials or commemorations.

In contrast the demand for skilled labour has increased, with wages in the high tech engineering sector rising to levels usually associated with more middle class professions such as teaching or social work. Those employed by Rolls-Royce or BAE Systems also live in the relatively affluent suburbs on the edge of towns and cities. Their skills are much in demand, with the result that their lives are far removed from those that struggle to find well-paid work because they lack the qualifications or experience required.

Historically it was assumed that both working class groups would vote Labour, although there has always been a sizeable working class Conservative vote. Increasingly, however, the unskilled have become disillusioned with politics with no trade union to guide them, with no work to go to, they have dropped out and stopped voting in ever larger numbers. When UKIP came on the political scene there was finally a party that claimed to represent both their views and interests – although no political party has the answer as to how the unskilled are to earn a living in an increasingly technological and sophisticated country.

More than anything, this explains why Labour's support has been steadily eroding in what were once thought of as being safe Labour seats. It was also a major factor in explaining the large turnout in the EU Referendum. People who had not voted in years found an issue that was theirs. They blamed globalisation for the loss of their jobs and the influx of lower paid European workers for hoovering up what unskilled jobs were still available.

I watched these economic and social changes in Ashfield over the eighteen years that I represented the constituency. When I was first elected, I was always invited to give out prizes at the annual Chrysanthemum and Dahlia Show. Not being much of a gardener, I had little idea of what to expect. I was amazed by the rooms full of flowers, timed and grown especially for the show, often by miners who after a shift underground liked nothing more than to work outdoors in their garden or allotment. The villages had their own fêtes and summer events. I would often see the same people that I met at Labour Party events. All would be heavily involved in the fabric of life of their local communities.

That slowly but steadily changed. The number of events reduced. They were kept going mainly by older people. Fewer and fewer people attended Labour Party meetings and events. Those that did were generally much less involved in their local towns and villages, other than perhaps as councillors. There was much more interest and competition for seats on the councils than any other aspect of politics. In 1992 Labour held every single council seat at every level in Ashfield. That perhaps not entirely healthy situation continued well after the election of a Labour government in 1997. Inevitably, Labour in power was forced into taking unpopular decisions. Council seats were lost as people used their local council votes to protest against the national government. The local councillors in turn blamed me and the government. An outsider would have concluded that most Labour councillors seemed to prefer a Tory government that they could attack and publicly complain about, rather than a Labour one that they would have to work to defend.

I went to every event in Ashfield that I could manage. I visited factories and schools. I helped local charities and fundraising. I might not have been born and brought up in Ashfield but I tried to make up for that by getting to know every part of the constituency in detail. At the same time I had always believed that the real job of an MP is at Westminster.

The Tide is Turning

There is no real job description for a newly-elected Member of Parliament. In one sense it is only that an MP must represent the constituency and its constituents. Most MPs are elected on a party ticket and are therefore expected to vote with the party whip at the end of most days' business. Some MPs, but by no means all, will be on Select Committees if they have some speciality or Bill committees as legislation is scrutinised in detail. In between, however, there are many hours for most MPs to fill. In my early days in the House of Commons I remember being advised to specialise in something but was given little indication of what that should be. As an Opposition backbencher I soon realised that it was entirely up to me to decide what I was going to do with myself in the House of Commons.

After the General Election in April 1992, it was clear that the issue of Europe and the Maastricht Treaty were going to dominate the early years of the new Parliament. A short European Communities Amendment Bill was introduced immediately after the election to give effect to the Treaty changes. John Major's government had a majority of 21, but given the number of euro-sceptics on the Tory back benches, the government's ability to win on European issues was continually under threat.

Although I made my maiden speech on the Second Reading of the Bill, I initially decided that as a still-sitting Euro-MP, I should try and stay away from the debates on the Maastricht Treaty. I didn't want to be typecast as someone who was always banging on about Europe. The committee stage of the bill to implement the Treaty was being taken on the floor of the House and was due to last many months with sittings often late into the night. Given what I had decided, I deliberately missed sitting in for the first few debates but, coming in one night to wait for an expected vote, I started listening to the speeches. The debates were dominated on both sides of the House by anti-Europeans and I had rarely heard such flights from reality. There were people who claimed to be experts on the subject who didn't appear to know the first thing about how the European Union worked. There was a real sense that 'Britain knew best', and that our constitution and democracy were somehow superior to anything developed elsewhere in Europe. Indeed people talked about 'Europe' as if it was somewhere else, somewhere foreign which did not include the United Kingdom. It reminded me of the probably apocryphal signal from a Victorian British naval commander:

'Fog in the Channel; Continent isolated.'

Provoked by speeches on both sides from the anti-Europeans, I began to participate in the debates, asking questions and trying to intervene on those talking the most nonsense. Jack Cunningham was the Shadow Foreign Secretary, and I began helping him prepare questions and work out the best line for Labour to take. On more than one occasion I found myself in the office of the new Labour leader, John Smith, as he was preparing for Prime Minister's questions, discussing the best way to cause divisions between the Conservative Government and some of their backbenchers. I was pleased to be there but it was obvious that John Smith did not need any help from me when it came to the art of asking questions. He was a natural and brilliant advocate, and all I could do was to suggest areas in which he might develop his arguments.

As a lapsed barrister and law lecturer I sensed that there was something legally flawed about the Maastricht Treaty. The legal implications obviously did not get as much attention as the politics. As an MEP I had been surprised when the Maastricht Summit, originally scheduled for three days of difficult negotiations, had ended in agreement on the second. The reason was that the other member states had surprisingly given John Major and the UK an opt-out on the Social Chapter; in an addition to the Treaty that extended qualified majority voting in certain limited areas of EU social policy. The combination of more qualified majority voting and the possibility of extending employment rights were too much for the Conservative government, and certainly for their euro-sceptic backbenchers. Yet to me it simply did not make sense legally. How could all of the other member states legislate to change a law which previously had applied right across the EU, but now would apply everywhere apart from the UK? Moreover what would be the legal effect of the decisions of the European Court of Justice when interpreting social chapter legislation? Would those decisions apply in the UK or not? How could you possibly have two different sets of laws in the EU applied by the same court?

However legally and academically interesting that might be, it was the politics that mattered. This was a great political opportunity for the Labour Party promoting the rights of those in employment, whilst at the same time highlighting the divisions in the governing party. The big question for Labour MPs at the time was working out how we could actually secure a vote on the Social Chapter.

I spent a great deal of time therefore working out ways to amend the Maastricht Bill to include the Social Chapter. For an ordinary Bill this would have been entirely straightforward; the necessary words could have been drafted and tabled as an amendment that could then have been voted on. The Maastricht Bill however gave effect to a Treaty previously agreed by all of the governments of the EU. It was not possible under parliamentary rules to amend the bill if that meant in practice having the effect of appearing to amend the treaty. Parliament acting alone could not change the terms of a treaty agreed by all EU member states. I became a regular visitor to the Public Bill Office behind the Chair in the House of Commons, where the clerks would politely but firmly reject my many early efforts as being contrary to the procedural rules.

Eventually, by a process of trial and error, and the benefit of expert guidance from the clerks, I did manage to find the right formula. In due course it became an official opposition amendment requiring an explicit vote by both Houses on a motion 'considering the question of adopting the Protocol on Social Policy' before the bill could become law. George Robertson, the Labour Shadow Europe Minister, described it as a 'ticking time bomb' under the government. This amendment became section 7 of the European (Communities) Act 1993, which in turn lead to a debate on the required motion. The Government's motion simply stated that the House should take note of their policy in relation to the Social Chapter. Labour's amendment to this sought to prevent ratification by the UK until the government had agreed to adopt the Social Chapter. This was deliberately designed to appeal not only to opposition MPs, but also to Tory euro-sceptic rebels who were fundamentally opposed to the Maastricht Treaty. The amendment was defeated but so was the government motion, which immediately gave rise to a confidence vote approving the policy of the government on the Social Chapter. Although the government was successful, it was generally thought that these debates and votes had knocked John Major's government off course. It exposed to public view the profound split in the Conservative Party on Europe. These divisions were to grow ever deeper over the years. It certainly meant that the government was extremely reluctant to legislate on any issue that would threaten its fragile parliamentary majority.

One personal consequence of all of this was that, together with George Robertson, I was nominated by *The Spectator* magazine as joint Parliamentarian of the Year for 1993. Having been in the House of Commons for only a few months, the presentation at the Savoy Hotel was for me a curious affair, since at that stage I knew very few of the journalists involved. The award was presented by former PM Jim Callaghan, who I didn't know but who I had always admired. George Robertson, on receiving his award first, spoke for so long that there barely time for me, the new boy, to say much other than 'thank you'. The award came with six bottles of malt whisky, one of which I presented to the House of Commons clerk who had given me the most help in drafting the amendment.

George Robertson's success in the Maastricht debates meant that for the first time, after many years of trying, he was elected to the Shadow Cabinet. He then generously passed on to me various positions that he was required to give up following his promotion. These roles helped me to develop a broader understanding of the different ways in which parliamentarians carry out their professional work. I became Vice Chair of the Westminster Foundation, a government-funded organisation set up after the collapse of the Soviet Union to promote democracy around the world. I was also Deputy Chair of Japan 2000, a small group of politicians and people from business established by Margaret Thatcher to promote political and economic ties between Japan and the UK. Additionally on a personal level, I was also able to indulge my passion for cinema and music by becoming Vice Chair of the British Film Institute and Chair of the all-party group

Friends of Music, which I had helped to set up thanks to friends from the music industry. I played regularly for the House of Commons football team, scoring a goal at Wembley and cricket for the parliamentary team, managing to hit a four at the Oval. In one match against the MCC played at Vincent Square I was required to bowl against a then current Pakistani test batsman. They are still looking for the ball that I bowled to him.

Golf was to provide one of the most embarrassing sporting moments of my life. I was asked to provide a team for a charity golf tournament at the Holinwell golf course in my Ashfield constituency. I had never played golf at the time, and rather than tear up one of Britain's best golf courses, I decided to be non-playing captain for a group of friends who did play. I walked the first couple of holes with the team and since it was a Friday, went off to carry out some constituency engagements. I was due back that evening to present the prizes. By that time it was dark and since the car park was full I parked my car on the grass near the clubhouse. I presented the prizes and thanked everyone for their efforts. Reversing my car in order to get out of the space, I felt the back end drop dramatically. I had parked on the practice green next to a bunker and had dropped well and truly in it. Despite my best efforts the car could not climb out. I had to go back into the clubhouse and sheepishly announce that I had put my car into a bunker. It cost me a round of drinks and a very red face to get a tractor to pull the car out.

This enjoyable and varied parliamentary life changed when a heart attack killed John Smith in May 1994. Jack Cunningham had tried to persuade him to promote me to the front bench but John Smith was old school. He had had to wait four years for his first promotion and believed that it was better to first get a good grounding in the House of Commons before speaking from the front bench.

By chance in July 1992 I had walked back from John Smith's coronation as Labour leader with Gordon Brown and Tony Blair. As a newly-elected backbencher I simply listened to their ideas about how they saw the modernising way ahead for Labour. I use 'they' because although there was a conversation between them there was no doubt at the time that it was Gordon Brown who was fizzing with new ideas and who seemed to be to be very much the senior partner in their relationship. I am sure that explains why when John Smith died, Gordon Brown was so angry about

Tony Blair's decision to stand for the Labour leadership. There could only be one 'modernising' candidate, and when it became clear that Tony Blair was going to get more support from Labour MPs, Gordon Brown stood aside with some considerable bad grace. This resentment and the 'deal' that the two men did over dinner at the Granita restaurant was to fatally damage the Labour government throughout its period in office, and arguably the Labour Party thereafter. As a moderniser, I believed at the time that by standing aside Gordon Brown deserved credit for not endangering the reforms that would soon put Labour into power. Some of my colleagues were much less charitable. They argued that if Gordon Brown had stood against Tony Blair he would have been comprehensively defeated and the later battles between them might have been avoided.

The election of Tony Blair as Leader started a period of rapid transformation in the policies and organisation of the Labour Party both inside and beyond Parliament. I was immediately affected as he promoted six of the 1992 intake into the Whips' Office, on the basis that we would learn about parliamentary procedure before becoming shadow ministers. At the time it seemed a brilliant idea; albeit one copied from the Conservatives who expect high flying ministers to first spend time in their Whips' office. In contrast Labour whips tended to stay put, with the inevitable result that they were generally older than most colleagues. The arrival of six of the modernising 1992 intake caused some tensions with the older guard of Labour whips, not least on the basis that we had been told that we were only passing through on the way to shadow portfolios.

I decided to keep my head down and learn what I could from my new colleagues. In addition to my departmental responsibilities as the Shadow Treasury Whip I was also the East Midlands Labour Whip, which proved a great deal more demanding. I was responsible for a number of very prominent left-wing Labour MPs including Dennis Skinner and Tony Benn. One of the younger whips, Gordon McMaster, who only a few years later was sadly to take his own life, routinely sent out a note to his Scottish group of MPs, explaining what he knew about the forthcoming business. This was in addition to the terse pink whip sheet that simply set out when MPs were required to vote. I copied the idea and received a very positive response from my group with even Tony Benn thanking me for my efforts. It may have been useful to all concerned but it did not seem to have any effect in preventing them from voting against the Labour whip.

As the shadow Treasury whip, I was part of Gordon Brown's team. At the time, despite the difficulties of the leadership election, I had no sense of the personal tensions between Tony Blair and Gordon Brown. Indeed, I was often in Gordon Brown's office in Millbank when Tony Blair would be on the other end of the telephone as the two of them worked their way through day-to-day issues. They had jointly created New Labour and even when the later infighting between their supporters was at its worst, I still had the impression that at a personal level they attempted to sort things out between themselves.

Although the modernisers were in control of the Labour Party at Westminster, there was plenty of resistance to New Labour policy changes elsewhere, including in the Ashfield Labour Party. My predecessor, Frank Haynes, himself a former miner, had managed to maintain an uncomfortable neutrality between UDM and NUM members of the Labour Party in Ashfield. However, by the early nineties most UDM members had drifted away, at least from any attendance at party meetings. In contrast, a new and younger generation of NUM members had been politicised by the strike and wanted the Labour Party to support their cause. Some of them came regularly to party meetings and although I managed to maintain friendly personal relations, it was obvious that we had very different views about the Labour Party's future political direction.

These differences came to a head over the local NUM's insistence that Arthur Scargill should be invited to speak at a meeting in Ashfield. This proved a popular idea amongst most Labour activists, although some did recognise the impact this could have on an Ashfield electorate that still remembered how the NUM leadership had organised massed flying pickets in the Nottinghamshire coalfields. One of those pickets had been Kevin Hughes, by 1992 the MP for Doncaster North and one of my closest friends in the House of Commons. Although elected as an NUM member, he recognised the mistakes made by the NUM and its leader. He suggested that instead of giving Arthur Scargill a personal platform from which to influence his audience, I should take him on in a debate so that both sides of the argument could be heard. That certainly made political sense, save for the fact that Arthur Scargill was a brilliant orator and I wasn't.

Nevertheless, the meeting was organised and Arthur Scargill came to

Ashfield and delivered a lively and provocative speech, winning over most of the large audience to his demands for the nationalisation of the top 1,000 companies. I responded with a predictably measured speech about the benefits of moderation and the mixed economy, as ever arguing against the domination of ideology. I am sure if there had been a vote at that point I would have lost by a landslide. We were then, however, invited to ask each other questions and I asked him whether he thought that Marks and Spencer should be nationalised. He said of course and without any prompting added many more well-known British companies to his list. I have rarely seen an audience so obviously change sides so quickly. They concluded that his ideas were mad and amazingly when the vote was taken I won comfortably.

At the end of my year in the Labour Whips' Office, I became a Shadow Minister in Margaret Beckett's Trade and Industry team, responsible for science and technology. I was not entirely comfortable in the role. I was never a natural opposition politician. I could always see the other side of the arguments that I was required to put forward. Moreover the rapid developments in the computer industry required a more detailed understanding of the subject than I could offer. I vividly remember arriving at a huge computer industry conference held at Olympia to set out Labour's policy. I had arrived by tube continuing to write and edit my speech on the way. Just as I got to Olympia, the Minister, Ian Taylor arrived in his ministerial car and later gave what seemed to me to be a superbly presented, well-argued and thorough speech, carefully prepared no doubt by a team of civil servants.

I spent a great deal of time in the role visiting companies that had invested in new computer technology, often in the process securing a photograph with the Labour candidate in the local paper of what was probably a marginal constituency. As a result I developed a collection of pictures of large metal boxes with lots of flashing lights. This continued right up to the 1997 General Election, as I had to combine campaigning in Ashfield with travelling the country as part of Labour's national campaign.

The only debate in 1997 centred on the likely size of Labour's majority in the forthcoming General Election. Although John Major was a thoroughly decent man who had survived a series of parliamentary rebellions to take his government through to the last possible election date of 1 May 1997, he appeared old fashioned and tired in comparison with Tony Blair, who clearly to many in the electorate represented a newer and more exciting future for the country. This feeling was palpable in the run up to election day as Tony Blair won votes from all parts of society, not only galvanising the Labour vote into turning out but at the same time attracting former Tory voters who believed in combining a strong economy with progressive policies of social justice. The resulting Labour landslide gave it a majority of 179, its largest ever, winning 418 seats out of 659, the largest number in its history and the highest proportion of seats achieved by any party since the Second World War.

THE MINISTER
Say the Word

The election in Ashfield could not have gone better. I had campaigned across the country but managed to get back to the constituency for the final few days. On the Wednesday evening there was a sense of excitement amongst Labour voters that I had never experienced before. They wanted the party to win and they wanted me to win. The Labour majority in Ashfield was 22,728, not quite the largest ever but only a few hundred votes short of the record.

Would-be ministers waiting by the telephone has become a modern cliché. But it does actually happen, and if you are likely to be a relatively junior minister it can be a long wait as the TV is full of news about Cabinet appointments and speculation about who is going where. When I eventually got the telephone call from Tony Blair on the Sunday after the 1997 election, I was in truth more than a little disappointed by what he told me. There had been rumours that I would be a minister in the education department as part of a Blairite team to deliver his 'education, education, education' election commitment. Instead he told me that he wanted me to go to the Lord Chancellor's Department to work with Derry Irvine as his junior minister. I was probably one of the few people in Labour politics who knew that the Lord Chancellor's Department administered the courts. It hardly seemed likely that the job would be at the cutting edge of the new politics. I felt that as a lawyer I had been typecast into a political backwater. I had never even met Derry Irvine, who at that time had very little political background or public profile. Although a Labour member of the House of Lords, he was still practising as a very successful barrister.

I learned later that the rumours had been right. I had been pencilled in to be the Minister for Higher Education, reflecting my previous university teaching career. At the last minute, however, a problem had arisen with the allocation of government ministerial jobs; Derry Irvine had categorically refused to work with Paul Boateng who had shadowed legal issues in opposition. Jonathan Powell, Tony Blair's Chief of Staff, had apparently resolved the situation by suggesting that Derry should ask for me which he duly did. It was probably just as well that I didn't go to education. New Labour policy changes there might have caused my marriage to a teacher to come under considerable strain.

Another disappointment for the true believing Blairites was the composition of Tony Blair's first government. He didn't really seem particularly interested in who got ministerial positions. In contrast Gordon Brown and John Prescott seemed to have lobbied hard for jobs for their closest supporters. Nick Brown, Gordon Brown's long time bag carrier and cheerleader was given the key job of Government Chief Whip. Tom Clarke became a Minister of State at Heritage alongside Richard Caborn, a strong supporter of John Prescott. Doug Henderson from the Brown team was in the Foreign Office, as was Gavin Strang at Transport. The general consensus amongst the Blairites was that Gordon Brown had a shadow government in waiting, with at least one of his people in every departmental team, ready to report back to the Chancellor of the Exchequer rather than the Prime Minister.

My perspective on the job in the Lord Chancellor's Department was not improved by my first meetings in the Department immediately after my appointment. It was a Bank Holiday Monday but I decided that I should go to London to meet Derry Irvine and try and find out what I was supposed to be doing. Although there had been the usual meetings between some very senior Labour figures and civil servants ahead of the election I was never involved. In truth I had hardly met a civil servant or been to a government department before. There was always a Foreign Office diplomat assigned to the European Parliament and although he was always around, he was very much in the territory of MEPs, meeting in the Bar or dining room. I had only a slight sense of the considerable civil service structure that lay behind government. Once or twice MEPs were given detailed briefings by the British Permanent Representative to the EU but this was always about detailed financial matters given the Parliament's role in the EU budgetary process.

When I arrived at the Lord Chancellor's Department, then mostly in a modern office building on Victoria Street opposite what was then called the Army and Navy store, I really had very little idea of what I would be doing. What ideas I did have turned out to be wrong; not helped by the kindly but out-of-date advice from my first private secretary. He had stayed on in the job for what was to be a short period to help the transition to the new government. His experience as a private secretary was based on the final years of John Major's administration when the Conservative government, unsure of its majority, introduced very little legislation. The private secretary told me therefore that the biggest challenge for me would be actually to get any real ministerial work to do. He suggested that the Lord Chancellor would be doing most things and that I would be very fortunate to get any policy scraps from his table.

My first meeting with Derry Irvine later that afternoon seemed initially to confirm that view. He was a formidable figure, intellectually powerful and obviously not lacking in self-confidence. At that first meeting he was also clearly very dubious about elected politicians, wondering out loud whether they could actually do a ministerial job. It wasn't exactly the most diplomatic of welcomes.

Nevertheless, having asked for me he was stuck with me. He noticeably mellowed when he learned that I had been at Jesus College, where for a time as a young barrister, he had been a law supervisor. It might also have been important that I proficiently opened the first bottle of his always excellent white burgundy. The opening of the wine became a regular feature at the end of our early evening meetings together. When my successor, Keith Vaz, arrived for his interview, Derry also expected him to open the wine. 'But I don't drink,' stammered the embarrassed Keith. 'You don't what?' replied the astonished Lord Chancellor. He had clearly failed to ask a crucial question before agreeing to his new deputy.

It soon became obvious that my private secretary's warnings based on his experience of the outgoing government were completely misplaced. Derry Irvine chaired five Cabinet committees and was a member of five more, all set up to thrash out the details of the new government's legislative agenda. These meetings took up the time that he might otherwise have spent in the department, meaning that I quickly became responsible for most of its day-to-day detail.

Derry Irvine also quickly made himself very unpopular with many of his new colleagues, who like me had probably had little to do with him previously and resented both that he hadn't been elected, and in particular what they took to be his negative attitude towards their pet projects. The entire government, from the Prime Minister down, was beginning to realise that talking about policy in opposition was much easier than developing practical proposals for radical change in government.

Although his Cabinet colleagues didn't always realise it, Derry Irvine was actually trying to help, although not in a way they recognised, understood or appreciated. Anyone like me who watched Perry Mason as a child on television will have grown up with the idea that lawyers win their cases by brilliant cross-examination of the other side's witnesses. That is very rarely true in practise. Lawyers win cases by cross examining their own side sometimes pretty harshly. In my days at the Bar, if I hadn't got my client at some stage in our interview to say 'whose side are you on then?' I probably hadn't been doing my job properly. Only by making sure that your own side was prepared for the questions they would inevitably face could you hope to win your case. Derry Irvine had a reputation at the Bar for his attention to every aspect of a case, working phenomenally hard to chase down every last detail. He brought these formidable qualities to bear as he looked at his new colleagues' plans for legislation, knowing that once they were published they would be torn into by the media and every affected interest group. Derry Irvine believed that by asking the tough questions early he was saving Cabinet colleagues from later problems. Too many of them however believed that he was making personal attacks on their competence. As a result, stories began to appear quite quickly accusing him of arrogance and indifference to the democratic process; those stories came of course from his own side, from his own colleagues. It was something I never got used to. Briefing against the Conservatives was one thing, but for too much of the time it appeared that ministers and MPs briefed against their own side.

Derry Irvine of course did not always help his own cause. It emerged that it had cost £650,000 to refurbish the Lord Chancellor's apartment inside the Grade 1-listed House of Lords, when not very long before Parliament had spent millions on the restoration of other parts of the same building. The media focussed on the cost of the Lord Chancellor's wallpaper. Derry Irvine was forced to appreciate that being a brilliant barrister was no preparation for dealing with the British media. By then we had all had experiences of how words could be taken out of context and twisted to make stories for the newspapers. It is probably one of the reasons why most ministers eventually end up sounding bland and uninteresting.

Derry was never bland and uninteresting as far as the journalists were concerned. In defending spending £59,000 on Pugin-style wallpaper for the flat at the £350 a roll price that the planners required, he told a Commons committee,

'You are not talking about something down at the DIY store that might collapse after a year or so.' The DIY industry was affronted, as were Labour voters who spent their hard earned wages at DIY stores. It was a gift to the sketch writers and cartoonists.

Worse was to follow when one day he came back from a lunch with Frances Gibb, *The Times'* legal correspondent. By chance I happened to be waiting in his office for his return from what had clearly been a very good lunch. He was positively beaming, believing that he would get a good story out of briefing a senior and well-respected journalist about his plans for legal reform. He was very keen to show that he had the political skills and abilities of his Cabinet colleagues and that moreover he could actually bring about political change.

He began to run through the various ideas he had highlighted, at one point saying that he had given Frances Gibb a draft copy of a speech in which he had compared himself in his reforming zeal to Thomas Wolsey. At which point he must have realised that my head was not only proverbially, but also physically, in my hands. The Press Office was alerted, as was Downing Street. But no amount of spinning could avoid the press that followed. The story made headlines everywhere. Worse were the cartoons, with Derry often portrayed in a red gown with a Cardinal's angular hat. For someone with such a formidable intellect, who was pushing through some of the most important changes in British legal and constitutional history, it was undoubtedly a difficult period. All politicians are used to debates about their ideas and policies. Indeed, most welcome the argument; but ridicule is much harder to bear, not least because unlike arguments which are quickly forgotten, cartoon images linger on in the public consciousness.

Derry Irvine was inevitably preoccupied with trying to recover from these PR disasters. Some civil servants took advantage by getting him to sign off on details of the practical implementation of the 1996 Family Law

Act which implemented a Law Commission report on reforming the law of divorce. It was generally the case that Law Commission proposals went through Parliament without much political debate. In the dying days of John Major's government, however, the Bill implementing the report had run into difficulties in the Commons. It was perceived to be making it easier to obtain a divorce, by removing the need to prove one of the four conditions previously required to prove that a marriage had irretrievably broken down. Most lawyers knew that these conditions were side-stepped by collusion between two parties who simply wanted to get away from each other. The proposed reform was to give effect to this practical reality of the divorce process.

There was however a strong sense amongst some Conservative backbenchers that the problem of too many failing marriages was caused by divorce being too easy. If not quite 'I divorce thee, I divorce thee, I divorce thee', it was nevertheless a process said to be entered into without much thought, with obvious negative consequences for any children. As a result Conservative backbenchers, led by the husband and wife team of Ann and Nicholas Winterton, tabled amendments requiring divorcing couples to attend what were described as 'Information Meetings' before they could secure a divorce. These meetings were to be organised by a trained professional and designed to check whether the couple were really serious about divorce and warning them of the adverse consequences; both financial and for any children. John Major had no reliable parliamentary majority towards the end of his government and was unable or unwilling to prevent these amendments from passing.

My first job as a Minister in the Lord Chancellor's Department was to work out how to set up the Information Meetings as required by the new law. It quickly became obvious that they would cost tens of millions of pounds at a time when the Legal Aid budget was under pressure and when the government was trying to stay within the previous government's strict financial guidelines. I was in any event profoundly unhappy about the very idea of such meetings. It had not been my personal experience that divorcing couples went through the process without thought. When my closest friend, Mark Smith, had divorced it was only after years of agonised personal debate as he tried to avoid the consequences of what he knew would have a massive impact on his daughter. I made my reservations clear to the civil servants responsible. The civil servants understandably argued back that they were only implementing the law. In a *Yes Minister* manoeuvre, they simply stopped sending me the relevant papers. At a considerable risk to his civil service career, my new private secretary, Jonathan Freeman, managed to keep me informed of what was going on.

He told me that the final sign off had gone to the Lord Chancellor and therefore the Government had approved the creation of the new system of Information Meetings. The timing could not have been worse from my point of view. Derry Irvine was rattled by his bad press and did not want further media controversy. Nevertheless, in the course of one of our regular meetings I set out my objections to what he had just signed off. Lesser men would have thrown me out, standing on their dignity and the fact that it had already been decided. Derry Irvine to his considerable credit listened to my arguments and conceded his haste in signing off something without discussing it with me first. He then said that since it had already been agreed across government, I would have to repeat my arguments in front of the Prime Minister. I was struck by the fact that the newspapers at the time were full of stories about Derry Irvine's alleged arrogance. He was in fact inviting me to tell the Prime Minister in his presence that he had got it wrong. That is exactly what happened when we subsequently went to Downing Street and Tony Blair's study. I rehearsed my arguments about why I thought Information Meetings were a waste of time and money, and I never heard about them again.

Not long after, I had my own problems with the press. As I had promised the Ashfield Labour Party, I opened an office right in the centre of the constituency in the small town of Kirkby-in-Ashfield. At the time, allowances for parliamentary offices were very limited and did not extend to having both a staff member in London as well as the constituency. I knew that I would need someone in London and I had promised during my selection to have a constituency office. We therefore bought a run-down building in Kirkby-in-Ashfield with some money left to Elaine and had it converted into a constituency office.

After the election I claimed rent for the premises, as the parliamentary rules then permitted. In addition to employing someone there, I also had a full-time researcher in London, Louise Pieros, who later was to become an extremely successful government lawyer. Louise had always done a tremendous job for me, working long hours and watching my political back in Westminster. In contrast the office in Ashfield was quiet for most of the time, with very few people calling in or getting in touch. In order to save some money, therefore, I cut back slightly on the opening hours with a small reduction in the staff costs there. A disgruntled constituent found out about this and took the story to *The News of The World*.

The first we knew about this was when the school where Elaine was teaching was asked in a telephone call whether 'Mrs Hoon' was working there. The secretarial staff said no but did mention it to the Head who was the only person there who knew that Elaine was married to me. The secretarial staff had no idea about who Elaine was married to because she had always kept her own name for all purposes, including in her work as a teacher.

When *The News of the World* contacted me, it was clear that they had all of the details about how much I was paying staff and what was being claimed in rent for the office. What the journalist was most interested in was the fact that Elaine was being paid the rent in her maiden name. I explained that this was because she had, throughout our marriage, always kept her own name. At the time he seemed satisfied by this explanation; not least because he had obviously already called her school to check.

Nevertheless when the story appeared the following Sunday the emphasis was on the fact that she was receiving the rent in her maiden name despite being married to me, implying dishonesty on our part. I learned a great deal from my first close encounter with the tabloid press; the facts really do not matter if journalists believe that they have got hold of a story they can embellish. Moreover, they can get access to information from even the most secure of sources. I knew this because apart from the House of Commons Fees Office, I was the only person who knew all of the details of my staff's salaries and the rent for the office. My claims were always made by me personally; the details were never shared with anyone else, other than the officials of the Fees Office. I explained this later to the Head of the Fees Office and an investigation was apparently carried out but hardly surprisingly no-one admitted to having sold sensitive information to *The News of the World*.

Reshuffles were an annual feature of Tony Blair's premiership, and often proved quite comprehensive. The 1998 changes were seen as significant because it allowed the Prime Minister to remove some of those that he had inherited as the result of the Labour Party's system of voting for the Shadow Cabinet in Opposition. In addition it gave him the opportunity of cutting Gordon Brown's team down to size and promoting for the first time some of his own people. Peter Mandelson, previously a Minister without Portfolio, was the most obvious beneficiary, becoming Trade and Industry Secretary with a seat in the Cabinet.

I found myself on the sidelines of what had clearly been a major row between Tony Blair and Gordon Brown. On the train down to London on Monday morning I was called by Derry Irvine to congratulate me, because I was about to be promoted to the position of Paymaster General in Gordon Brown's Treasury team. One of Derry Irvine's great strengths was his willingness, perhaps at a cost to himself, to recommend and promote people that he had worked with successfully. Other senior ministers with able juniors were often inclined to try and hold onto them. He was enthusiastic about my prospects. More enthusiastic than I was, deep down, because as I completed my journey to London I wondered what it would be like as a card-carrying Blairite working with Gordon Brown.

In the absence of any official contact, I went to my office in the Lord Chancellor's Department and got on with the job. Details of what was a significant reshuffle ran from time to time on the news. I was not surprised on the Monday that my name was not mentioned, since there were big changes around the Cabinet table. On the Tuesday, however, as the reshuffle reached down into the lower ministerial ranks there was still no mention of my position and no call from Downing Street. I carried on with my various meetings, beginning to wonder what on earth was going on. As the reshuffle seemed to have been completed, my private secretary said that the Prime Minister would be calling. Tony Blair was extremely apologetic, indicating that he knew that I was expecting something else but saying that he wanted me to stay in the department but as a Minister of State, one rung up on the ministerial ladder. The next day's *Morning Star* ran a story saying that I was going to be paid more for doing the same job, which was of course quite true.

Later it became clear that Tony Blair had wanted to remove Geoffrey Robinson from his position as Paymaster General at the side of Gordon Brown. Gordon Brown categorically refused to agree and after some serious political arm-wrestling Tony Blair backed down. This state of affairs lasted only until Christmas, when both Peter Mandelson and Geoffrey Robinson were forced to resign over the emergence of a £373,000 home loan that the wealthy Geoffrey Robinson had advanced to Peter Mandelson whilst in opposition. Although it crossed my mind that I might then have gone to the Treasury, I knew that my position would have been impossible given the in-fighting that had taken place.

The prospect of at least another year with Derry Irvine was actually a good one. I had far more responsibility than most other junior ministers. Derry Irvine was heavily involved in Cabinet Committees which meant that I substituted for him in most areas of the work of the department. When he was away I would also attend Cabinet Committees on his behalf. I sat through a long presentation by Chris Smith, the Culture Secretary, on the plans for a Millennium Dome which was a key part of the government's plans for celebrating the new century. It had become controversial, and at the end of the presentation I had no idea whether Chris Smith was for or against the proposal. I also got to speak regularly from the dispatch box as if I was a Cabinet Minister, because when the Lord Chancellor made a statement it had to be repeated in the Commons. I got plenty of experience therefore of dealing with awkward questions on the floor of the House of Commons.

This increasingly comfortable ministerial existence was interrupted by the sudden death in early May 1999 of Derek Fatchett, a Leeds MP who was a Minister of State in the Foreign Office. I had known him from Leeds politics and from the University where he was also a lecturer in the early 1980s. I was to be his replacement, responsible for countries in the Middle and Far East. Derek Fatchett was known as a strong supporter of Robin Cook, the Foreign Secretary. I was fairly confident that I would not have been Robin Cook's choice for the job.

I was appointed on a Monday morning, when by chance Foreign Office questions were to take place that same afternoon. After some brief housekeeping in my new very grand FCO office I went straight to the Foreign Secretary's even grander office for a team meeting to prepare for questions. I discovered that the team only prepared and discussed the questions that the Foreign Secretary was planning to answer. On my very first day in the job I had not really expected to be much involved, but at some stage in the meeting Robin Cook turned to me and said that I could do a question on Iraq, which happened to be first on the order paper. It was only one question, but it was a hot topic and one that required careful handling. It was not exactly the best introduction for a new minister on his very first day in the job.

I have no particular recollection of the question, the supplementaries or of my answers. Hansard says that I referred to disarmament but there was no specific mention of weapons of mass destruction. It was not without significance that I began my time in the Foreign Office on the subject that was to haunt the rest of my ministerial career and well beyond.

The Middle East peace process had been revived by Bill Clinton with the Wye Memorandum, signed somewhat reluctantly by both Yasser Arafat for the Palestinians and Benjamin Netanyahu for Israel in October 1998. In May 1999 Netanyahu was comprehensively defeated in a General Election by the Israeli Labour Party led by Ehud Barak. The British Labour Party had given some help on presentation in the course of what was a tight election campaign. The negotiations with the Palestinians after the agreement at Wye had not been going well and Ehud Barak had promised as part of his election campaign to change the terms of what had previously been agreed.

This was the background to my visit to Israel and Palestine in July 1999. I was to play a small part in trying to move forward the Arab/Israeli peace process. I met leading Israeli politicians before setting off for a meeting with Yasser Arafat in Gaza. As I waited for the formalities to be completed to allow us to cross into Gaza I was lectured by a young Israeli soldier as to why I was wasting my time by going to Gaza and talking to the Palestinians. It was a curious conversation. I was a minister, part of an international effort to promote peace in the region, being lectured by a young conscript who clearly had a very poor, almost certainly racist, view of the Palestinians.

Gaza was a dreadful place. After the affluence of Israel, people were obviously desperately poor, living in breeze block shelters often with only a tarpaulin as a roof. Many homes had a key prominently displayed on the wall. I was told that this was the key to what had been their family home in Israel. These families had fled during the 1948 war when the Arab world had tried to destroy the new state of Israel. I was in full visiting politician mode as I held a baby, only to discover that it didn't have a nappy. It was not a mistake I made again.

I had a long meeting with Yasser Arafat which was peppered with his frequent emotional and angry outbursts about the Israelis. It was clear that he could not deal with the new Israeli government's efforts to adjust the terms of the Wye memorandum. He did not seem to understand the way in which democratic elections could affect government decision-making. At the same time I recognised that he had probably taken a risk with his own side in reaching the agreement at Wye and could not be seen to lose face by accepting a unilateral change imposed by the Israelis.

As a result I agreed with the Foreign Office team that I would try to speak to Tony Blair to see what influence he might have with his Labour counterpart in Israel. However there was a problem with this since we were staying at the Gaza Hotel and assumed that any outgoing calls would be listened to by the Palestinians. It was nevertheless decided to make the call on the basis that if it was overheard it would do no harm since the Palestinians would see that we were making efforts on their behalf with the Israelis.

A further practical problem was the three hour time difference and the fact that there was no direct dialling. We would have to wait for a telephone line to become available. After dinner I went to bed, only to be awoken by my private secretary, Frances Luff, at around two in the morning saying that the Prime Minister wanted to speak to me. I was pretty disoriented in a strange bed in a strange place and as soon as Angie Hunter from Tony Blair's political office came on the line I started burbling about what we had happened that day in Gaza. When I paused for breath she said, 'What on earth are you talking about Geoff?' I said 'The Middle East Peace Process'. She said that she wasn't calling about that – 'I'm calling about the reshuffle'.

It became clear that there were some serious crossed wires. I had set off for Israel knowing that there was likely to be the annual summer reshuffle but assuming that since I had only been in the job for a matter of weeks, I would not be affected. The Downing Street switchboard had got hold of me through my private office, not telling Angie Hunter where I was. To her credit she did ask, and when I explained she apologised for waking me up, but said that Tony Blair wanted to speak to me. He then came on the line to say that he wanted to move me again, this time to the job as

Minister for Europe in the Foreign Office, replacing Joyce Quin, another former MEP. I then explained why I had wanted to speak to him and after what seemed to be a long discussion given the time of night, he agreed to raise the various questions with the Israelis.

The next morning after breakfast we were collected by our minder, a close confidante of Yasser Arafat. He took my arm and discreetly said, 'Thank you and congratulations.' We were at least right in the assumption that the Palestinians would be listening in on our calls.

More seriously, when the following year the Camp David meeting failed to further the peace process, it was generally Yasser Arafat who was blamed for not accepting what was said to be a historic Israeli offer by Ehud Barak. I thought back to my meeting in Gaza with Yasser Arafat and wondered whether the real reason for his refusal was his failure to understand the fundamentals of democracy. Political parties make promises before elections that they try to keep and as a result new governments might well have to change the policies of their predecessors. Yasser Arafat had led the Palestinians from 1967, and in the absence of any kind of democratic process simply outmanoeuvred or removed his critics. It was not the best preparation for dealing with democratically-elected politicians. But as a result, the Middle East missed what has since proved the best chance for a lasting peace.

Back in the UK I moved offices for the third time in six weeks. Although only around the corner and along the corridor in the Foreign Office. I was given a magnificently appointed room – the old India Office which was ornate and somewhat intimidating. It was also slightly strange in that it overlooked the Durbar Court, regularly used for receptions. The noise from below made it impossible to work when a reception was taking place in the early evenings, so I either joined in or more often went across to the House of Commons.

With the summer recess and school holidays I was not in the office much until September when I made an official visit to Russia. The idea was to visit the three British diplomatic posts in Russia; Moscow, St Petersburg and Yekaterinburg. It was during the dying days of Boris Yeltsin's administration, marked by the start of a bombing campaign that arguably changed the course of Russian history. Before the first bomb on 4 September 1999, Russia was still striving to be a democratic country.

A family portrait (Author's collection)

*With (L to R) Spanish Foreign Minister Miguel Angel Moratinos
and Gibraltar Chief Minister Peter Caruana* (Alamy)

With US President George W. Bush (NATO Photos)

With Tony Blair and Jack Straw at a Party Conference (Alamy)

With Tony Blair (Alamy)

An 'equipment' shot (Alamy)

Secretary of State for Defence (Author's collection)

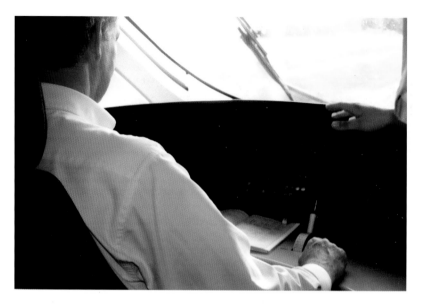

Driving a High Speed train in Germany (Author's collection)

High Peak Railway – train driving with a contrast! (Author's collection)

Speaking in the European Parliament (Author's collection)

With former Defence Secretary, Dennis Healey (Author's collection)

Ashfield School with Headteacher, Ian Fraser (Author's collection)

On patrol in Ashfield (Author's collection)

The new hospital at King's Mill, Sutton-in-Ashfield (Author's collection)

Playing in the band at Ashfield Show (Author's collection)

Whips' Office, 1994 (Author's collection)

The new minister – Lord Chancellor's Department, 1997 (Author's collection)

On board HMS Chatham (Author's collection)

Flying with the Red Arrows, March 2004 (Author's collection)

With 'friends' at Hereford (Author's collection)

Target practice in Sierra Leone, 2000 (Author's collection)

I met members of opposition parties in the Duma. There was about to be a contested election for Moscow's Mayor and I met more than one of the likely candidates. I was in Moscow for the first bomb, but as the attacks against apartment blocks continued through the early weeks of September, killing hundreds of people, the attitude of the administration became much harsher. The bombings were blamed on Chechen separatists and were used by the Russian government as a pretext for a second war in Chechnya. They also marked the point at which Vladimir Putin went from being a relatively unknown Prime Minister to being the clear favourite for the Presidency in the 2000 Presidential elections.

The impact of the September bombings in Moscow on Russia has sometimes been compared to the impact of 9/11 on the United States. Yet the aftermath was profoundly different. The US set up a series of inquiries to establish what had happened and who was responsible. The Russians have always refused to follow suit, leading to strong suggestions that the bombings and the bombers were orchestrated by the Russian Federation's security service, the FSB, the main successor organisation to the KGB, where Vladimir Putin had been a foreign intelligence officer for 16 years. I never saw any intelligence material that proved definitively that the Russian government was complicit, but the circumstantial evidence was strong, as it has been in a series of killings in the UK and elsewhere involving Russian citizens.

For a lapsed historian, the visit to Yekaterinburg was fascinating. Almost 900 miles to the west of Moscow on the Asian side of the Ural Mountains, it had been a closed city in Soviet times as it was a centre of the military-industrial complex. Yekaterinburg was Boris Yeltsin's home and the capital of the economically successful Swerdlovsk region. Under Yeltsin, the Regional Governors had become powerful as they recycled the local tax revenue. One of Vladimir Putin's first decisions as President was to ensure that this money was returned to the centre, breaking the power of the Russian regions.

Britain was at the time represented by a single Foreign Office official, living there alone as it was not considered suitable for his wife and family. He had arranged for me to meet local officials and to have dinner with the Governor, Eduard Rossei. A great deal of vodka was consumed; something which continued at 6 am the following morning as I was about to board the plane back to Moscow. I had never previously (nor since) had vodka for breakfast, but I realised as I slept on the flight back to Moscow that it gave me a real insight into Russia and in particular how Boris Yeltsin felt on most days.

On the 11 October I flew very early in the morning to Luxembourg for the regular monthly meeting of the EU's Foreign Affairs Council. Robin Cook was in the lead but I was expected to attend to cover for him in case he had to return to the United Kingdom or was engaged in bilateral talks with European colleagues. Since I was in Derby for the weekend I had flown commercially whereas Robin as Foreign Secretary had one of the Queen's Flight jets at his disposal.

Not long into the meeting, Robin Cook said that he had to leave the room. On his return I was then told by my private secretary that I had to speak to the Prime Minister. It was a short conversation. I was to be the new Defence Secretary, replacing George Robertson who was to become the NATO Secretary General. It was my fourth ministerial job in six months. When I returned to the meeting room, I apologised to Robin Cook that I was going to have to get back to the UK. My private secretary had already started looking for flights. Robin Cook, who already knew what was happening, insisted that I took his plane back, saying,

'It's your plane now anyway,' referring to the fact that the Queen's Flight which ferried ministers and members of the Royal Family around, was the responsibility of the Ministry of Defence and its Secretary of State.

At Your Command

I had a brief handover with George Robertson in the MOD office of the Secretary of State for Defence, shortly before he was to become the new NATO Secretary-General. At the time he seemed not entirely certain about really wanting this new job in Brussels. I got the impression that Tony Blair had wanted the job for Britain and that George was the obvious, indeed, the only candidate. Whereas George Robertson himself, having spent more than half a lifetime working to bring about a Labour Government, was not entirely sure that he wanted to give up on elected politics after only two years in government in return for a seat in the House of Lords and a possible future as an international civil servant.

He nevertheless assured me repeatedly that he had sorted out all of the main problems facing the department, and that all I would have to do was implement the various policy changes that he had set out in the 1998 Strategic Defence Review White Paper. He certainly made it sound straightforward. In the years ahead as we met at NATO meetings or various conferences, I routinely reminded George about his comments that he had sorted out all of 'the big issues' for me. I am sure that he got very bored with my repetition of the comment and that he had by implication somehow overlooked the major events that were about to occur in Afghanistan and Iraq.

For the first few months in the new job, George Robertson seemed to be right, as I attended a series of follow up departmental meetings aimed at putting the SDR into practise. It was just as well that things were quiet because I had a great deal to do to get up to speed. Defence is not a subject that most modern politicians have to deal with. Health and education both feature in every MP's experience because every constituency has schools and doctors. However the reduced footprint of defence across the country means that only a handful of MPs have any constituency experience of the subject. At the time an even smaller number had had actual military experience either on short service commissions or as reservists. Long gone are the days when the Secretary of State for Defence could have earned a Military Cross as Beachmaster for the Anzio landings in the Second World War, as Denis Healey did. I am sure that experience of war shaped that generation's attitudes – not least in respect of Europe, and the necessity to build institutions that would prevent another world war. There is an interesting irony about attitudes towards the European Union; those that actually fought in the Second World War like Denis Healey or Edward Heath were strong supporters of greater European integration, believing that this would prevent any further European war. In contrast I have heard countless comments about 'remembering the war' from those who could not possibly have been personally involved.

The sum total of my military experience was three years in the school combined cadet force, where my key learning was the ability to read an Ordnance Survey map. I had, however, grown up in the 1950s in a household still dominated by the Second World War. Although my Dad said little about his wartime experiences in the Far East, I was and remain proud of his courage in volunteering when he could easily have stayed at home in his reserved railway occupation. My mother had grown up around the corner from the Rolls Royce factory in Derby where the Merlin Spitfire engines were made. Derby was an occasional target for German bombers, and she often talked about the nightly blackout and the day that a German plane machine-gunned people in the nearby streets. Both of my grandfathers had served in the army, my paternal grandfather was a Sergeant Major, mentioned in dispatches in the First World War while my maternal grandfather was the right (or wrong) age to have served in both world wars; in a railway regiment. He almost certainly visited Umm Qasr in southern Iraq, as I did many years later. Both of us, for very different reasons and in quite different times, were concerned about the railway line linking the Persian Gulf to Basra and Baghdad.

In a debate in the House of Commons in 2003, trying to explain its military and geographical significance, I rashly compared Umm Qasr to Southampton. I learned later that this had not gone down well with British troops suffering the heat and sand of the Iraqi desert. One soldier is supposed to have commented,

'There's no beer, no prostitutes and people are shooting at us. It's more like Portsmouth'.

Immediately after arriving in the MOD, I was asked about my military experience by Sir Charles Guthrie, Chief of the Defence Staff. Not having any of my own, I was forced to refer to my family, and in particular my Dad. I am sure that he was unimpressed. Like many in the armed forces, he may have wondered why he had to accept the decisions of a civilian politician with no military experience and, at the time, very little actual military knowledge. Nevertheless, he was always completely correct in his dealings with me. Coming from what seemed to be an aristocratic background, he told me many times that he was the very last soldier in the British armed forces to have joined the army as part of his National Service. He of course stayed on for a long and distinguished military career.

From day one all ministers are assumed to be experts, even though they might only just have been appointed to a department completely new to them. This is true for all government departments but the military dimension adds still more complexity and potential difficulty for a new minister and in particular for a new Secretary of State. The MOD main building itself was intimidating. At the time it was a huge rabbit warren of small, near-identical offices spread across six floors of similar looking corridors. It was also symmetrical along its centre, with lifts on both sides. This meant that when one of the four lifts arrived at the ground floor it was not immediately clear whether to turn left or right when I arrived at the sixth floor where the ministerial and senior military offices were located. If I had turned the wrong way, I simply affected to be on a tour of the department, eventually making my way back to my office as if I had deliberately taken a detour. The office itself was similarly intimidating as the furniture had been used in the Second World War by Sir Winston Churchill. As I suspect was the case for most of my predecessors, sitting behind the great man's enormous desk did sometimes make me feel like a complete impostor. After the interior of the main building was comprehensively gutted and modernised, I discussed with Nicholas Soames, Churchill's grandson and for a time the Conservative Shadow Defence Minister, what should happen to his grandfather's furniture. He hoped that it might feature prominently in a Churchill museum.

The initial policy and practical briefings in the MOD were excellent, as they were in all of the departments I worked in. Given the number of reshuffles and resignations, civil servants must get used to the constant merry-go-round of ministerial changes. Discreetly hidden away somewhere there is always a big briefing pack marked 'For new ministers'. I often wondered whether Prime Ministers realise that regular reshuffles simply hand power to civil servants as new ministers take time to understand the complexities of their new department?

I have never understood the criticisms made of civil servants, often coming from new ministers with only a superficial grasp of the ministerial job. I always found civil servants to be highly professional, loyal to their minister and department as well as showing the highest standards of competence and integrity.

The MOD inevitably focussed on current operations and the detailed high level issues the department was then facing. As lawyer I was used to absorbing that kind of detail but I worried much more about some of the basics which never featured in any of the briefings. What if someone asked me about the different ranks in the different services? How did a Wing Commander in the RAF compare to a Colonel in the Army or a Captain in the Royal Navy? I had absolutely no idea at the time and no-one told me. After a while I was too embarrassed to ask anyone to explain. Yet like the awarding of campaign medals, which are of relatively little concern to civilians, these were issues that were vitally important to serving members of the Armed Forces.

The gap between the civilian and military understanding of the rank structure always came into sharp focus when newspapers ran defence stories. They would for example feature a critical quote about MOD policy from a retired colonel. The rank sounded seriously impressive to any lay reader. Yet I spent my time surrounded by Generals, Admirals and Air Marshals who were every bit as much involved in policy making as any politician or civil servant. The *Daily Telegraph* routinely ran stories justified as being from 'senior military sources'. It was suggested by the cynical MOD Press Office that this meant someone in the Sergeants' mess. 'A very senior source' might well be a Warrant Officer.

Another joy of those early briefings was the regular use of a variety of acronyms to describe all aspects of the military. George Robertson had launched 'a war on acronyms' and I followed his example by insisting that any initials were always fully spelled out. At least I would then have some sort of a chance of understanding what was being discussed.

Given that going to the Ministry of Defence involved my fourth ministerial job in five months, I was well used to the introductory processes. I added one of my own. I had developed the habit of 'walking the floors', trying to visit as much of the department that I could in the first few days. That obviously did not mean travelling around the country to far-flung military bases – that would come later – but I could walk around the six floors of the MOD main building, its headquarters in Whitehall, meeting as many people as possible. There were of course aspects of the MOD that were very different from civilian departments, not least the cramped flats at the very top of the building for the duty clerks on call twenty four hours a day, seven days a week to ensure that the country is never taken by surprise. Deep under the building is the shelter that would become part of the country's headquarters in the event of nuclear war. I was taken around and shown the sleeping cots for all of those who would need a protected space, including of course one for the Secretary of State for Defence. When I got back home to Derbyshire at the weekend this must have been something that stuck in my mind about my first few days. I told the children about the rows of bunks built into the wall. My nine year old daughter, Nathalie, asked innocently, 'Where would we go, Daddy?' I rapidly changed the subject.

I was fortunate in the timing of my arrival in the MOD given that the fighting in Kosovo had stopped the previous June. Although we had significant numbers of troops deployed there, it was in a relatively benign environment, at least as far as our soldiers were concerned. I was also fortunate in having very recently visited Kosovo as a Foreign Office minister. At least that meant that I was up to speed with the broader political picture.

I had discussed this at length on a visit to General Mike Jackson, then in charge of NATO's rapid reaction force in Kosovo, based in Pristina. In fact our conversation went on so long that his ADC was forced to interrupt to indicate that his next visitor was already waiting. Mike Jackson expressed his view that he was still busy, in typically forthright terms, much to the embarrassment of the next visitor who was standing just behind the ADC, and clearly heard every, not entirely polite word. Mike Jackson was a larger-than-life character who was also another highly intelligent and talented military figure who featured prominently throughout my time in the MOD.

Britain can count itself fortunate in having such clever and capable people at the top of its armed forces. I often wondered why they seemed so much better than their counterparts in other similar countries. I came to the conclusion that it was the result of family history. Many of Britain's senior officers have followed in their father's footsteps and are now, both men and women, carrying on a family tradition. No doubt the next generation might be following in their mother's footsteps.

As well as the complexities of the armed forces, a new Secretary of State also has to deal with the defence industry, their trade unions and those MPs who are convinced that every defence order should automatically come to their constituency. Privatisations in the UK mean that the MOD is probably the last government department that can have a direct effect on industry and the wider economy. Trying to buy the right equipment at the right time and the right price inevitably means that defence ministers spend time dealing with the defence industry.

On my third day in the job I was given an invitation to attend the launch of an exhibition of scientific drawings by Leonardo da Vinci, sponsored by the Italian defence conglomerate Finmeccanica, at the Science Museum. I managed to spend fifteen or twenty minutes on my own looking at the amazing drawings before someone from the company noticed and I was immediately surrounded by their most senior Italian executives.

A key issue for me in all defence procurement decisions was whether and to what extent it was possible to support British industry. I have heard it said the Armed Forces are convinced that political decisions to favour British companies mean that they get second rate, often unproven equipment, that no other country is likely to buy. They much prefer that defence equipment should be bought off the shelf from an established source, because it not only has a track record but it will also be used by other countries that we have to work with. In short, that almost always means buying American kit. The United States can usually offer the full range of military equipment and the chances are they will have sold the same kit to other NATO countries that we might have to deploy alongside, significantly improving close military cooperation.

Whilst there is real force to this argument, my overriding concern was that since I was spending the hard-earned money of British taxpayers, many of whom worked in the defence industry, I had to take account of their interests as well. By not buying British, I was doubly disadvantaging the domestic workforce. Not only was I spending their taxes abroad, providing jobs perhaps for their direct competitors but the chances were, given the irregularity of large defence orders, I was actually also putting them out of work. Without an order from their own government, the likelihood of British companies winning any other defence business was distinctly limited. Years later, travelling the world trying to sell British-built helicopters, I never had an effective answer to the question 'if your helicopters are so good, why hasn't your own government bought them?'

Other countries, particularly the United States, take a very protectionist view of government spending and particularly in relation to defence, almost always favouring their domestic industries. Most of the bigger continental countries, especially France, also follow this approach. There is a pervasive myth in the UK that there is real and open competition for defence orders, and that somehow Britain gets the best value for money by putting defence work out to tender. It may be true of small repetitive orders for standard products like bullets. However, for significant large equipment like ships, tanks or planes, the reality is that the equipment will be made to order, not least because Britain's sophisticated Armed Forces have their own very specific requirements designed to suit their advanced concept of operations.

There was no doubt that, as Chancellor of the Exchequer, Gordon Brown shared my view of looking after our own; or at least in his case looking after Scotland. Although always reflecting the Treasury's general view of the wastefulness of much of MOD spending, he was at pains to ensure that where possible Scotland – and in particular Scottish shipyards – should be looked after. As part of the Strategic Defence Review, the government was committed to building the two largest aircraft carriers ever in service with the Royal Navy. There was also a commitment to replace the Type 42 Destroyer fleet with up to twelve brand new Type 45 ships. It was clear that Gordon Brown wanted to ensure that Scotland would benefit from the huge shipbuilding work being considered. He was particularly keen as a constituency MP to highlight the virtues of the Rosyth Dockyard in Dunfermline East, his then constituency, as the best place for the assembly of the aircraft carriers.

The Treasury was however badly caught out over defence spending when it introduced a new resource accounting system for government departments. It was supposedly modelled on the private sector and treated capital assets as part of the overall income of government departments. I assume that this was intended to ensure that departments behaved as carefully with their fixed assets as they did with their annual expenditure. What the clever civil servants in the Treasury had overlooked however is that those departments with huge tangible assets like the MOD could write off their old equipment and claim new cash as part of their annual budget. Kevin Tebbit, the highly intelligent and astute MOD Permanent Secretary, started to claim more and more cash for the MOD, significantly increasing the annual budget available to spend on new equipment for defence.

When Gordon Brown found out what was happening, he wrote to me trying to stop this practise. I was able to quote word for word from the original Treasury letter sent out by Paul Boateng as Chief Secretary to the Treasury, explaining exactly how the new resource accounting system was supposed to work. The MOD had followed his correspondence to the letter. There was thereafter more and more acrimonious correspondence from the Treasury until at last Gordon Brown appealed to Tony Blair, who instructed that the MOD had to restrict its annual budget in line with the Chancellor of the Exchequer's instructions. There was no doubt at the time that the MOD was seeking to benefit from an enormous loophole in Treasury spending rules – a loophole of the Treasury's own making – but I never forgot these exchanges when in future years both Tony Blair and Gordon Brown claimed to be protecting the Defence budget.

From day one in the MOD I had inherited a much delayed decision about which missile to buy for the Eurofighter/Typhoon jet. It was supposed to be a completely new generation of missile, with its capabilities going well beyond what was then currently available. The US missile company Raytheon proposed what seemed to be a safe and cost effective solution, offering their existing very capable missile for the short term but with a defined programme to develop it to the new advanced standard. As I read the background briefings and sat through a series of meetings I gradually came to the conclusion that the US solution was the safest and most cost-effective option.

The rival European solution offered by a consortium led by MBDA, a joint British, French and Italian company, proposed a completely new missile that would achieve the higher required standard as soon as it came into service. There were obvious financial and developmental risks, which although the company indicated it was willing to absorb, still meant that I would be taking a significant risk in choosing the European solution.

As the date for the announcement drew near, I had a one to one off the record discussion with the then Chief of Defence Procurement, Robert Walmsley. He indicated that the US decision was certainly the safest and probably the least risky financial choice. It was strongly favoured for that reason by the Treasury. He invited me to consider however the impact on the European missile industry of allowing such a significant technological order to go to the United States. In his opinion it would effectively mark the end of the development of any future European missile capability. I spent the weekend working through the issues and the following week decided on the European solution, with the proviso that the financial and developmental safeguards offered were written into the contract in the most unambiguous terms.

Not very long after, I was summoned across to Downing Street to see the Prime Minister in his study. He waved a letter at me, which I could see from the letter heading was from the White House. President Bill Clinton just about stopped short of saying that I had taken leave of my senses in not choosing the US offer but he was certainly distinctly unimpressed by my decision. To Tony Blair's considerable credit he accepted my explanation and the decision stood. The Prime Minister had, as far as I was concerned, an entirely unjustified reputation for wanting to interfere in every government department and every government decision. On the contrary I found that he generally left me to get on with the job; only occasionally asking me to justify what I was doing. Providing that I had a thought through and coherent explanation, he was happy with my judgement. Fortunately for me, and the MOD, MBDA achieved all of the missile developmental stages successfully and their Meteor missile is today in service, offering a capability claimed by the manufacturers of six times the performance of its predecessors.

I learned a great deal in working through this process. I insisted that I should have at least a summary of all of the relevant information to be able to make a decision. The previous practice of the MOD had been to set out the arguments and come to a conclusion that I was invited to either accept or reject. The lawyer in me wanted to see both sides of the argument before reaching a conclusion. Moreover, it was always likely to be difficult to reject a decision that procurement experts had reached particularly if I wanted to do so for employment reasons, often then characterised as political interference. I also learned a valuable lesson about the United States. I had lived there, worked there and had a large family there. Few people are more sympathetic and supportive of the United States than I am. However, in business the US system is completely ruthless in delivering the right result in the interests of the United States, by engaging each and every part of their political system from the President down. The US will use every argument it can, often relying on impossible-to-challenge 'security' arguments to justify favouring its own industries, which in turn it ruthlessly protects from foreign competition.

A related issue later arose out of our commitment to help build and develop the Joint Strike Fighter, now known in service as the Lightning II. The UK had signed up to be the only 'Tier One' partner to the United States, paying over £1 billion for 10 per cent of the planned development costs; the work to be carried out by BAE Systems. The company soon found however that it was unable to carry out its share of the work because its US industrial partners blocked access to the relevant technology, apparently on security grounds. I raised this with Donald Rumsfeld, the US Defence Secretary and Tony Blair raised it with President George Bush, but initially to no avail. We sought what is known in the US system as an ITAR waiver to allow technology transfer out of the US. Although the US President was strongly in favour, Congressman Henry Hyde, Chair of the House of Representatives Committee on International Relations, refused to agree. I had to explain to Tony Blair the complexities of the checks and balances inherent in the US constitution. He had understandably assumed that if the President supported something it would necessarily happen. He was used to having a secure and reliable parliamentary majority and didn't understand the US separation of powers and congressional independence. It took five more years to agree a deal that would pass the US Congress and allow the UK access to the relevant software technology. Exactly the same issue is likely to arise in relation to any post-Brexit trade deal with the United States. The President and his administration may well be strongly in favour, but it will still have to be approved by Congress. Moreover members of Congress, whatever they might say, will not be looking exclusively to their national interest; they will also be looking to protect the interests of their constituents in their own districts. The pork barrel is alive and doing very well in the US political system.

The UK's close defence relationship with the United States through NATO involved also the wider and more difficult issue of European Defence, and the extent to which the countries of the European Union could and should co-operate militarily. It was a sensitive subject politically, because the moment the question was raised publicly there would immediately be newspaper headlines condemning the very idea of a 'European Army', even though the European co-operation in question had absolutely nothing to do with the army. It was also sensitive with the Armed Forces. They rightly saw NATO as the real guarantor of European security and, given limited defence resources, were nervous about the EU trying to duplicate military capabilities that were already available through the Alliance.

On the other hand, there needed to be some means of encouraging European nations either to spend more on defence or at least to spend what they had more effectively. It was necessary to avoid the inevitable duplication of defence capabilities caused by national prestige and national sovereignty, where several European countries would spend their scarce defence budgets on the same or similar equipment. At one time neighbouring NATO members, Greece and Turkey had large numbers of tanks; not for any benefit to NATO, but in case they needed to fight each other. Clearly this was not exactly the best basis for international military cooperation.

If European defence meant that some countries were politically more inclined to take these difficult spending decisions through the EU than through NATO, the end result was still positive. My first official visits as Secretary of State for Defence were to Berlin and Paris, where the French in particular were keen to push European defence co-operation at every opportunity. Tony Blair was also keen to project the image of his government as being pro-European. Given the difficulties he faced with Gordon Brown over the euro, encouraging more European defence co-operation was obviously a way of burnishing his European credentials.

What has never really been understood in Britain is that most continental countries actually believe in the 'ever closer union' enshrined in the text of the Treaty of Rome, and that this applies to questions of defence as much as it does to those matters originally set out in the Treaty. Given the nature of global threats, whether from hostile states, or parts of states or from terrorist groups, the UK has to be very confident that it can afford to ignore the contribution that the EU can make to dealing with such threats. There is no doubt that NATO should and will remain the keystone of Britain's military security, but during an increasingly irritated and isolationist US administration, the European dimension may become increasingly important. Without the drag anchor of British antipathy towards the concept of EU defence it may well gather momentum. With what seems to be a growing reluctance for the United States to deploy its forces overseas, Britain could find itself seriously isolated militarily.

Northern Ireland was not seen as a European issue at the time. It was still, however, a significant responsibility for the Defence Secretary. Although Tony Blair had very successfully built on the peace process inherited from John Major, many of the military security arrangements in Northern Ireland and along the border with the Republic were still in place in 1999. On an early visit to Crossmaglen, still then described as being 'bandit country', I was helicoptered into the province before having to run the last fifty yards to the reinforced concrete sangar where British troops were based. I was still regularly running quite long distances at the time, but I did wonder what would have happened if the Defence Secretary had been a portly, unfit Member of Parliament.

In addition to these fortifications, the watchtowers and border posts between the north and south of Ireland were all still in place. I peered through high powered binoculars into the farmhouse home of Thomas 'Slab' Murphy, believed to be the Provisional IRA's Quartermaster, and said to be responsible for securing the funds through smuggling that financed their terrorist activities. The Provisionals leadership were demanding, as part of the next stage of the peace process, that these security facilities should be taken down and permanently abandoned. The local Northern Ireland police and the British Army were extremely reluctant to do this, fearing that any return to violence by the para-militaries would go undetected and leave the security forces in an impossible position. I believed that I had no choice other than to put forward their view, based as it was on the need for security, in the discussions with Downing Street. Tony Blair was determined to push the peace process through; seeing the watchtowers as symbols of the surveillance of the past, he wanted them removed. He proved to be right. As a result, the watchtowers and other aspects of border security were taken down and removed. Given that this helped to preserve a lasting ceasefire, it would be a massively retrograde step if, as a result of the uncertainties over Britain's future relationship with the EU, controls at the border with the Republic of Ireland were reintroduced.

On one occasion I was invited across to Downing Street to discuss the border security arrangements with Tony Blair. As I waited outside his study, the door opened and there were Gerry Adams and Martin McGuinness. It was a surreal experience because for me at the time they represented what I still thought of as the enemy; but there they were, emerging from what had clearly been a very friendly chat sitting in the armchairs in Tony Blair's small study. There was easy-going laughter as they came out of the study; the three men were obviously very comfortable with each other. Years before, right at the start of the peace process, I frequently stayed in the same hotel in Strasbourg as SDLP leader John Hume. We would often have a late-night whisky together as we sought to put the world to rights. I asked him why it was that, after so many years of hostility towards the British State, the Provisionals were willing to enter the peace process. His explanation was that both Gerry Adams and Martin McGuinness had sons. Without the peace process they both expected their sons to die in the armed struggle, either blowing themselves up or being killed by the army.

It was clear by then that the real negotiations were being pushed through by Downing Street in the form of Jonathan Powell, Tony Blair's Chief of Staff. Mo Mowlem, the Secretary of State for Northern Ireland, had been moved to one side. In December 1999, after leaving the Northern Ireland office, she spoke at a big MOD Equal Opportunities Conference at the arena in Birmingham. I was the warm-up act, delivering the usual carefully crafted, civil service drafted speech. As far as I could see, she had made no preparation – she certainly had no speech to hand. I realised that there was something wrong when she talked genially for half an hour or so without ever really addressing the subject of the event. I saw her brilliance as a politician and a human being when afterwards she went round the building thanking everyone personally who had been involved in the organisation of the event.

Having been involved at the periphery of both the Middle East peace process and its counterpart in Northern Ireland, I was always aware of a remarkable contrast. In Northern Ireland there was a real process, with significant compromises made by all sides. There was however no agreed end state; indeed, it is difficult to imagine how there could ever be one, as the Unionists will never agree to a united Ireland which is precisely the ultimate ambition of Sinn Féin and its supporters. In stark contrast, in the Middle East there is broad agreement that there should be a two state solution, with the Palestinians finally getting a homeland for their people. What is lacking is any kind of process to bring the parties together. The focus on the process in Northern Ireland has been remarkably successful. A generation of young people have grown up without their lives being devastated by the fear of intimidation and the threat of violence. Sadly, the absence of a process in the Middle East seems to have further entrenched hard and uncompromising attitudes.

The Falklands involved a similar historical background, although getting there was more demanding than the short flight to Belfast. The 'Air Bridge' to Stanley in the Falklands Islands involved an eight hour flight from the RAF base at Brize Norton on a Sunday night to Ascension. After a short stop for refuelling and breakfast, there was another eight hour flight to our ultimate destination. I was told that when Mrs Thatcher made the trip, a specially designed container had been built in the hold of a cargo plane to allow her to do some work and to get some rest. We live in more egalitarian times, so I sat up for 16 hours not entirely sure where I was and what time it was when I eventually arrived.

The Falkland Islands are spectacular, with horizons that seem to go on forever. That first time, I was only there for a few days. I learned that one of the biggest problems for those stationed in the islands was sheer boredom, with very little to do other than watch videos. I was able to do some walking to see the vast crowds of very smelly penguins; in the wonderful wildlife documentaries, it is just as well that the smell does not get across. I was also able to fire off some surplus Rapier ground to air missiles. The missiles required a manual element in firing which needed split-second aiming as the missile approached the target. I was pretty poor at this last minute course correction. I was told that it was the youngest soldiers who were the best at this because they had grown up playing computer games where precisely the same skills were required.

It was also a period of relatively good relations between the UK and Argentina. I became the first British politician to lay a wreath at the Argentine cemetery at Darwin on East Falkland. Like all such places it made me think of all the young men who left their countries to fight in war and never came home. Argentina had conscripted raw recruits and sent them to their deaths in a war fought purely for reasons of national prestige. They were up against highly capable professional British soldiers who knew exactly what they had to do to win. On a later visit in 2002, I was walked through some of the battlegrounds by NCOs from the Parachute Regiment who had been young soldiers in the 1982 Falklands War, twenty years before.

I then made a convoluted journey to Buenos Aires for meetings with senior Argentine politicians. Argentina would not allow direct flights by a British Government aircraft, so I had to make a short stop in Uruguay complete with South American honour guard and a meeting with my counterpart. I was well briefed on the close connections in history between Argentina and the UK, particularly with Wales. Those that I met, despite the Falklands War, seemed to have genuine affection for the UK and in many cases strong personal ties. The Defence Minister was called Ricardo Lopez Murphy, whose name seemed to sum up the ambivalence of the Argentine people and its politics to the United Kingdom.

I continued to have some contact with the Falklands through the practice that I introduced of making Christmas calls to deployed service personnel. I spent each Christmas morning whilst in the job making telephone calls to a variety of people who were, unlike me, spending their Christmas on duty far from home. Through the MOD switchboard I was able to speak to a sailor on board a ship in the Indian Ocean, to an RAF pilot stationed in Kandahar, and perhaps most memorably to a soldier serving in South Georgia who was able to describe the penguins that he could see from the hut where they would be eating their Christmas dinner.

Inevitably given events, most of my time in the MOD was focussed overseas. However, in March 2000, I found myself at the centre of Britain's worst outbreak of foot and mouth disease since 1967. Nick Brown was strictly the Minister responsible at the Ministry of Agriculture, but that department had no spare resources to devote to the complex task of controlling animal movements, and an understandable reluctance to oversee the culling of millions of cows and sheep; many of which were completely free of the disease.

Tony Blair decided that I should chair the emergency COBRA committee set up to deal with the crisis. I read the government paper produced on lessons learned from the 1967 outbreak. It evidenced how much the world of agriculture and food had changed in the intervening years. In 1967, the outbreak was essentially regional, because farmers sent animals to their local abattoirs and on into the local food chain through independent butchers and small supermarkets. Yet by 2001 animals were being moved many miles for slaughter and large supermarkets had national distribution arrangements which meant that animals and their carcasses were moved sometimes many times right around the country. As a result, what began as a small outbreak in Essex soon spread to Northumberland, Devon and the Lake District, which was particularly badly affected.

Animal movement bans were put in place to try and control further eruptions of the disease but it quickly became clear that more radical measures were required. The COBRA meetings took place in a dark and windowless committee room in the Cabinet Office building just off Whitehall. As I sat in the chair the main protagonists were to the left and right of me in what seemed as the arguments developed, to be an increasingly small room. The Government Chief Scientist, Professor David King, argued that it was necessary to cull all animals within three kilometres of known cases whether or not they had the disease, in effect creating a 'firebreak' through which the disease would not spread. This tough and uncompromising policy was challenged by the Chief Vet, Jim Scudamore, in what evolved into emotional, tense and difficult exchanges. It was clear that the Chief Vet simply could not contemplate the killing of disease-free animals on the scale that was being recommended. He probably realised that he would have to defend the government's policy in meetings with farmers who would be understandably angry about the effect on their farms and livelihoods.

In more recent times, when I read about the government acting on 'scientific advice' during the COVID-19 pandemic, I was extremely sceptical about whether there was any such single stream of scientific opinion. I had had to resolve such scientific differences, and I suspected that modern ministers did exactly the same.

Eventually I came to the conclusion that the only way of getting the disease under control was to come down in favour of the cull, which the army then was involved in carrying out. I went up to Cumbria to see what was happening for myself. I doubt that I will ever forget the sight, smell and heat of burning cows stacked on an enormous pyre. Legs and heads stuck out at peculiar and impossible angles, with the constant sizzling and small explosions of fat as the carcasses melted from the intense heat. Some six million animals were slaughtered across the country, as the outbreak of foot and mouth was gradually brought under control and the disease eventually eradicated.

The rapid spread of the disease right across the United Kingdom as the result of 21st century food distribution networks reminded me of a briefing I received about the country's vulnerability to an attack by a sophisticated biological weapon, contained perhaps in a test tube or similar small receptacle. Such weapons can be designed to facilitate human-to-human contamination, with the weaponised disease being passed on before people even realise that they have been infected and are carriers. I was taken through a scenario in which a biological weapon was introduced into a London railway or underground station after lunch on a Friday afternoon. People would be travelling home – perhaps quite long distances, as they came to the end of their working week. They would spread the disease as they mixed with their fellow travellers in crowded stations and on busy trains. The following morning those first infected might be feeling the early effects, calling their doctors or perhaps making their way to their nearest accident and emergency department, in turn infecting still more people in different parts of the country. Without the ability to actually know what was going on elsewhere, the smaller number of doctors and nurses on duty at weekends treating the first few patients might not recognise what was happening, thinking initially perhaps that this was a new strain of influenza. They might send people back home suggesting they rest and take paracetamol; all the time adding to the number infected as the disease proliferated. By Monday the most vulnerable, the elderly or those with pre-existing health problems could be seriously ill, overwhelming the emergency services as they called for ambulances or arrived at hospitals in increasing numbers. The first of these would begin to die as only then nationally was the scale of what was happening fully appreciated. By that time, millions might have been infected with a disease that initially might have no known antidote or cure.

I was invited to imagine what could happen if such a biological weapon fell into the hands of a fanatical terrorist group or was used by an enemy state. The capability and sophistication of our armed forces would count for nothing against such a terrifying threat. Indeed, a single individual armed with such a weapon could do incalculable damage. Years later I did wonder whether that and very similar terrifying briefings had made me hyper-sensitive to the possibility of such threats being developed.

That came later. My first military challenge came from an unexpected source deep in the African jungle, and was very much a hangover from Britain's colonial past.

MOD – SIERRA LEONE

As someone growing up in the 1960s on the political left, I necessarily thought of colonialism as being a bad thing. It never crossed my mind that developing countries could actually benefit from a close connection with a former colonial power like Britain, and certainly not that they could become reliant on its armed forces. Yet that is exactly what happened in Sierra Leone, and with the connivance and support of the United Nations, which is usually fundamentally hostile to any hint of colonialism.

Sierra Leone was one of Britain's first colonies in Africa, and its capital Freetown was for many years a useful base and stopover on the long sea voyage to India in the days of the British Empire. The winds of change lead to its independence in 1961 and despite remarkable natural resources – abundant rain and sunshine, white sandy beaches and mineral wealth in the form of diamonds, bauxite and rutile – political instability meant that its GDP at the turn of the 21st Century was actually lower than at the time of independence. Within a few years of independence, a series of military coups lead by one rebel general after another, together with regional and ethnic tensions, ensured that economic and constitutional progress proved impossible.

In the 1990s, the Revolutionary United Front (RUF), with a leadership trained in Libya, fought to gain control of the diamond mines in eastern Sierra Leone. Their determination and ruthlessness proved successful, and eventually the territory controlled by the lawful government consisted only of the capital Freetown. The government's response was to hire foreign mercenaries from a South African company, Executive Outcomes. Although militarily very successful – the RUF was pushed right back to the Liberian border – it proved controversial in the West, and the government was pressured into replacing the mercenaries with an international peace-keeping force that, in comparison, proved militarily ineffective.

Following elections in 1996, a UN diplomat, Ahmad Kabbah, was elected President of Sierra Leone. Despite negotiating a peace treaty with the RUF, he was quickly overthrown before being restored to power by a Nigerian lead force operating under a UN mandate. In April 2000, the RUF again sought to control the country, taking a number of UN observers prisoner, including a British major, Andrew Harrison. At the beginning of May 2000 it seemed as if the UN operation had failed and there was little to prevent the rebels taking control of Freetown.

The UN was, however, determined to protect its mandate and its reputation. For curious historical reasons, the UN, and in particular its Secretary-General Kofi Annan, believed that Britain was best placed to sort out the problem. His approach seemed to be based on no better reason, that Britain as the former colonial power, had some sort of an historical obligation to the country. This was clearly a very weak justification for deploying British forces, but Robin Cook as Foreign Secretary was enthusiastic. Similarly, in his Chicago speech only the year before Tony Blair had talked about a moral duty to intervene in appropriate circumstances to restore the democratic order; using Britain's military as a 'force for good'.

The challenge, therefore, was to try and find a way in which the situation in Sierra Leone could be resolved, the democratically elected government restored, and the UN mandate upheld without involving British forces in yet another long term military commitment. When the MOD was asked for its view, there was some understandable concern from the military about the risks of overstretch and the likely effect of a major undertaking in Africa to add to continuing commitments in the Balkans, in Bosnia and Kosovo where substantial numbers of British soldiers were already stationed. Yet at the same time the military wanted to be involved; to show what British forces could achieve, especially in what was a difficult area of the world where many others had failed.

In the first place it was necessary to find out what exactly was happening on the ground, since very little was known about the situation in the country beyond Freetown. Brigadier David Richards, later Chief of the Defence Staff, was dispatched with a small military reconnaissance team to assess the situation and report back on what was needed and what might be effective. As well as being down to earth and straightforward, he was an outstanding officer, who simply got on with whatever job he was given.

The first priority was the safety and security of British citizens in Sierra Leone. Working closely with the High Commission team in Freetown, it was estimated that there were around 1000 British citizens, who would have to be evacuated before the capital fell to the rebels. The rebels had a long history of brutality, which included chopping off the arms of children as a warning to the local population not to co-operate with the lawful government. Given the geography of Sierra Leone and the absence of secure land routes through neighbouring countries, an evacuation by sea or air was the only practical solution. The geography of Freetown and the location of its airport at Lungi, on the edge of the surrounding jungle, also significantly complicated the required operations. The airport was close to rebel lines and would have to be secured once the evacuees had been assembled on the beach in Freetown. They would then be helicoptered out to the airport and flown to safety.

With the security situation deteriorating by the hour, all of this had to be planned and prepared quickly. What is known as the Spearhead Battalion was always kept ready at very short notice for just this kind of emergency. It was the turn of 1 Para who were quickly deployed to Sierra Leone, both to secure Lungi Airport and to help with the evacuation from Freetown. The rebel advance on Freetown continued, and as rebel forces approached Lungi there was a fierce firefight during which the RUF suffered heavy casualties and were forced back by 1 Para. This skirmish had very significant longer-term consequences. It emphasised the superiority of western trained forces, but also showed the local population that Britain was once again standing by to protect them. What was a fairly short military engagement seemed to become symbolically important to the people of Sierra Leone in terms of their confidence in the UK and their reliance on and respect for its armed forces.

Around 500 British and EU citizens were actually evacuated; confirming a view that, for a significant number, it was better to stay in their long-term homes in Sierra Leone rather than return to a country they might not have lived in for decades. There was also the outstanding question of Major Harrison and other UN peacekeepers held by the rebels. He had a satellite phone, and incredibly I was able to speak to him in the village where he was still surrounded by rebel forces. He accepted pragmatically that it would be difficult to mount a rescue operation so far from Freetown in a village still in rebel hands. He stoically expressed his disappointment that the BBC World Service had not broadcast a commentary on England's very recent European Championship game against Portugal. He had had to listen in Portuguese and could not make out the score. I pointed out that he was probably better off not knowing since England had managed to squander an early two goal lead, actually going out of the competition, losing 3-2 to Portugal. It is perhaps typical of the remarkable qualities of the British military that I was able to have a conversation with a British officer who was thousands of miles away and in effect a prisoner, but still talk mostly about football.

To prevent the risk of a continuing commitment Britain was at the same time beginning the process of handing over control to local forces. The key was to train an army that would be loyal to the democratically elected government. A training team was sent out, based ironically at a former British base at Benguema. I was able to visit the camp a few weeks later; the British built barracks seemed to have been left untouched since 1961 but was soon brought back into use.

Arriving in Freetown, I had what to me were an embarrassing number of conversations in which the main concern of the local people that I met was to ask when Britain would come back to run the country again. There seemed near consensus that we would do a better job than successive governments had managed since independence. A neutral observer would have found my discomfort amusing. Here was a British minister who had just helped to save the country from rebel forces arguing with people from the same country that they would be better off running their own affairs rather than having Britain back. They did not seem to be persuaded.

It was my first visit to tropical Africa, and I began to realise why people became frustrated with Africa's lack of political progress. For a continent rich in natural resources, its chaotic politics held it back from much-needed economic development. Sierra Leone seemed completely typical. At first sight it seemed to have everything going for it, apart from the fundamental matter of political and constitutional stability. Yet the political stability taken for granted in democracies was not so easy to secure.

Sierra Leone had largely gone out of the news when, late in August 2000, a small British patrol was captured by the West Side Boys; a well-armed group who used their considerable arsenal of weapons to intimidate the local population. Their name was modelled on New York street gangs, and they probably had some contact with the RUF, although essentially they were a local militia force, independent of any outside control. The British patrol had been visiting Jordanian forces when their commanding officer decided to visit the village of Magbeni to try to improve their knowledge of the area. Unfortunately they ran into a heavily armed group of West Side Boys who took them hostage, moving them across a nearby creek to the nearby village of Gberi bana.

When it became clear that they had been captured, I was initially persuaded that efforts should be made to negotiate their release. I asked in addition that discreet military preparations should be made in the event of a military rescue being required. The West Side Boys first of all demanded a satellite phone, which was made available; not least because it meant their movements could be tracked remotely. Five British soldiers were then released. They reported back that the entire group had been abused and subjected to mock executions. This added to my determination that the situation could not be allowed to continue for much longer. I had always admired the 'leave no-one behind' mantra of Israel's armed forces. It emphasised to the world that their people would not be held prisoner if there was a military way out. I wanted British forces to know that the British government valued them just as highly.

I spent the night of Thursday 31 August considering the military options and approved the plan in principle for an assault. The CDS, General Guthrie, then asked for a private word. Although he fully supported my determination to rescue the soldiers, he said he wanted to be sure that I understood how difficult the military operation was likely to be. It was a risky and hazardous mission to rescue British soldiers, reaching deep into the West African jungle. It was a curious conversation for me; I had been in the MOD as a civilian for little more than nine months. He had been a soldier for more than 40 years, rising to the very highest military position that he could achieve. Although by then I had approved a number of clandestine operations, this was the first public attack that I had authorised. He pointed out to me that if it went wrong and there was significant loss of British lives, I would have to resign. I am sure that he had in mind the failed US rescue operation of US Embassy staff in Tehran in 1980. I had been living in the US at the time and that failure had probably cost Jimmy Carter the presidency. Because of that background, I had already worked out for myself what the consequences of failure would be, but was grateful that he was sufficiently concerned to point it out. It was generous of him to take such trouble with a relatively inexperienced Defence Secretary. From his perspective, after an entire career serving a series of Defence Secretaries, he knew that I would be replaced immediately and it probably made little difference to him which civilian occupied the position. From my point of view I was left in no doubt that the succeeding next few days could bring my ministerial career to a sudden end.

It took some days to get the required troops into position, together with the necessary helicopter equipment. There was a real concern that if the West Side Boys learned of these preparations, through seeing or hearing helicopter movements, they might take it out on their British hostages. I approved a plan to launch the assault on the West Side Boys at first light on Saturday 9 September. In fact, it took much longer than planned to get the ground forces into position. I learned later at first hand that they had had to crawl through jungle swamps to be ready for the attack.

The assault was launched at first light on the Sunday morning. Chinook and Lynx helicopters flew in at very low altitude as the ground troops attacked. In a coordinated operation across the nearby creek, A Company of 1 Para landed by helicopter to clear Magbeni and ensure that the West Side Boys' heavy weapons could not be used against the attackers. The risks involved in this kind of operation were shown when the paratroopers found themselves in swamp-like conditions, wading 150 yards to get into position. They came under mortar attack, with their commanding officer suffering serious injuries early in the engagement. I was told later that the mortars would have done much greater damage but for the soft conditions, which had absorbed much of the blast effect. Had the ground have been harder there might well have been more casualties and General Guthrie's cautious warning would perhaps have come to pass.

The main assault involved two Chinooks flying over the huts where the hostages were being held. The rotor blades blew the roofs off, allowing the attackers a clear view of their target as they descended by rope. As they went down, Bombardier Brad Tinnion was hit by enemy fire. Brilliant flying by a Chinook pilot allowed him to be picked up and taken out to the hospital ship, RFA Lancelot, lying off the Sierra Leone coast. Despite the incredible skill of the helicopter crew, he died of his wounds on the journey to the ship. All of the hostages were freed, together with a number of other prisoners held by the West Side Boys.

In a later statement I emphasised the powerful messages sent by the operation; Britain would not allow its soldiers to be held hostage, and would not do deals with hostage takers. A few days later I visited the forces who had been involved, at their bases on the south coast and in the west of England. On arrival at their headquarters, I was initially anxious about their reaction to the death of one of their comrades, but it was made very clear to me that they had all appreciated my decision to see through the rescue and that Bombardier Tinnion would have expected people to come after him if he had been taken prisoner. I was flown back to Derbyshire in an Agusta helicopter captured from the Argentinians and brought back to Britain after the Falklands War.

On a visit to Sierra Leone shortly afterwards, I went out into the jungle area previously controlled by the West Side Boys. Following the rescue operation, newly-trained elements of the Sierra Leonean army had swept through the nearby Occra Hills, eliminating the last remnants of the West Side Boys. One of those captured had been their leader, Foday Kallay, who I met in a hospital unit where he was being treated for his wounds. It seemed curious that, not very long before, Britain had been trying to kill or capture him and by then we were giving him expert medical assistance. Lying in his hospital bed he looked like a skinny teenage thug; certainly not someone capable of standing up to highly-trained professional British soldiers. I learned that he had not even tried; on hearing the helicopters he had run away, leaving his followers to their fate.

I went to Sierra Leone on a number of occasions, initially only to Freetown but then further out into the jungle. I came to understand why sub-Saharan Africa both frustrates and yet also obsesses people. Sierra Leone should be a rich and successful country, and probably would be if its population could agree on how it should be governed. We in Britain take democracy and the rule of law for granted. We have regularly tried to export those principles, but without the backing of British soldiers those ideas came to nothing in Sierra Leone. Yet there are obvious limitations as to how often Britain can be involved in such overseas operations; they will only be supported in Britain if they are short, successful and involve few British casualties. No British Defence Secretary can give such assurances, not least when international crises dominate the news.

MOD – AFGHANISTAN

As I listened on the radio in the ministerial car to the account of the second aircraft flying into the World Trade Centre, I knew as we drove at speed back to the MOD that British troops would soon be operating in Afghanistan. I already knew that Al Qaeda was based there. I knew that the terrorist organisation had long held ambitions for a further attack on the United States. I knew as well that any American administration of whatever political complexion would hit back hard. And I knew that Britain would want to stand by its closest ally militarily.

On the morning of 11th September 2001, I had opened the first Defence and Security Exhibition to be held at the Excel exhibition centre near to the City Airport in East London. I had made a speech, toured the stands and had a quick lunch, before getting back to my ministerial car. As I did so, my driver, Dave, said that there had been what was initially thought to have been a terrible accident in New York, as a civilian airliner crashed into the World Trade Centre. Minutes later of course we learned of the second aircraft and began an urgent drive back to the MOD. Meetings in the MOD were being organised as we drove.

As well as some slightly ad hoc MOD meetings with the senior military leaders who happened to be in the building, or who had been able to get back when the news from New York came through, an emergency COBRA meeting chaired by the Prime Minister was organised for early that evening. That was less concerned with any military preparations but much more about the fact that intelligence warnings suggested that events in the United States could simply be the precursor of worldwide terrorist attacks, with London being a prime target. Looking back at those events, it is easy to overlook the sense around at the time that the West faced a series of terrorist attacks. That was the way that Al Qaeda had previously operated, and what we expected.

International airspace was closed and countries around the world went into lockdown. As the details of what happened that day became clearer, in particular the third attack at the Pentagon, staff and service personnel in the MOD were in direct contact with friends and colleagues in the United States. The British military had regularly worked alongside their

American counterparts, sharing equipment, training and expertise. This network of exchanges produced personal friendships, but also a profound understanding of each other's military capabilities. It meant for example that as the military coalition was being assembled to attack Afghanistan, the Americans already knew which specialist British military capabilities they would be asking for.

In the meantime the MOD went through a collective crash course on the history and geography of Afghanistan, working out the practical problems of attacking a landlocked country two and a half times the size of Great Britain, yet with only with around half its population. It seemed that every invader, from Alexander the Great, through Genghis Khan to the British in the nineteenth century and the Russians in the twentieth, had got into military difficulty in Afghanistan. It was the Russian failure and withdrawal in 1989 that set the scene for the eventual takeover by the Taliban, who in turn provided Al Qaeda ('The Base' in Arabic) with an operations centre and training grounds. After the Russian withdrawal the country had quickly disintegrated, as rival warlords and ethnic groups seized control of territory, launching destructive attacks on their rivals. On my first visit to Kabul I asked why it was that almost every building seemed damaged in some way. I was half expecting to be told that it was the result of British and American bombing. I was actually told that it was neither us nor the Russians; the destruction was the result of the civil war between rival warlords and the anarchy that followed the Russian withdrawal.

Because of this chaos and confusion, the Afghan people initially welcomed the Taliban's apparent determination to restore a degree of stability and order to the country. What they had not appreciated was that the Taliban shared a common belief in an extreme form of puritanical Islam with Al Qaeda, and that they would repress and abuse the Afghan people whilst at the same time providing a base for Osama bin Laden and his followers. He and his supporters had arrived in Afghanistan to fight the Russians but stayed on to continue their 'Holy War' against other targets, most notably Saudi Arabia and the United States. Following their attacks on US embassies in East Africa in 1998 where over 200 people were killed, President Clinton ordered cruise missile attacks against training camps in Afghanistan. That attack demonstrated the difficulty of military operations in remote Afghanistan. An American general wryly observed to me later that all they had succeeded in doing was 'to turn some very big rocks into some smaller ones'. His rueful observation was always in my mind when later the allies bombed targets in the country. There was not that much to bomb.

At the time of 9/11, Afghanistan was still divided. The Taliban, largely ethnic Pashtuns from the south, essentially controlled Kabul and the centre and south of Afghanistan. The north was still controlled by Tajiks and other ethnic elements from the former government, loosely arranged into what was to become known as the Northern Alliance. They were to provide a significant element of the ground forces when the allies attacked Afghanistan.

The world was shocked by 9/11. The UN immediately passed a resolution condemning the attacks. For the first time in its history, at the urging of Secretary-General George Robertson, NATO invoked Article 5, setting out the mutual guarantee at the heart of the Alliance, that an attack on one member state should be considered an attack on every member state. Given Al Qaeda's responsibility, Afghanistan was given a two week warning to surrender Osama bin Laden. The Taliban refused and by October 7th, a coalition organised by the United States, and with a prominent role for the UK, began military operations in Afghanistan.

There had been a series of lengthy discussions inside the MOD about the best way to respond to 9/11. The devastating attacks had been carried out by a terrorist group, not a country. Al Qaeda occupied no obvious territory. What exactly was the coalition going to attack? The refusal of the Taliban to hand over Osama bin Laden meant that in effect the target was to be the leadership of the country as well as the forces of Al Qaeda that were stationed there. This was to have significant implications later when the longer term future of Afghanistan had to be considered.

Afghanistan's landlocked geography meant that the attacks could only be by air or through neighbouring countries. We therefore needed their help. Meetings were arranged with all of the neighbouring countries to secure their support. I flew to India where a plane had been pre-positioned to take me to Uzbekistan for a meeting with President Karimov. He was one of a number of leaders of former Soviet states who had managed to make the transition to independence and a very controlled form of democracy, in one of the many new countries that emerged after the collapse of the Soviet Union. Given the time difference I had not been able to sleep on the way to India, and after arriving in Tashkent I was taken straight to the Presidential palace. President Karimov knew that I was there to ask for basing rights for coalition aircraft to launch missions into Afghanistan. After some short introductory pleasantries, he then spoke to me (or possibly at me) for two hours without a break. He reviewed the world as he saw it for my personal benefit, finding time to comment on what he thought of as the relatively poor result the Labour Government had achieved in the June 2001 General Election; noting that we had only got around 40 per cent of the vote. 'I got over 90 per cent last time,' he observed. I refrained from pointing out that he had something of a reputation for boiling his opponents in oil, which might well have contributed to his election success. I actually said nothing for the two hours, and was so tired that the only way of staying awake was to take my own notes. Given that my private secretary and the British Ambassador were doing the same, it must have looked very strange as we all sat there apparently writing down what he was saying. It at least helped frame my response when he finally seemed to have finished. I spoke for about ten minutes in reply and, for my temerity, we got another half an hour of his detailed views on the world situation. I did not speak again other than to thank him and leave. After all that time it wasn't even clear that he had actually agreed to my request.

Not surprisingly, the Americans were willing to throw their considerable military power into the campaign. More than 300 aircraft, two dozen warships and over 28,000 military personnel were quickly assembled within range of Afghanistan. Submarines and surface ships equipped with Tomahawk missiles were deployed to the Indian Ocean and long range bombers based both in the US and Diego Garcia were prepared. This created a practical problem for the UK and all those other countries desperate to show their solidarity with the US. What military capabilities could they offer that the Americans did not already have in abundance? The answer most of the time was more of the same. The UK had Tomahawk-equipped submarines which were also sent to the Indian Ocean. In addition, there were some gaps in the US military arsenal. The US Navy strike aircraft used the same mid-air refuelling system as the British. A different system was used by the US Air Force which meant that British long range tanker aircraft became vital components of the US attack on Afghanistan. Additionally, Britain's ageing but very capable

Canberra aircraft provided detailed ground photography. These and other niche capabilities were identified early on by US planners and were willingly offered by Britain.

One of my responsibilities was to approve all British bombing targets. We had relatively little detailed knowledge about Afghanistan. At one stage I looked at an ancient guide book which was being used to ensure that we avoided targets of historical significance. There had been a worldwide outcry when the Taliban had destroyed the two enormous Buddha statues in the Bamiyan valley, and we did not want to do anything that could be seen as being similar. Military operations actually began with a combined US-UK cruise missile strike on 7 October, aimed at the terrorist training camps and the military installations of the Taliban regime. In the days that followed, other military buildings and infrastructure were targeted and destroyed.

It soon became clear there were relatively few strategic targets worth bombing, and that the only real means of controlling the country was to put troops on the ground and take and hold territory. Getting invading foreign forces there in large numbers would take time, so the Americans decided to use a small number of specialist soldiers alongside the ground forces of the Northern Alliance. Britain also contributed its specialists.

The overwhelming US technological superiority in terms of information and intelligence was used to support local soldiers, often on horseback, fighting in ways that their ancestors might have recognised, albeit that they had expert assistance in the form of laser designation of targets. In effect, as the Northern Alliance advanced, their path was cleared by the coalition's devastating precision bombing of enemy positions. By early November 2001 the Northern Alliance was moving rapidly south, taking control of key towns and cities. By mid-November, the Taliban had been defeated on the road to Kabul and a small British force was sent to secure Bagram, the only operational airfield close to Kabul. Ironically, the coalition bombing had very comprehensively cratered the runway at the main airport for the city, rendering it unusable.

As the military operations proceeded, there was a growing concern in the western world about a possible humanitarian crisis in Afghanistan. The UN Security Council organised a meeting of all non-Taliban groups in Bonn in early December. It was decided that a Loya Jirga or tribal council would be held within six months to decide on the composition of a Transitional Council to run the country. In the meantime an interim authority would take charge, subject to the presence of an international force based in Kabul, to ensure that no single ethnic group or faction could dominate proceedings. Tony Blair made clear that Britain was willing to provide the initial lead for such a force.

This marked the beginning of a real difference in emphasis between the United States and other countries involved in the international coalition. The US was understandably entirely focussed on capturing those responsible for 9/11 – bin Laden and the leadership of both Al Qaeda and the Taliban. They saw the British approach, and that of the UN, as peacekeeping and nation building, which was simply not on their immediate agenda. It was equally obvious that, after the previous anarchy, some longer term stability had to be established – and quickly.

I spent the Christmas holiday fielding military offers from countries around the world wanting to show their support for the United States. Given later events, and in particular the military challenge of operations in the south, it has always seemed ironic that the main problem I faced at the time was politely turning down large numbers of offers of infantry battalions. It was clear as I spoke to a series of Defence Ministers on Boxing Day 2001 that they had been instructed by their President or Prime Minister to make sure that they were seen to be supporting the Americans with their troops. Some were quite irritated when I explained that we simply could not cope with still more infantry.

There was an obvious willingness at the time to deploy troops into Afghanistan, but unfortunately they were generally the wrong sort of soldiers. The UK had already committed the infantry backbone of the International Security Assistance Force or ISAF. What was actually needed were all of the ancillary elements required to support such a force in the field – one where there was virtually no local capabilities. In a statement to the House of Commons I explained that we had to 'construct a balanced and capable force able to get to Afghanistan quickly, support itself and do its job. The ISAF needs logistics support. It needs Explosive Ordnance Disposal troops. It needs signallers. It needs engineers. It needs medical units. It needs helicopters. And, given that it will deploy and be supplied by air, it needs air transport.' One of the most popular deployments was a

Bulgarian mobile shower unit, allowing the soldiers to remove the dust of Afghanistan which certainly in my experience seemed to get into every pore.

This final requirement, air transport, was a cause of further friction with the United States. It was vital to have an emergency escape route in the event of mission failure. The UK had a limited number of leased C17 aircraft that could do the job providing they were not operating elsewhere. Only the United States had sufficient capability to be always available for a rescue operation in the event of an emergency. After a certain amount of prevarication about the risk of diverting resources from their war fighting operations, the Americans did agree somewhat reluctantly to assist in any evacuation.

I flew into Kabul at the beginning of February 2002 under cover of darkness. I had flown from Bahrain in the back of a Hercules transport aircraft in what proved to be a very bumpy flight. I felt as if I had been inside a tumble dryer for three and a half hours. I was then taken in the early hours to a bombed out factory which was next to an old house designated as ISAF headquarters. I had a couple of hours sleep on a camp bed before washing in a bucket of hot water and trying to make myself presentable in my rather rumpled suit. Defence ministers who try and get away with wearing combat clothing inevitably attract media ridicule, but getting into a suit and tie in the middle of what had until quite recently been a war zone was equally absurd. I was saved by sitting down in a large tent with British soldiers to a full English breakfast. Afterwards I thanked the chef, who remarked, 'It's just like home, sir.' I refrained from pointing out that in my home if I ever wanted a full English breakfast I would probably have to cook it myself. The chef was obviously of the opinion that officers and Defence Secretaries had cooked breakfasts every morning.

Even so soon after the end of the fighting, the Afghan traders were already back on the streets, selling anything they could. I visited Chicken Street, famous for its carpets, coats and souvenirs, where I bought Elaine an Afghan coat. Later in a meeting with Hamid Karzai, who was in effect already acting as Afghan President, I tried to explain why for my generation, influenced by the fashions of the 1960s, such coats were the thing to have. He disappeared from the meeting room only to return with one of his own trademark coats, which he generously presented to me. He was famous for wearing it over his shoulders, which I decided might not work for me. My mother later very expertly converted it into an impressive dressing gown.

I also met my counterpart, the Defence Minister, 'Fahim Khan' (properly named Mohammed Fahim). In our discussions the tension between the Pashtuns led by Karzai and the representatives of the Northern Alliance became clear. Fahim, a Tajik, was the military commander of the Northern Alliance. He had supported Karzai for the top job but expected his own troops to be in control of Kabul. That was precisely the unbalanced situation that the ISAF was designed to avoid. After some difficult discussions, he accepted that, providing there was a limit of 5,000 soldiers, ISAF could in fact deploy. This had been agreed by the time we met, but he remained morose about the presence of foreign troops in his country. There were some suggestions in the background that this was because they might have threatened the lucrative drugs trade in which his brother was said to be a major player.

I left, again under cover of darkness, to be taken to Bagram airbase in the back of a Toyota Land Cruiser. That may not sound unusual except that the Land Cruiser was itself loaded onto the back of a Chinook helicopter for what was a short but exciting flight. The back door was down to allow a rear gunner to keep an eye out for any enemy action. I spent the journey wondering what it would be like if the ropes holding the Land Cruiser in place gave way. Bombing Kabul with a Toyota Land Cruiser was not anywhere in my instructions – and especially not with me inside.

Given some difficulties with other allies, British troops led ISAF for longer than originally planned. The operation proved a real success. The main runway at Kabul airport was quickly repaired, security was established and preparations were made for the Loya Jirga, at which Hamid Karzai was confirmed as President of the Transitional Authority, whilst plans were also drawn up for future elections.

Meanwhile the Americans pushed south, taking Kandahar; a previous stronghold of the Taliban. The retreating Taliban and what was left of Al Qaeda's leadership fled into the mountains in eastern Afghanistan near Tora Bora, where they had an extensive network of tunnels and caves. On a visit to the Pentagon soon after, Donald Rumsfeld the US Defense Secretary, showed me remarkable footage of the American attack on one cave complex. The satellite images showed the huge explosions triggered by American bombs as weapon dumps exploded. Then miles away I was able to see people escaping from the other end of the tunnels. He was convinced that this was when Osama bin Laden escaped.

I was then asked to deploy British troops to the south in what was expected to be a field combat role. A force of 1700, mainly commandos and helicopters, was sent to conduct 'sweep and clear' operations in the south-east. This noisy and relatively heavy force demonstrated the difficulties that coalition forces were to face in the next stage of operations in the south. They had no actual contact with enemy forces, who could see and hear them coming at a distance. Even had they made contact, the Taliban could blend in with the local people, who were according to the local code of behaviour, honour bound to afford hospitality. Although large amounts of weapons and equipment were discovered and destroyed, the exercise was typical of what was to follow, as conventionally organised forces found it difficult to deal with a fast-moving enemy that could quickly blend into the local population.

I went again to Afghanistan in July 2002 and had a similar round of meetings as before. The previous temporary leadership was about to be formally recognised on an interim basis, pending the holding of democratic elections. I visited British troops still operating as the lead element of the ISAF, although soon to be replaced by Turkish forces. I also saw something of the US war fighting machine. One part consisted of an enormous tent, full of soldiers sitting at desks with laptops open in front of them. This was digitised warfare, with the US 4th Infantry Division communicating through computers and handheld digital devices. They were way ahead of anything that Britain had at the time, or any other NATO forces, and indeed even most other parts of the US Army. But it showed what was about happen to the modern soldier. In the future he or she would carry a digital communicator along with a rifle.

The underlying tension between the allies' ideas for nation building in Afghanistan and the Americans' determination to capture and kill Osama bin Laden, and all of his senior associates, continued throughout the rest of my time dealing with the country. The British view, and that of other allies, was that if we were to avoid any further involvement in the country, it was necessary to help to create robust and permanent institutions and organisations that could prevent still more conflict. Given the history of Afghanistan, and its ethnic and tribal divisions, that was perhaps at best a naïve view, but one which was consistent with Britain's historical approach. Winning the war meant more than just winning the fighting. We had to rebuild the country and its institutions to provide longer-term stability. In stark contrast the Americans simply wanted to capture or destroy the man and the organisation that had inflicted such enormous damage on their country. That continued to be their primary focus even after Osama bin Laden was tracked down and killed. In a sense, neither side of the debate has ever proved successful. The Americans and their allies continued for many years to prosecute a war against the Taliban and a range of resistance fighters before eventually concluding belatedly that perhaps it could never be won militarily.

After the withdrawal of the coalition forces that had been propping up the government in Kabul, the rapid and complete collapse of all of the institutions that had been established there in the twenty years since 9/11, showed just how little progress had actually been made on nation building. It had naively been assumed that the huge quantity of US dollars poured into Afghanistan would at the very least allow some parts of the country to avoid Taliban control. Yet, even the Afghan army, the main beneficiary of US financial support, simply melted away in the face of highly motivated Taliban forces.

Afghanistan and the West will once again face the threats that follow from the risks of allowing a country to offer a safe haven for terrorist training. No one knows exactly how many foreign fighters contributed to the Taliban's military re-conquest of Afghanistan. What is known is that the Taliban have continued to have close connections with Al-Qaeda and its various successor organisations. It is difficult to believe that those fanatical foreign fighers will be content with victory in Afghanistan. They will continue their campaign against the West.

The US and its allies are simply the latest foreigners to have failed to control Afghanistan over its long and violent history. Both war-fighting and nation-building, promoted by outsiders, have proved incapable of moving Afghanistan from its tribal, ethnic and religious roots. It remains to be seen whether the people of Afghanistan can ever find a way of re-building a country and its institutions capable of surviving the religious fanaticism of the Taliban and its adherents.

MOD – IRAQ

One hundred and seventy nine service men and women were killed in the course of military operations in Iraq. Many more suffered life-changing injuries to their minds and bodies. As Secretary of State for Defence, I was ultimately responsible for those casualties. I had supported the attack on Iraq and the war that followed. That responsibility will always be with me. It was what my Dad was getting at, when he said that for him going to war was easier than what I had to do. I never really accepted his view because for those actually fighting a war the risk of death of injury is ever present. Nevertheless I was always aware that when I took decisions it could result in deaths and injury. Those decisions were never taken lightly.

At some stage in my time in the Ministry of Defence I learned that some of the bodies of service personnel killed in the Falklands had been brought back in containers many months later. In contrast I had seen in the United States the way in which their fatal military casualties were repatriated with flag-draped coffins and slow marched down an aircraft ramp in a short but dignified ceremony. I was determined that the same honour should be accorded to Britain's military fatalities.

Early on the morning of Saturday 29 March 2003, I went to Brize Norton airbase in Oxfordshire as the first ten bodies of servicemen killed in Iraq were returned to Britain. I was there on behalf of the government; Prince Andrew represented the Queen. As each coffin was slowly carried down the ramp of the huge C-17 aircraft that had brought them back from Iraq, I was very aware of the grief of the families standing immediately behind us. Their grief was fresh and raw. Only a matter of days before, they had lost a husband – or a father or a son – for them, perhaps the most important person in their lives. I met many of those families again later at the various events organised to commemorate their loss. By then many were able to put on a brave face and talk about their feelings to the various dignitaries they met. That was not the case early that Saturday morning.

One by one, each of the ten coffins was marched down the aircraft ramp and placed into a series of black hearses standing waiting immediately in front of us. As the long and difficult process concluded, the MOD had set aside a large room for all of the families to be given tea and sandwiches. I am sure that those families would have been comforted by speaking to Prince Andrew, not only because he was representing the Queen but also because as someone who had served in the Falklands War he knew the shattering reality of what it was like to lose a close friend or family member. Unfortunately he had to leave for another engagement, although I was not told what it was. As he disappeared at speed with his entourage, I walked slowly towards the building where the families were taking tea. I knew that it was my personal responsibility to meet and talk to each of the families. As I walked through the door, I realised that it was going to be one of the most difficult things that I had ever had to do in my life.

It could not have got off to a worse start. Each family was seated in a group around low tables. As I approached the first family a young woman stood up crying, saying that she was never going to speak to me and stormed off. I stepped back, hoping that the floor might open up and swallow me. I was saved by the dead soldier's mother, a kindly Scottish lady who said that I should come and sit down next to her. She explained that the young woman was the soldier's fiancée and that she had taken his death very badly. I learned a lot about people that morning. The young woman had fallen in love with a handsome soldier not very long before and planned to spend the rest of her life with him, perhaps not having the time to think about the real nature of his job. In contrast, any parent whose son or daughter has joined the military must at some stage have thought of the possible consequences. The mother had lived with those possibilities over many years, from the first time that her son, still in his early teens, had said that he wanted to join the army. That did not in any way lessen her grief, but as with other parents she had thought about what military service just might possibly mean for her son, and for her, on very many occasions.

As I went to each family group, I had similar difficult but at the same time moving conversations with parents, partners and family members. The smallest group consisted of a very dignified South African lady and her two equally impressive daughters. She could see on my face that I was having a difficult time, but said that I should not take it personally as her husband had died doing what he loved. The family lived in South Africa but her husband had chosen to join the British Army and had always fully appreciated the opportunity that he had been given to serve. She said again that he had died doing what he loved, and that I should not reproach myself for his death.

Another family, from Wales, explained that following their son's death they had received letters of condolence from their local council, from their County Council and even from the Welsh Executive; but had heard nothing at all from the government that had sent their son into action. Back at the MOD I wanted to know why that was. I was never given a particularly satisfactory explanation other than it seemed to be based on history, going back to those wars when thousands of men might have died in a single day's military action. Despite misgivings from officials and senior military figures, I decided to do something about it. From then on, until I left the Department, I hand-wrote letters to the next of kin of every service man and woman who died on active service. Part of the reason for the official misgiving was the difficulty in deciding who should receive such a letter. Death on active service covered large numbers of fatalities, including road traffic accidents, actually the largest single cause, and suicides. I wrote to every family.

What every family that lost loved ones wanted to know was that the death had been for a reason. They wanted to feel that the sacrifice of their loved one had not been in vain. For my Dad's generation that was straightforward. In the Second World War they were liberating the world from the evil of fascism in the course of a war of national survival. Modern conflicts are not usually as straightforward as that; Iraq was not like that. Saddam Hussein's regime was not an immediate threat to the home territory of the United Kingdom. Although it had been a threat to its neighbours, the first Gulf War and the war with Iran seemed to have eliminated any risk of any immediate further Iraqi expansionism. What was certainly the case was that Saddam Hussein was a direct and immediate threat to his own people. He led a vicious and brutal regime that had used chemical weapons against its own citizens. It was his failure to renounce such weapons, and his failure to comply with UN resolutions that was the immediate justification for the war. At the same time the underlying concern was that leaving him in place with such capabilities risked further conflict. I accepted at the time, as did most people, that after 9/11 the Americans were justified in identifying further potential threats to global security and that Saddam Hussein was high on their list.

I have of course to recognise and accept that successive inquiries have shown that he probably did not have any substantial stocks or even any current programmes for reconstituting chemical or biological weapons. This was at odds with the consistent and detailed intelligence that I was shown. It was at odds with what US Secretary of State, Colin Powell set out to the United Nations in a presentation that focussed for example on trailers said to be mobile weapons laboratories. Those trailers turned out to have been supplied by Marconi, a British company, and were actually for filling hydrogen balloons for use on artillery ranges. Colin Powell has since acknowledged that the presentation was a 'blot" on his career and the result of a significant intelligence failure. At the time however almost everyone, including the United Nations, and even those countries that subsequently refused to join the war in Iraq, believed that Iraq had weapons of mass destruction.

This seemed also to include senior figures in the Iraqi regime. Why else did Saddam Hussein and his supporters go to such great lengths to frustrate the work of the UN chemical weapons inspectors? Why did they do so if they had nothing to hide? I do not know the answer; nor, I suspect, does anyone else. It may be that the programmes were quietly abandoned by Iraqi officials, but no-one responsible dared tell Saddam Hussein given his brutal reputation for dealing savagely with those that he perceived to have let him down. It has also been suggested that it was the chemical and biological programmes that gave the regime credibility in the eyes of its enemies. Admitting that they had been abandoned would have been a significant sign of weakness. What is not in doubt is that Iraq's failure to co-operate with the inspection regime was seen by almost the whole world at the time as evidence that the regime was concealing continuing chemical, biological or even nuclear programmes.

It was this confusion that led to the allegations that the war was fought on a lie. The suggestion was that the US and UK governments knew that there were no weapons of mass destruction, but nevertheless went ahead with the war perhaps only because Saddam was regarded as unfinished business by the Americans after the first Gulf War. In my meetings with all of those involved – on both sides of the Atlantic – I never once had a sense that I was being lied to, and that in turn I was lying to the people who lost their lives.

I first started seeing intelligence about Iraq in my short spell as a Foreign Office Minister responsible for the Middle East in May 1999. I cannot now recall the precise detail of those briefings or intelligence reports, but I am quite confident that there was a clear assumption by the intelligence community and by civil servants in the Foreign Office that Saddam Hussein had stocks of chemical weapons. When six months later I started seeing similar material in the MOD, it did not come as any great surprise. Right up to the invasion of Iraq there were lines of reporting suggesting that the regime had stocks of chemical weapons. I accept with the benefit of hindsight that I could have challenged those assumptions more vigorously and sought to establish the basis for the belief that he had such weapons. I was not the only person to fail in this respect; it seemed that all of the relevant departments as well as the intelligence community believed it as well.

In the final few days before the attack on Iraq was to be launched, I was with Tony Blair in his small study in Downing Street together with Richard Dearlove, then 'C', the head of the British Secret Intelligence Service. Tony was sat at his desk, with Richard Dearlove on the sofa, next to me. Tony Blair asked him quite specifically and unambiguously whether Saddam Hussein had chemical weapons. His answer was unequivocal; the regime had them and would use them to defend Iraq if attacked. We spent a lot of time and effort in the MOD trying to determine when that time would come. Would it be as soon as coalition forces crossed the border into Iraq or later as they threatened Baghdad? Soldiers in Kuwait waiting for the attack were required to put on their chemical suits at very short notice. I did it myself; it was hot, sweaty and distinctly uncomfortable, and not something you would do unless it was thought to be absolutely necessary.

Given that Saddam Hussein had used chemical weapons frequently in the war with Iran and in attacking the Shia in the south and the Kurds in the north, it simply came to be assumed that he could and would do so again. It was those attacks on his own civilian population that led to the creation of the no-fly zones over Iraq after the first Gulf War. British aircraft were patrolling the southern no fly zone on a daily basis. My first meetings about Iraq in the MOD were concerned with those operations and the risk to the British pilots and crews involved. The Iraqi regime had a number of mobile surface-to-air missile launchers that were a direct threat to the aircraft patrolling the zones. They were frequently hidden in centres of population, making them difficult to target without risk of civilian casualties. They operated in a way that came to be known as 'shoot and scoot', firing a missile at coalition aircraft before moving on quickly to a new concealed site.

There was an acceptance that at some stage the Iraqis would be successful in bringing down a coalition aircraft, and that the Americans would make significant efforts to rescue any surviving crew; even, if necessary, to the extent of putting troops on the ground if any crew had been taken prisoner. It was thought at the time in the MOD that this might itself lead to a rapid escalation and war with Iraq.

This was one of many contingencies that US planners worked through as they prepared for the invasion of Iraq. That planning was initially conducted on a 'US eyes only' basis, although there was a great deal of speculation amongst the British military as to what was going on. One of the most intellectual of the senior British generals, Anthony Pigott, talked me through how he thought a successful invasion of Iraq could be achieved. He was adamant that it would have to be on two fronts, with simultaneous attacks from the north and from the south, to divide what were seen as Iraq's highly capable and professional armed forces.

Very shortly after Tony Blair's visit to Crawford, George Bush's home in Texas, an invitation came from the Americans for British involvement in the planning. There was no sense at the time, as far as I was concerned, that this was the result of any agreement that he had entered into with the Americans. I was never aware that he had given any kind of a commitment to George Bush. Even on the day of the parliamentary vote many months later, I still believed that British participation in the invasion of Iraq was conditional. The Crawford meeting has in retrospect assumed much greater significance, and involved much greater controversy than was apparent at the time. Tony Blair had regular calls and meetings with George Bush. At the time Crawford seemed to me to be simply part of that continuing dialogue.

As a result of the invitation from the Americans, I agreed that General Pigott should go to Florida to join the US planning at Centcom, the US headquarters for operations in the Middle East and Central Asia. After a good deal of discussion, he was then able to persuade the Americans to change their previous plan, an attack only from the south, to the simultaneous attack concept that he had outlined to me. As the planning developed, it was assumed that the UK would actually lead the attack from the north, even to the extent of having large numbers of US soldiers under direct British command.

There was however a significant political problem with this planning: Turkey, which at the beginning of November 2002 had seen the election of a radical new force in Turkish politics, the AKP, a party led by Recep Erdogan, which was known to be moderately Islamist. Most people in the west were taken by surprise by the success of an Islamist political party in a country that had a secular guarantee in its constitution. Their leader was not even initially able to take up his parliamentary seat, having been previously convicted of a public order offence that was said to have breached secular principles.

The Americans in particular were unprepared for what was to prove a significant change in Turkey's political direction: they had been used to a degree of influence either directly on the politicians or through Turkey's military. On previous visits to Turkey I had visited Turkey's MOD where the Chief of the General Staff, commander of the Turkish armed forces, had a grand and imposing office; in sharp contrast to the office of the Minister of Defence, tucked away in a much smaller corner of the building.

The new Iraq invasion plan needed Turkish support, or at the very least, their acquiescence, because in order to get to northern Iraq, the invading forces would have to cross almost the entirety of Turkey, west to east, from the Mediterranean to the Iraqi border. In discussion with Kevin Tebbitt, the MOD's Permanent Secretary who had previously served in the British Embassy in Ankara, I decided in early January 2003 that we both needed to visit Turkey to discuss the plan. I arrived in Ankara on the 8th, knowing that we had very little time before the invasion would likely take place. I was not prepared for what I found. Although I like to think of myself deep down as a historian, my studies had never included the impact of the post-World War One Treaties on Turkey, which having sided with Germany in the conflict, was severely punished by Britain and the other winners. The old Ottoman Empire was broken up and crucially, Turkish-speaking territories in the south of Turkey were transferred to the newly-created state of Iraq. This had never been forgotten by the Turks and the British had never been forgiven. I found myself on Turkey's equivalent of Newsnight being grilled by their equivalent of Jeremy Paxman about the perfidy of Britain in the 1920s. Turkey's military activities across the border in Syria have mostly been interpreted as being about controlling Kurdish ambitions; there may also be an element of Turkey seeking to restore at least some of its former Ottoman territories.

I then had discussions with all of the leading Turkish political figures, from the President down. The mood of the meetings was good; I got on extremely well with my Turkish counterpart, Vecdi Gonul. The problem was, however, that although no-one ever said that we could not take coalition forces across Turkey, no-one equally said that we could. I came back to the MOD with a very clear view that it was never going to be allowed. The new Turkish government was political; it was no longer in thrall to the military and in turn to the Americans. I asked myself what it would be like if we were asked to allow tens of thousands of French soldiers to march across England; even for peaceful purposes it could cause political problems. As a result, the invasion plan had to be re-engineeered. British soldiers would, like the Americans, be going in from the south. Although British soldiers and their equipment were already on their way to Turkey, their ships had not by then passed the Suez Canal so it was relatively straightforward to divert them towards Kuwait.

This decision was not exactly warmly welcomed when I went to Washington at the beginning of February, primarily to discuss post-conflict planning. The Americans were convinced that I was wrong, that the Turks and especially their military would eventually cave in to US pressure. As a result, the US 4th Infantry Division, and all of its equipment, was left bobbing about in the Mediterranean all through the earliest stages of the invasion, only joining the fighting later as a follow-on force.

In the course of the Washington visit, I was briefed at Donald Rumsfeld's request by Doug Feith, the Pentagon's Under Secretary of Defense on aftermath planning. The British civil servants that were with me were far from convinced that the Americans were taking the issue sufficiently seriously.

The British military had had their own problems in preparing for the invasion of Iraq; the UK had nothing like the military resources that were available to the United States, and these were already stretched given existing commitments in the Balkans, Sierra Leone and preparing Fire Service cover in the event of a likely fire strike. Around 19,000 service personnel or one in ten of the entire military were at the time on standby for fire cover.

In addition, Tony Blair was leading the international calls for the US to secure a second UN resolution explicitly authorising the use of force against Iraq. He made clear to me in the early autumn of 2002 that he would not welcome overt military preparations as he attempted diplomatically to secure support for the second resolution. That proved to be a very practical problem because the MOD had by then adopted what is known as an 'Urgent Operational Requirement' system for items of equipment that might be needed only in times of war or other unforeseen emergency. It also allowed the acquisition of new equipment to deal with new and unforeseen threats.

Previously, the MOD had held stockpiles of almost everything that might have been required to cover almost every emergency eventuality. The problem was that expensive kit would have to be disposed of as it reached the end of its shelf life, often without ever having been used. It seemed much more sensible to order the new equipment as and when it was needed. This was a policy that probably assumed, as in the Cold War, a long build up to a possible conflict. That long build up was simply not available in relation to Iraq, and some vital equipment, such as body armour, was ordered very late in the day. It did all actually get to Iraq in time; the real problem was that the MOD had no effective tracking system to ensure that the right equipment reached the right place in the right quantities. I was told that, as a result, when containers arrived various units took what they thought they might need, leaving other units short of what they actually required. When shortages were reported I kept being told by the Defence Logistics Organisation that the equipment had been sent. Willy Bach, the Minister for Defence Procurement, was given the task of working through the equipment pipeline to ensure that what had actually been sent reached its destination. Nevertheless the shortcomings in logistics management meant that deaths and injuries resulted, for which I and others were inevitably criticised.

When I set off for the United States on 8th September 2002 to attend the Remembrance Ceremony at the Pentagon, one year on from 9/11, the question of whether President Bush would 'go the UN route' was still very much open. I argued the British case to a sceptical Donald Rumsfeld. I then found myself in a curious position. During a courtesy visit to the State Department, I was formally received by Richard Armitage, the formidable Deputy Secretary of State, and a distinguished Vietnam veteran. We were soon joined by his boss, another former distinguished soldier, Colin Powell, who wanted to impress on me the importance of Tony Blair continuing his efforts to persuade the US President to take the UN route. Here was the US Secretary of State wanting a foreign Prime Minister to lobby his own President. I of course passed the message on.

I arrived in New York to visit Ground Zero at around the same time as the President was due to address the UN General Assembly. He had by then decided to ask for a second UN resolution. Tony Blair's diplomacy with the US President had been successful, although their combined efforts subsequently failed to secure an agreed further UN mandate for military intervention.

This caused clear legal problems for the UK, and in particular for me in the MOD. British troops, like all parts of the British government, must act in accordance with the law. I was under pressure from Mike Boyce, the Chief of the Defence Staff, to provide him with clear legal authority allowing him and the forces under his command to take action. Without a clear mandate in the form of a second resolution actually authorising the use of force from the UN, the UK's participation in any invasion depended on a complex interaction involving several not entirely consistent UN resolutions. It was the responsibility of Peter Goldsmith, the Attorney General, to resolve the question. He produced a very long and very detailed legal opinion that I suspected only sophisticated scholars of international law would entirely understand. I was sent a copy from Downing Street under conditions of considerable secrecy. I was told that it was for my eyes only and that I should not discuss its contents with anyone else. I actually had no idea at the time who else had received a copy. I read the opinion several times; it was not an easy read. This may simply have been the inevitable result of the sheer complexity of international law; although it did cross my mind at the time that the Attorney General was not unhappy about producing a document that only lawyers would understand; and then only after a great deal of detailed study.

Eventually I came to the view that the Attorney General had decided that invading Iraq would be lawful if the Prime Minister believed that it was in the UK's national interest to do so. It was not exactly the ringing legal endorsement that the CDS was looking for, and in any event, I was not strictly allowed to show it to him or even discuss it with him. Moreover, when my Principal Private Secretary, Peter Watkins, called Jonathan Powell in Downing Street and asked what he should now do with the document, he was told in no uncertain terms that he should 'burn it'. Peter Watkins was the very model of a principled British civil servant, and that instruction worried him greatly. He asked me what we should do and I agreed that we should lock the document securely into an MOD safe to which only he at the time had access. For all I know it is probably still there.

As the likely date for the invasion drew closer, I spent more and more time at the MOD, working through weekends in the Old War Office building. We had been relocated there because of a massive programme of internal reconstruction at the MOD main building on Whitehall. The last Defence Minister to have occupied my office in the building was Jack Profumo. I sincerely hoped that his resignation would not be a precedent.

One Saturday evening I was in the bowels of the building, having something to eat in the temporary canteen still serving those who were working through the weekend. It was downstairs and well away from my office and my private secretary, which meant that I was unusually alone when I went to eat. I fell into conversation with the only other person eating there at the time. He didn't introduce himself but said that he knew Iraq and that we were doing the right thing by invading and bringing down Saddam Hussein. I did not often get the chance to talk to people in the department without a formal meeting having been arranged, so it was fascinating to talk to someone who knew Iraq. He was quietly spoken but clearly very knowledgeable about the country and the activities of the regime. He did not specifically tell me that he had been a UN weapons inspector, even though it was very clear from his words that he knew in detail what he was talking about in relation to Iraq and its various weapons programmes. I mentioned the conversation to my private secretary when I got back to my office upstairs, but he had no idea about the identity of the person that I had met. I only learned later from his wife and daughters that it was David Kelly. He had gone home that night and told them that he had had a long conversation with the Secretary of State about Iraq.

On the day of the crucial parliamentary vote on Iraq, the 18 March 2003, I had one of my regular telephone calls with Donald Rumsfeld. It was just before lunch UK time, early morning in Washington. We went through the detailed questions that I had been instructed to raise in the very practical kind of discussion that I always had with him. However, towards the end of the conversation I believed that I needed to say to him that if we lost the vote later that day, then Britain would not be able to join in the invasion. I was not expecting to lose but thought it appropriate to explain the political and constitutional significance of what was happening in the House of Commons. He went straight from the call to his morning press conference where he referred to our conversation, stating that it would not affect US preparations, that they had 'work-arounds' to compensate for a possible British no-show. He was firmly making the point for his US audience that the invasion would still go ahead. The British media audience present took it as meaning that the UK was not really needed; a story that ran through the lunchtime news bulletins. As they concluded, I received a comprehensive Prime Ministerial bollocking over the telephone.

Despite what he clearly thought was an unnecessary diversion from his preparations, Tony Blair's speech at the start of the Iraq debate that afternoon was outstanding. He set out clearly and factually all of the detailed steps that the international community had taken to try and persuade Saddam Hussein to co-operate with the United Nations and the international community. Given the failure of the regime to respond positively, there was simply no alternative other than to remove Saddam Hussein and his supporters from power. The logic was in effect the same as for Afghanistan, where there had been a series of steps designed to allow compliance with the international community's requests. A failure by Iraq to agree would lead inevitably to war. The House of Commons agreed; the anti-war amendment was defeated by 396 to 217 and the government's motion was carried by 412 to 149. Three ministers resigned, including the Leader of the House and former Foreign Secretary, Robin Cook. Immediately the vote was passed, I had given authority for certain British units to begin to deploy in advance of the anticipated air campaign.

Given the controversies surrounding the war in Iraq, it is generally overlooked that the invasion and subsequent advance on Baghdad by US forces was a remarkable military success. A country almost the size of France, possessing apparently capable and professional armed forces, was defeated in a matter of weeks by a comparatively small attacking force. One of the mission-critical differences between the two sides was technology. The fighting showed the crucial difference that smart weapons could make. A relatively small number of aircraft could deliver guided munitions from a safe distance; perhaps even aimed simultaneously at different enemy positions, with a near guarantee of hitting the target. In the early phases of the air campaign I had to authorise each target personally. Together with senior RAF advisors, I spent many days poring over detailed reconnaissance photographs of military targets in Iraq.

I was inevitably nervous about civilian casualties; the American phrase 'collateral damage' was banned from use in our conversations. The bombing task was made still more difficult by the way in which Saddam Hussein would co-locate military command bunkers alongside schools or hotels full of foreign journalists. Initially I was probably over-cautious, preferring to pass on the more difficult targets, leaving them for later if they were still relevant. As the post-operation photographs came back showing the kind of damage inflicted, I became much more confident in the accuracy of the weapons. One reconnaissance photograph showed a bunker next to a hotel which had beach umbrellas on some sort of a roof terrace. The senior RAF advisor suggested that the weapons were so precise that the bunker could be destroyed without disturbing the umbrellas. He was mostly right; the later photographs showed the beach umbrellas on their sides, blown over by the blast, but otherwise intact.

Despite these efforts, there were inevitably civilian casualties; estimates of the actual numbers range from the low thousands in the early war fighting period to over a million following the insurgency and its aftermath. I was left in no doubt about the human cost of war, with the crash of a fully laden Chinook helicopter on the first night of the invasion as British and American forces were being ferried ashore to the Al Faw peninsula. Eight British and four American personnel were killed. I was awoken in the middle of the night with the terrible news. I had never had any lack of understanding about the risk to service lives, but somehow in the small hours of the morning those deaths really brought home to me the reality of war; I lay awake thinking about the families that might also soon be awoken with the same bad news.

I learned later that families were getting most of their information from 24-hour news programmes; each of which had embedded journalists alongside military personnel. We had taken the decision to embed journalists because we knew otherwise that some would make their own way to Iraq, massively complicating the military task on the ground as efforts would have to be taken to protect them. As British troops went ashore in Iraq it was quickly realised that the television live footage might show soldiers being injured or killed. Fortunately the TV companies involved had also recognised the problem and agreed to insert a short delay in their broadcasts to allow for the screening out of any casualties.

As British troops consolidated their position in the south, US forces were advancing at remarkable speed north towards Baghdad. Their initial pace was for a short time slowed by the need for sleep and the re-supply of food and equipment. Occasionally they encountered resistance from irregular Iraqi forces, known as Fedayeen, which were completely loyal to Saddam Hussein and could blend in with the local population. In contrast, regular Iraqi forces lining up for battle in their uniforms were destroyed by precision bombing from the air. Regular Iraqi soldiers had previously been bombarded with leaflets in Arabic inviting them to desert. As they saw the destruction wrought by smart weapons, many of them did just that. By the time that the Americans soldiers actually reached Iraqi positions, the enemy military units had pretty much ceased to exist as effective fighting forces.

The follow-on British task of consolidation was every bit as demanding. Before the conflict, it had been estimated that around 60 per cent of Iraqis were dependent on UN food supplies. Those supplies were inevitably halted by the fighting, and as a result there were predictions of a possible humanitarian catastrophe. The opening of the port at Umm Qasr allowed vital supplies to be brought in. British forces built a pipeline carrying fresh water from Kuwait to the south of Iraq. I talked about this with the Kuwaiti Defence Minister. He was amused and puzzled as to why a country that had no natural water sources was supplying one that had several major rivers.

The primary target for British forces was Basra, which inevitably as a large city had a diverse population ranging from diehard Saddam supporters through to his hard-line Shia opponents. It was eventually taken on 6th April by a carefully-targeted campaign against Saddam's remaining loyalists thereby avoiding an all-out assault on the city, which could have cost very many lives in what might have involved hand-to-hand street fighting. It was a clever and sophisticated operation by British commanders on the ground.

The Americans reached the outskirts of Baghdad by 5 April, and after a series of 'thunder runs' into the city decided that they could advance to the centre. Saddam Hussein's regime was toppled symbolically on 9 April as his statue was dragged to the ground in Firdos Square. By the beginning of May, President Bush was able to state that the war fighting was officially over. What was not fully appreciated at the time was that the hardest part of the conflict was still to come.

When I first visited Iraq in April 2003, I flew in a helicopter from Kuwait. I had made a similar short flight previously up to the border with Iraq and I can recall how strange it seemed when we just kept on going all the way to Umm Qasr. The helicopter flew tactically, which involves flying at speed close to the ground with the back open for the rear gunner to keep watch for any threats from the ground. There was in fact no sign of resistance or hostility. Nor at the time would I have expected to see any; the coalition had liberated a largely Shia area that had suffered greatly at the hands of Saddam Hussein's regime. During that visit I walked around Basra with British soldiers who were wearing berets not metal helmets. We talked to the local people and gave out sweets to the curious children, who were more interested in the soldiers' rifles than the sweets. The city itself was a mess, but not as the result of anything that British forces had done. The Shatt al-Arab waterway, which links Kuwait and Iran, was littered with abandoned and partially destroyed ships; I assumed these probably dated from the Iran-Iraq war. As I walked along the path by the water side I could see palm trees in the distance and commented that Basra, with some investment, could become a tourist destination. I was told that the city had once been known as the 'Venice of the East', and under the Ottomans had been a thriving cultural centre. At this distance and given what has happened since, it seems absurd but it was how Basra was seen by almost everyone at the time. There were even talks with other Arab countries about investment and how they could help to rebuild the Iraqi economy, financed by the huge supplies of readily available oil that could for the first time in a generation be properly exploited.

That at least was the thinking. The reality was of course very different. The reasons for the subsequent descent into anarchy and opposition to foreign forces were the culmination of a set of circumstances that would have been difficult to predict. Conventional wisdom suggests that the coalition failed to prepare for the aftermath of the fighting. That is not how I remember it; I seemed to spend far more time in meetings discussing what would happen after the fighting than actually planning the fighting itself. Clare Short, as International Development Secretary, had given Cabinet colleagues regular and long lectures on how we needed to avoid a humanitarian catastrophe in Iraq. We listened to her, and the British military in turn devoted its efforts to ensuring that there would be food and fresh water in the areas that were Britain's responsibility.

It is clear, however, that British assumptions about the aftermath proved wrong, at least in part because the Americans took certain significant decisions without any kind of consultation. It was thought that the occupation would be relatively brief, that there would be little or no opposition, and that the Iraqi professional classes would emerge from the shadows to take over the running of the country. Critically, as happened at the end of the Second World War in Germany, lower ranking members of the ruling party would remain in post. Many had probably joined the Ba'ath Party in the first place because it was a requirement of their job, not out of any enthusiasm for the regime. Similarly the British believed that the Iraqi army could be a force for stability. Instead the first two Orders from the Coalition Provisional Authority removed all members of the Ba'ath Party from their positions, banning them from future employment in the public sector, and disbanded the Iraqi army. The first Order was aimed at the staunchest supporters of the regime but it also hit many people who had joined the party simply to be teachers or civil servants. Many of them were likely to be Sunni, further dividing Iraq along religious lines. In both cases of course Iraqis were effectively deprived of an occupation and any income. Most of them were Sunnis who became increasingly resentful as the majority Shia population gradually took control of the country.

At the stroke of an American pen, a determined and angry opposition was created. It was one that had significant military expertise that was later put to use in planning and executing attacks on coalition forces. The British military had grave doubts about the decision because the Republican Guard had been seen as a potentially stabilising force within Iraq, without having any particular loyalty to Saddam Hussein. Both decisions meant that large numbers of otherwise law-abiding Iraqis were deprived of their role in Iraqi society. In the months of violence and anarchy that followed, there was a growing sophistication about the deadly attacks on coalition forces that was thought to be the result of former members of the military joining the ranks of the opposition and deploying their military expertise.

What was also not anticipated was the scale of Iraqi expectations. The Shia south had been denied resources all through Saddam's time in power. There was only one ancient power station that regularly broke down, and an electricity grid that was routinely interrupted with power outages in what is the hottest city in Iraq, with temperatures regularly exceeding 50C. As the Americans assumed control of their country, Iraqis expected that they would soon enjoy an American standard of living. When after weeks and months nothing seemed to improve, they became increasingly restless and angry. If anything, matters got worse as it was impossible to repair the decaying infrastructure to acceptable standards. In the event, the power station had to be shut down and completely replaced. Its replacement would take years, which was time the coalition forces simply did not have.

On that visit in April 2003, I also noticed on every street corner platforms that looked a little like the podium that an orchestra conductor might use. I thought initially they were for directing traffic, but it was explained that they were for the local Iraqi militia, positioned across the city as a visible demonstration of the regime's power. By the time that I arrived they were of course empty, and before long the liberated population across the country looted buildings associated with the regime, which included hospitals and museums.

Law abiding Iraqis blamed the foreigners for this failure. They had been used to the regime exerting significant control over their lives. They expected coalition forces to do the same and be visible on every street corner in the way in which Saddam's people had been. There were simply not enough soldiers to do this. Those British soldiers involved in the invasion had to be quickly rotated out of Iraq as they reached the end of their tour of duty. Although there was a United Nations mandate to restore and rebuild Iraq, the controversies of the invasion meant that many countries, like France or Germany, were never going to send their troops. Some countries like Australia and Italy did send significant contingents but other countries, whilst willing to send some soldiers, were not able to take responsibility for major sectors of the country. Iraq was simply too big to control from outside.

That became tragically obvious during the 24 June, when six British military policemen were murdered by a mob in the remote town of Al Amarah. They went there, lightly armed, on a humanitarian mission to advise the local police in respect of establishing law and order. As the result of a complete communications breakdown, they had not been warned that only hours before the Parachute Regiment had been involved on the other side of the same town in a serious firefight. It had been so violent that they had been forced to withdraw. The six military policemen were overwhelmed and brutally killed. I made a statement that night to the House of Commons after the close of normal business at 10pm. For many MPs it was an obvious indication that winning the peace was going to be much more difficult than winning the war.

The fact that the majority of the dispossessed were Sunni in a country where the majority were Shia only added to the instability. The first democratic elections in a generation in January 2005 inevitably favoured the Shia, with many Sunnis simply not participating. I had been aware before the invasion of the potential for violence between the Muslim sects. What had not been anticipated was that foreign fighters would deliberately provoke that violence by targeting Iraqis as they went to their mosques for prayer. Shia worshippers in the south were the targets as Al Qaeda and their affiliates sought to provoke a religious reaction against the Sunni minority. Iranian elements were also involved, as the places most sacred to the largely Shia population of Iran were located in Iraq. Although I was never likely to meet him, I viewed the Shia cleric, Ayatollah Ali Sistani, as the most remarkable force for toleration. After every outrage, with hundreds of Shias killed in terrorist bombings, he consistently called for calm and restraint, preaching that outright civil war was contrary to their faith and that it would lead to countless more deaths on both sides.

Ultimately, only Iraqis could resolve these issues; this process continues to this day. Britain began the long process of building new Iraqi police and military forces by establishing training camps for the new security forces.

On a further visit to Iraq I visited several of these camps, recognising that it was going to take time to make these organisations effective. Initially British soldiers went out on joint patrols with their Iraqi counterparts, gradually pulling back into a more mentoring role.

In the course of an interview with John Humphreys on the Today programme, I was asked whether an Iraqi mother who had lost her son in the fighting would ever thank Britain for what it had done in the country. He obviously knew that he was asking an impossible question. I am a parent, and like all parents I have imagined the life-changing pain involved in the loss of a child. I knew as a father that a mother would continue to grieve for her child to the end of her days. As Defence Secretary I could not be seen to be criticising British forces as they risked their own lives in a war that I supported. Struggling for an adequate response, I said that I hoped that one day the Iraqi people, freed from the brutality of Saddam Hussein's regime, might be able to decide on their own future.

I recognise that day has yet to arrive. When that might be, I simply do not know. No one knows what would have happened if Saddam Hussein had continued in power, just as no-one can be sure how many more deaths of his own people he would have ordered. What we do know is what happened in the course of the invasion of Iraq and the long period of anarchy that followed. There are some signs of growing stability in Iraq but at the same time there are still large scale terrorist atrocities. My 'one day' reply, however optimistic, still seems about right.

MOD – AFTERMATH

I have asked myself over and over again whether I could and should have done more to prevent David Kelly's shocking suicide. Although not a regular civil servant, he was employed by the MOD and with hindsight it should have done more to support and protect this rather shy and retiring figure through what was for him a period of unprecedented public exposure. It is perhaps all too easy to write that now some twenty years later. The real question is what I and others should have done at the time. It is much more difficult to look back and attempt to analyse each step that led to his untimely death and ask what could have been done differently, especially given the number of people and institutions involved and the intensity of the controversies. Irrespective of who else was responsible, I profoundly regret that David Kelly took his own life because of a lack of support from the MOD.

The sequence of events was set in motion by the row between the government, in the person of Alastair Campbell, and the BBC over a story that appeared on the morning of May 29th 2003 on the Today programme by former *Daily Telegraph* journalist, Andrew Gilligan, claiming that an intelligence briefing document had been deliberately 'sexed up' to bolster the case for invading Iraq. The background was the polarisation of the press for and mostly against the Labour Government. Alastair Campbell had robustly criticised the story.

I had strongly supported Alastair Campbell's complaint about the Andrew Gilligan broadcast, because it seemed in that particular report as if the BBC was heading in the same direction as the newspapers, ramping up stories for publicity effect rather than providing objective analysis. If, anxious about its ratings, the BBC behaved just like newspapers worried about their circulation, it would become difficult for any government to govern. As the circulation of newspapers continues to decline, the BBC is an increasingly important source of information for most members of the public.

The row became so toxic because the BBC was determined to defend what it saw as its editorial independence. That is perfectly right and understandable, although I felt at the time that the BBC went further than necessary because Greg Dyke, BBC Director General, and Gavyn Davies, its Chairman were both portrayed in the press as 'Labour luvvies'. Both were determined to show that they were going the extra mile in standing up to a government which it was generally known they had previously supported.

On the government side the stand-off was made worse by the involvement of both the MOD and Downing Street in separately trying to determine the right way to deal with a government employee who had apparently made critical comments 'off the record' to a number of journalists; with just one apparently embellishing what had been said to produce a sensational story.

I was first told by the MOD Permanent Secretary Kevin Tebbitt, on the evening of Thursday 3 July, that someone had come forward to his line manager, suggesting that he had spoken to at least one journalist. I was not told the name, only that he was an expert advisor employed by the MOD, rather than being a regular civil servant. Downing Street was informed immediately, although when I spoke to Alastair Campbell the next day, it seemed that he had been kept out of the loop.

The BBC Governors were due to meet to discuss the issue on the following Sunday, and I felt strongly that they should be told that someone had actually come forward suggesting that he might have been the source of the story. My view was that this would have taken the heat out of the situation, allowing both sides to say that they would look at what had been said originally and compare it to the broadcast. By then, however, it was in the hands of senior civil servants in Downing Street who understandably wanted to follow appropriate civil service procedures, which apparently meant that the information should remain confidential. I tried unsuccessfully to speak to Tony Blair more than once to set out my view on the Sunday morning. I learned later that he did not want to intervene in the due personnel processes of the civil service. Unfortunately, that meant that when the BBC Governors met that evening they had little alternative other than to back the Director-General and maintain their strong line regarding editorial independence. Sometime later I asked one of the BBC Governors what difference it might have made at their meeting if they had known that someone had actually come forward. She was convinced that it would have completely altered the outcome, as they could have then left it to the civil servants to establish what had been said to Andrew Gilligan and compare it to the broadcast. Instead without the relevant information, they continued to assert the BBC's editorial independence, a line inevitably followed by the newspapers.

There is little doubt that everyone involved on all sides simply failed to appreciate the impact on an intensely private man of being at the centre of such a huge public row. I visited Mrs Kelly and her two daughters at their home. Given the circumstances, they were incredibly generous and understanding. They told me about my meeting with David Kelly months before in the MOD canteen, and told me a great deal about him. They were equally generous to all of the people caught up in the events, including Tony Blair, Alastair Campbell and myself. They made it clear that they did not blame us for what had happened. By then, of course, the decision as to who was to blame was in the hands of Lord Hutton, appointed to conduct an official inquiry which was essentially an inquest into the reasons for David Kelly's death.

That summer, in 2003, we had planned a long family holiday in Arizona and California. Some people involved with the inquiry were surprised when I decided to go away but I could not face letting Elaine and the children down. It would not have been the first time they had missed out on a holiday because of my work. We had long wanted to take the children to the American West, revisiting many of the places we had been to on our long drives together in 1980. It did prove a good call to go. I was able to completely relax, mostly cut off from events in the UK, with the only information coming via members of my protection team as they changed over at the end of each week of the holiday.

When I arrived back, I was totally unprepared for what was happening. We flew back overnight in economy from Los Angeles, which meant that the photographs taken of me as we got off the plane were less than flattering. I complained to my protection team that my security was not exactly watertight if journalists and photographers knew exactly which flight I was on so that my picture could be taken literally as I stepped off the plane. Given the profile of the inquiry I was less surprised by the demonstrating crowds around the Royal Courts of Justice as I arrived to give my evidence to Lord Hutton. Having spent part of my life asking other people questions in court, it was more than strange to find myself apparently in the dock, and that is certainly how it felt with virtually every newspaper stating that I would be the fall guy, quoting Michael Heseltine's pithy comparison that I was 'toast'.

I was not entirely comfortable with the evidence that I gave because it felt as if I was being rushed through events that needed time and careful consideration. And, as the inquiry went on, I began to worry that the general atmosphere generated by the newspapers was so poisonous that the outcome could only be negative. On the other hand, I knew deep down as a lawyer that the decision was in the hands of a judge who was unlikely to be influenced by the newspapers and public opinion. As a result when I was asked by journalists to say how I thought things were going I refused to comment. Again I was given lots of advice that I should get my case across in the media but whilst that might have given me some respite from the journalists for 24 hours or so, I could not see how that could help with Lord Hutton, who might well resent my giving evidence outside of his inquiry.

I gave my oral evidence in the morning, with Alastair Campbell due in the afternoon. I was cross examined in detail by counsel for the Inquiry, with the result that by the lunch break I had not been asked in public about all aspects of the witness statement that I had previously prepared and submitted to the inquiry. Some days later when Richard Taylor, one of my Special Advisors, gave his evidence about the only relevant meeting that he had attended, I was accused in a front page headline by *The Times* of lying to the Inquiry because I had not mentioned this particular meeting in evidence. I had though dealt with it in my confidential written statement to Lord Hutton. After the Inquiry's findings were published, I complained about the ludicrous *Times* story to one of the journalists whose name was on it. He said that he had written only part of the story, and that none of the contributing journalists would have seen the full story before it was published.

The last question to me came from counsel for the BBC who asked why I had not sought to correct a newspaper story that had suggested that the so called '45-minute warning' referred to the possibility that Saddam Hussein could launch missiles against British bases in Cyprus. I had absolutely no idea what he was talking about at the time, and stumbled through a reply about how difficult it was to get newspapers to retract stories. I later found out that the question referred to two articles in *The Sun* and *Evening Standard*, which had included provocative photographs of missiles being launched. Only when I checked the date of their publication against my diary, did I establish that I had been in Kiev meeting President Kuchma of Ukraine at the time. I had been sent there to warn him off supplying any further advanced radar equipment to the Iraqis. Although Peter Watkins, my private secretary, had prepared a press summary for me to read that day in Kiev, he did not believe in including material from the tabloids or from regional newspapers.

I had obviously been aware of the '45-minute warning' issue. Indeed, when the draft dossier was circulated to relevant ministers and departments, I had specifically asked to speak to an expert from Defence Intelligence so that I could properly understand what the '45-minute warning' referred to. He told me that he assumed that it referred to the time taken to deploy and fire a chemical artillery shell. Since it was well known that Saddam Hussein had used such shells in the war with Iran (and against his own people), the explanation did not cause any great surprise. I had absolutely no idea at the time of giving my evidence to Lord Hutton that the '45-minute warning' issue had been deployed by the Press Office in Downing Street in a very different context.

The Hutton Report was published on 28 January 2004, and almost completely cleared the government of any wrongdoing. There was some mild criticism of the MOD for not looking after David Kelly better, but most of the strongest criticism was reserved for the BBC. Tony Blair was due to make a statement after Prime Minister's Questions and obviously I went into the chamber to listen. As I made my way along the front bench, the majority of the parliamentary party was cheering and waving their order papers in support of me. I was very grateful for their show of solidarity as I sat down in the middle of the row. After Tony Blair arrived, he insisted that I should sit next to him in prime position for the TV cameras. He demanded in the light of the report's conclusion that I should be left alone and allowed to get on with my job in the government.

The sour notes came the next day with newspapers claiming that the report was a 'whitewash'. These same papers had originally praised the appointment of Lord Hutton as an independently-minded, strong-willed Ulster judge, unlikely to be swayed from finding the truth by the government's views. Now he was described as a lickspittle who had slavishly followed the government's line. His treatment by the press was disgraceful. He had been asked to do a difficult job and had produced his considered opinion, but because it went contrary to what most newspapers wanted by way of a verdict, they then tore into him and his reputation. I was aware in the years that followed that it became increasingly difficult to persuade people to take on these kinds of high profile public tasks; the rewards were modest but the downsides were becoming unacceptable. After all, why should a public figure have their reputation trashed because they dared to disagree with the view the newspapers had previously decided on?

It was obvious that the media would use the opportunity afforded by public inquiries to make headlines. What I was surprised and disappointed by was the extent to which lawyers would also join in. As allegations were made about the mistreatment of Iraqi prisoners by British soldiers, a public inquiry was established to investigate. Two firms of solicitors in particular, Leigh Day and Public Interest Lawyers, led by Phil Shiner, had scoured Iraq for complainants. To generate still more headlines, these firms suggested that the mistreatment had either been ordered centrally or at least condoned or ignored at the very top of the MOD, thereby amounting to war crimes committed by the British State and its ministers. I again found myself in the dock giving evidence. I was told in detail in advance about which issues affecting me the Inquiry was concerned about. I was therefore able to prepare thoroughly to refute any suggestion that I or any other minister had been aware of any mistreatment before it had been properly reported to us. As I was about to leave the witness stand, counsel for the Inquiry asked me to watch a video. It appeared to have been filmed on a mobile phone and purported to show British soldiers ill-treating Iraqi prisoners. I was asked for my reaction. I was shocked, not only by what I had been shown but also that counsel for the Inquiry was trying to catch me out by staging a theatrical stunt at the end of my evidence. I had never seen the video before and had not been warned that it would be used.

The Inquiry had concluded in 2014 that allegations of war crimes were based on 'deliberate lies, reckless speculation and ingrained hostility' and that British soldiers had responded to an ambush by insurgents with 'exemplary courage, resolution and professionalism'. Public Interest Lawyers were closed down in August 2016, following a finding by the Legal Aid Agency that they had breached contractual requirements following a Solicitors Regulation Authority investigation. Phil Shiner was struck off the roll of solicitors in 2017 because of his misconduct in making false abuse claims against British soldiers with a finding that he was 'guilty of multiple professional misconduct charges, including dishonesty and lack of integrity'.

In January 2014, Public Interest Lawyers had submitted a claim to the International Criminal Court to prosecute senior British politicians and military leaders for war crimes in Iraq. That investigation continued until towards the end of 2021, notwithstanding that it was based on material supplied by a comprehensively disgraced lawyer.

These inquiries although difficult and time consuming were nothing compared to the Chilcot Committee Inquiry, set up after media pressure, by Gordon Brown in July 2009, eventually reporting in July 2016, with a report running to 2.6 million words in twelve volumes.

I was the first former Cabinet Minister to give evidence on 19 January 2010. I was fortunate not to be in full-time employment at the time, as ploughing through the piles of documents that had crossed my desk years before took up an inordinate amount of time. I should not have been surprised about the amount of paper involved, because most nights as Defence Secretary I would have two red boxes to read, and at weekends quite often three. It meant however that years later it was impossible to recall all of the detail or even some entire documents. There were very many documents with my name on that I had completely forgotten about. In March 2002, for example, as we were first learning about US concerns about Iraq, I wrote to Tony Blair pointing out that perhaps Iran was likely to prove a much bigger problem.

The time taken to produce the report attracted extensive criticism. It was delayed by a variety of factors, including the illness and death of one of its members, Sir Martin Gilbert, and the 2015 General Election. The Committee was also required as a matter of law to give all those criticised in its draft report the opportunity of responding to the criticisms. For some of those involved this appears to have been a further extensive exercise. It seemed to produce an odd imbalance in the final report, in that the executive summary was fair and balanced, presumably having been re-written in light of the various representations made by those who had been criticised initially. However, some of the background material appeared to have been published without amendment in light of relevant representations.

The Chilcot Report was difficult reading for all of those involved. No-one came out of the process particularly well, although a senior businessman commented to me that if his multi-national company had been required to hand over every document produced over an eight-year period and explain every decision taken by every senior executive during that period in detail it would make his business seem shambolic. He argued that although there were obvious mistakes made, the integrity of the process and of the individuals involved came through in the Report. I am not sure that I could construct quite such a positive perspective, but at least the conclusions clearly did not suggest that anyone told lies about Iraq.

Even today there are still further pending investigations about my time in the MOD. One such investigation, led by the former Chief Constable of Bedfordshire, is looking into allegations that the British state was complicit in IRA murders in Northern Ireland. Although the main events occurred long before I became Defence Secretary, I was asked to make a statement, which involved looking at MOD documents which again I had long since forgotten about.

I have often been asked about the difficult period I spent as Secretary of State for Defence. According to Peter Watkins it was just two weeks short of the longest period in that office, when Denis Healey held the position from 1964 to 1970. Because of our connection going back to my days in Leeds, he kindly agreed to come into the MOD on more than one occasion and I was able to ask his advice. He often found my requests for his advice amusing, pointing out that he had had comparatively little to do during his time in the job. Indeed there was one year in which not a single British soldier had been killed on active duty. Although he was too generous to mention it, the subtext of his remarks was that he and the then Labour government had refused to join the United States by sending British troops to Vietnam, whereas I had been part of a government willing to send British forces into Iraq. Sometimes what is not said is of greater significance. He had one of the most brilliant minds of any British Minister. Some years later I was invited to a dinner in his honour given by the Speaker in his rooms in the House of Commons. In his nineties Denis

Raising money for military charities (Author's collection)

On board the Queen's flight (Author's collection)

On board one of Britain's nuclear submarines (Author's collection)

On the front line of Arctic Warfare in Sweden 2001 (Author's collection)

Being welcomed as Chair of Twycross Zoo Trustees by Dr Sharon Redrobe, CEO of the Zoo (Author's collection)

A brief visit to North Korea 2000 (Author's collection)

In Afghanistan with my local regiment (Author's collection)

At the controls flying over Afghanistan (Author's collection)

In Nepal with Gurkha veterans (Author's collection)

In one of the villages in Sierra Leone (Author's collection)

Setting fire to drugs in Pakistan (Author's collection)

With President Karzai in Afghanistan (Author's collection)

With President Chirac in Paris (Author's collection)

NATO meeting Colorado Springs October 2003 (Author's collection)

With Donald Rumsfeld at a Press Conference in 2003 (Author's collection)

At the Despatch Box in the House of Commons (Author's collection)

With Gary Brooker of Procol Harum and Fran Nevrkla, Chair of the PPL in Abbey Road Studios (Author's collection)

Brian Clough launching my
election campaign in March 1992
(Author's collection)

With Jackie Chan at the Foreign Office
(Author's collection)

On the set of 'Lord of the Rings' in New Zealand (Author's collection)

With Steve Cram after Sport Relief fundraising (Author's collection)

Healey entertained the room by quoting spontaneously and at length from Shakespeare. There is little doubt in my view that he should have been the Leader of the Labour Party at some stage in his long and illustrious political career.

It is that contrast between two Labour governments that history will record; one that refused an invitation from the US President, the other that accepted. History will also record my part; although there were many other aspects of the job that I hope will also be remembered. White Papers in the days of Denis Healey were only a few pages long, setting out very precisely what the government proposed to do. I was responsible for a number of White Papers, often running to hundreds of pages complete with photographs, maps and diagrams, explaining not only what was proposed but in more enquiring times, why. The most significant was the so called 'New Chapter' to the 1998 Strategic Defence Review. It was in effect another strategic defence review to take into account the consequences of 9/11 terrorism on Britain's armed forces and the impact of modern military technology. It sought again to re-balance Britain's Armed Forces away from the slow moving build-up of the Cold War era towards rapid response and greater agility. The problem with all such reviews is that the people, their training and their equipment cannot be altered overnight. It can take decades to develop and implement a new strategy; by which time almost inevitably the world will have changed again.

Another decision that I trust will stand the test of time was my concern to establish a permanent memorial for all of those killed in military service. This arose in part because of a constituency coincidence. The parents of Stephen Restorick, the last British soldier to be killed in Northern Ireland on 12 February 1997, moved into my Ashfield constituency shortly after I became Defence Secretary. Mrs Rita Restorick, who in 2000 wrote a book arising out of her son's death by a sniper's bullet, was a tireless campaigner for some sort of public recognition for service deaths in Northern Ireland. I saw her and her husband on a number of occasions as their constituency MP and they rightly pointed out that the names of British service personnel who died in the two world wars were recorded on public monuments up and down the country, whereas those that died in Northern Ireland generally died in ones or twos and were not publicly recognised anywhere.

I tried to find ways of properly satisfying their justifiable concerns, but everything that the MOD came up with was less than they felt appropriate compared to previous generations. In the course of a family holiday on the East Coast of the United States, we spent some time in Washington visiting the various museums and monuments. I had not previously visited the Vietnam Memorial, two long black granite walls containing more than 58,000 names of American soldiers killed in Vietnam in date order. It is an immensely moving tribute to those that died and I realised that something similar could be done to record British service deaths since the Second World War. Britain had been involved in many conflicts where it was unlikely that the names of those that died would be publicly recorded; Northern Ireland was the most obvious example.

My initial idea was to have something similar in London on some open ground between the main MOD building and the River Thames. I felt that central London was the appropriate place for such a national memorial. However, in discussion with service charities and in particular the Royal British Legion it became clear that they would strongly oppose a central London site on the grounds that it might detract from the significance of the Cenotaph. I was then fortunately approached by David Puttnam, as a Director of the National Arboretum in Staffordshire, asking whether I would be willing to site the memorial there.

The Armed Forces Memorial was dedicated in the presence of Her Majesty the Queen on 12 October 2007. On a 43-metre diameter structure with two curved walls and two straight walls are recorded the names of more than 15,000 service personnel who were killed in the course of more than fifty conflicts and operations in which Britain participated since 1945. Stephen Restorick is one of those names.

LEADER OF THE HOUSE
Do What He Please

Throughout the 2005 election campaign I had an entirely irrational but very real sense that things were not quite right as far as my job in government was concerned. I had no evidence for this other than a feeling that I was somehow out of the loop. It was not that I had particularly expected to be in any loop – not least because I was busy enough in the Ashfield constituency, helping out in Erewash, the marginal seat where I lived held by Liz Blackman my PPS, as well as travelling the country as part of Labour's national political campaign.

The Ashfield General Election count always seemed to take forever, probably because it took time to get the ballot boxes in from the small outlying former mining villages. The result was finally announced at around four in the morning and on a much reduced turnout I had been re-elected by just over 10,000 votes; not a massive majority compared to the past, but nevertheless still comfortable.

When the call came from Tony Blair on the Friday after the election, I was still at home in Derbyshire. The fact that I was being called early was obviously bad news; Prime Ministers have to remove the dead wood before they can start on promoting the new faces in a reshuffle. I was not entirely surprised therefore when he said to me that he had to 'let me go'. I am sure that he chose the formulation because he thought that he was being kind – but I was seriously unimpressed by the entirely inaccurate convolution. After I'd done almost six years in what had proved to be one of the most difficult, demanding and unpopular jobs in his government, he had decided for whatever reason that he wanted me out.

I am sure that most of the time I would simply have accepted his decision – but I was sufficiently irritated after a long and tiring election campaign to protest that it was 'unfair'. My mood was not helped by having had only a few hours' sleep. I was also annoyed that he had not chosen to see me and tell me to my face. Again he was probably being kind in trying to save me from the humiliation of walking along Downing Street in front of the cameras having just been sacked. Nevertheless, I said that I wanted to see him and hear his explanation directly. Tony Blair said that I should 'come over' and was obviously surprised and irritated to discover that I was still at home in Derbyshire. Not for the first time I realised how London-centric Tony Blair was. I was told by a very grumpy Prime Minister that I had to get to his office by 6pm.

My protection team was then scrambled and we made what was certainly my fastest ever drive to London – using the hard shoulder when needed to avoid traffic queues, and travelling for most of the time at well over the motorway speed limit. The excitement of the drive down was almost worth getting the sack for. Less than two hours later, when I walked into the outer office at Downing Street, I saw immediately on Jonathan Powell's computer screen a list of Cabinet appointments that had me down as Leader of the House of Commons. When I went into his study, Tony simply told me that was what he had decided and since I wasn't in the business of pushing my luck, I agreed. There was no explanation or even any reference to our earlier conversation, which struck me as being distinctly odd.

I have no real idea as to why he had decided to sack me or indeed why he changed his mind. I was to be replaced at the MOD by John Reid who I knew had long wanted the job. John was certainly adept at the black arts of politics; I am sure that he had been lobbying behind the scenes. I have no idea what he was saying but I suspect it probably played on Blair/Brown tensions. It was possible that I was paying the price for Iraq, although at the time the public were essentially still onside, having just voted overwhelmingly for the government that had joined in the war. I did wonder whether it was a media scheme dreamed up by Alastair Campbell to distance at least part of the government from Iraq – but given that joining in the war had been driven through by Tony, that hardly made sense.

Whatever the reasons, there is no doubt that it was a turning point in how I saw my relationship with Tony Blair. Up until then I had been an entirely loyal Blairite – supporting his decisions – but more importantly essentially sharing his view about the positioning of the government politically and wanting us to continue in his phrase to be 'the natural party of government'. Indeed, in Andrew Roth's Parliamentary profile, I was described as being 'a Blairite before Tony Blair became Leader of the Labour Party'.

Although my political views remained the same, there is no doubt that my confidence in his ability to see them through was undermined. I had always had doubts about his handling and treatment of people. From the start of his government he seemed to have little or no regard for those that actually supported his political view of the world – but at the same time he promoted those who were actually working to undermine it. Now I seemed to be on the outside and thereafter I was even more wary about his judgements.

I had called Alistair Darling immediately after the telephone call from Tony – and almost immediately after that I was called by Gordon Brown. He made clear that he thought the decision was wrong and that he had played no part in it. He indicated that when he was Prime Minister I would be reinstated in his Cabinet. Up until that conversation, I had not had the easiest of relations with him. I was clearly a Blairite and my only one-to-one conversations with him had involved difficult discussions about the budget for the MOD. Gordon Brown consistently reflected the standard Treasury view that the department was wasteful, and that when it came to government financial planning the military always engaged in special pleading to get more than they needed. I had obviously resisted this argument, which had led to some sharp exchanges. Now it was clear to me that I was being recruited to the Brown team, having been sacked from the team that I had thought I was on; this put me in a very strange political place.

Nevertheless, I was still in the Cabinet – at least for a while – and I actually enjoyed being Leader of the House. I had always liked being around Parliament. I could never really get over the astonishing idea that I was actually there and part of the place. So being part of the team responsible for running Parliament was something that I thought I would enjoy.

There was one last wrinkle in the reshuffle. When it had seemed to be all over I got another call from Tony Blair. This time he began by asking me a favour – one that he said not entirely jokingly would 'upset' Alistair

Darling. He wanted me to take Nigel Griffiths as my unpaid deputy. It was immediately obvious that this request really came from Gordon Brown, fighting the corner for one of his people who would otherwise have been out of the government. I knew that Alistair would be annoyed; he and Nigel Griffiths were both Edinburgh MPs and did not get on with each other. Nevertheless, I had no particular objection to taking a deputy and in truth Nigel Griffiths carried out the limited tasks required in the job competently and, as far as I was able to tell, loyally.

What struck me strongly at the time, though, was the stark contrast in their approach to people showed by the two men at the top of the government. Gordon Brown was fiercely loyal to his team, fighting their corner when he thought that he needed to. In contrast, Tony Blair seemed to be completely uninterested in his strongest supporters. He had hung Alan Milburn out to dry in the course of the 2005 election campaign, and was obviously quite prepared to do the same to me. This sounds as if it was only about individual ministerial careers. It was about much more than that; it was about the future political direction of the Labour Party and the government. Only by promoting and supporting like-minded people could Tony Blair ensure the continuation of his ideas and policies. Margaret Thatcher had famously wanted to ensure that her successor was 'one of us'. Curiously, Tony Blair seemed not in the slightest bit bothered about this – which is why ultimately his ideas and policies were largely abandoned by the government and by the Labour Party.

This also showed how desperate most people are for ministerial appointments. I suppose that it is simply a tangible sign of success, although some perhaps foolishly believe that as junior ministers they are about to exercise power. There was one very notable exception to the usual rule. My PPS and local MP Liz Blackman was an outstanding MP; she had won a difficult marginal seat from the Conservatives, and at the 2005 election had continued to build her majority as the majorities in safer Labour seats like mine were falling back. I had strongly recommended her for promotion, and in the course of the reshuffle she had been offered a ministerial job. To Tony Blair's obvious amazement – and some considerable irritation when he complained to me about it – she turned down the job. She apparently told him that she did not believe that being a minister was right for her. I wish that I could have spoken to her first, but she was having a short break in Paris at the time and even the legendary No. 10 switchboard had had some difficulty in reaching her. It was entirely to my benefit in that she continued as my PPS – but she would have been an excellent minister. It might even be a good test of who would be a good minister – that they should have first genuinely turned down the opportunity.

After almost six years of serious day-to-day departmental activity in the Ministry of Defence, the job of Leader of the House came as a very pleasant interlude. It was not really a full-time job. There were regular committees to attend, dealing with the organisation of the business and planning of the work of both Houses; but there was no department and no departmental administration.

There was the tangled issue of House of Lords reform, which we spent a great deal of time discussing but ultimately failed to resolve. As a young university lecturer teaching constitutional law I had read the *Crossman Diaries* avidly – it was the first real contemporary insight into the internal workings of government. The second volume covers his time as Leader of the House and his protracted efforts to reform the House of Lords. It seemed slightly weird that I was doing the same job, dealing with many of the same issues, almost 40 years later. I re-read Volume Two of the Crossman Diaries and found some fascinating and highly relevant quotations:

'For the weekend I had no red box full of papers, no departmental chores.' (Friday 2 September 1966)

'... the risk of my dropping a clanger is quite high. I have no Department, I have no field to work except that I should cover the whole of government policy.' (Sunday 11 September 1966)

My first task in the new job was to chair the Legislation Committee, which was to determine what should go into the Queen's Speech. I had attended the Committee when I worked for Derry Irvine and witnessed some spectacular bust ups, as Cabinet Ministers insisted on getting their own particular priorities into the upcoming but crowded parliamentary session. I was fortunate in that the next session was due to run for 18 months, meaning that most of my colleagues' ambitions could be satisfied. Nevertheless, Des Browne as the new Treasury Chief Secretary made clear that there would be no money for a Housing Benefit Reform Bill that was strongly supported by David Blunkett. This looked like Gordon Brown using his financial veto to decide on political priorities; it could equally have been about striking down a potential rival for the party leadership.

There was also the Business Question to prepare for every Thursday, when I would announce the agenda of the House of Commons for as far ahead as possible; usually two weeks or so. Since the question lasted for up to an hour, when MPs could raise any issue they liked in the guise of asking for a debate or statement on the subject, it was in effect a subdued version of Prime Minister's Questions. There was obviously none of the pressure or media attention involved; indeed, sometimes the chamber was very quiet as individual MPs asked constituency based questions aimed at getting coverage in their local newspapers. It was nevertheless a good exercise for me; I had to keep up with policy developments and issues right across the government and learn to deflect or ignore those troublesome questions that I really didn't have an answer for.

The practice every Thursday of trying to deal with wide ranging questions from MPs from all parts of the House of Commons did at least come in useful when I found myself standing in at Prime Minister's Questions for the real Prime Minister when he was away on EU business. Strictly, of course, that job fell to John Prescott as Deputy Prime Minister. It was an open secret that he hated having to do it – not least because of the mauling he usually got in the next day's newspapers. After Cabinet one day he came up to me with a broad smile on his face, saying cryptically 'it's your turn now'. I had no idea what he was talking about; I am not sure that I even knew at the time that the Leader of the House stood in for the Deputy Prime Minister if he and the Prime Minister were both away at the same time.

I was distinctly nervous from then on. It was one thing dealing with questions in the relatively relaxed atmosphere of the Thursday Business Question session; it was quite another to crash and burn live on television in front of all your colleagues. I could quite see why John Prescott hated doing it. The sense of unreality was compounded when I went across to Downing Street for two hours of very professional preparation and was presented with a folder which said 'Prime Minister and First Lord of the Treasury' on the front cover. It was as if I had written into some television programme asking to be Prime Minister for the day and my wish had been granted. Alistair Darling pointed out in his dry Scottish way that my entire future could depend on how it went – that people would talk for years about what a mess I made of it, pointing me out as I shuffled by along a parliamentary corridor, 'There's the one who had that disastrous time at Prime Minister's Questions, the time that Tony Blair was away. They never let him do anything again after that.' I knew that Alistair was joking, but it showed that I had no need of enemies with friends like that.

I actually bumped into Tony Blair on the Wednesday morning, as I went across to Downing Street for the final briefing session. He was just setting off to go to Strasbourg to make a speech to the European Parliament on the British EU Presidency. At that point, with only a few hours to go, I would have very happily changed places. He made no comment about why I was there; he obviously had other things on his mind or he had simply forgotten.

I had been hoping that the House of Commons would be subdued given that my opposite number, Chris Grayling and I, were not exactly the first team. Someone on the television brutally, but entirely accurately, pointed out that we were actually the third team. In fact the Commons seemed as noisy as usual, with Tory MPs looking to impress with the prospect of a newer and younger leader. I got through the half hour of PMQs in the same way that I had dealt with the Business Question week in week out; short answers to the questions that I knew about, and attempting to deflect anything that I didn't. It was school half term and Elaine, Julia and Nathalie were on holiday in Tenerife. They apparently watched it at their hotel; I never found out what other British holidaymakers thought of them sitting watching parliamentary proceedings in the bar when they were supposed to be on holiday.

Being Leader of the House reminded me a little of my early days as an MP; I was free for a lot of the time to pursue the subjects that most interested me. I was also often used by the Government to meet and greet visiting politicians and dignitaries, often from other parts of the EU, or people that I knew from my days in Defence. President Karzai came on a state visit from Afghanistan and I was able to show him around Parliament and get him a ringside seat in the Chamber. Several Tory MPs noticed his presence, and made points of order congratulating him on the remarkable work that he was doing in Afghanistan. As I showed him around Parliament he was fascinated by the building and its history; we discussed what it might take to create something similar in Afghanistan.

I had also had time to pursue my European interests, both inside and outside the House. I tried to improve the parliamentary scrutiny of European legislation, which seemed largely to be in the hands of euro-sceptics from both of the main parties. I knew from my time in the European Parliament that the views of national parliaments were usually set out far too late in the European legislative process, with the result that they had very little impact on the proposed new legislation. I was also keen to involve British Euro-MPs, since they were likely to be much better informed about what was happening in respect of individual proposals. I devised an elaborate series of subject-based committees which was probably simply too complicated to succeed. The only real objection at the time, however, came from my friend Bob Ainsworth as Deputy Chief Whip. He pointed out that the fundamental problem with my proposal was that it assumed that MPs actually wanted to be more involved in the scrutiny of legislation, and wanted to be more involved around the House of Commons. His cynical view, no doubt borne out of long experience in the Whips' Office, was that modern MPs no longer wanted to do serious work on parliamentary committees; what they actually wanted to do was to be in their constituencies, appearing in their local media to ensure their subsequent re-election.

I also raised these questions on a visit to Strasbourg, nominally as part of the 2005 British EU Presidency, meeting many old friends from across the different countries and political groups. It was a measure of how much time I had available, freed from departmental administration, that I was able to drive to Strasbourg, spending some time with Elaine over a weekend revisiting places that I had not been to since being a Euro-MP. It made me think about what might have happened if I had turned down the chance to become an MP. We discussed that over dinner with an old friend, Gary Titley, Leader of the Labour group of Euro-MPs. Like many Euro-MPs, he had originally wanted to be an MP but had taken full advantage of his position to develop a very successful career in the European Parliament. He was quite sure that I had taken the right career path. Ironically, I was the one who had the doubts.

I made a visit to Australia to discuss compulsory voting. I had never understood why we legally require the wearing of seatbelts but do not expect people to vote at least once every five years. Even for elections to the European Parliament, countries like Belgium and Italy had compulsory voting. Australia was the country most like ours which expected people to vote with the sanction of a small fine for those who failed. What that achieved was an expectation that people would vote, whether or not they faced a sanction – in exactly the way that seatbelt legislation for cars has lead most people nowadays to buckle up. I even met someone from Australia's Country Party that traditionally represented farmers and other rural voters. I was told that their voters would think nothing of driving 150 miles to cast their vote, going to the polls and back in a single day. It would be interesting to see the turnout in the UK if such journeys were ever required. I made a speech at the IPPR which was interpreted by *The Times* and *The Guardian* as new government policy on the subject of compulsory voting. That evening I was a hero in our division lobby – Labour MPs know that apathy about voting is a much bigger problem for them than their Conservative counterparts. It is perhaps surprising that the Labour Party has never followed this through.

I was able to attend the grandly-titled Bosphorus Conference in Istanbul. As Defence Minister I had always had a good relationship with Turkish politicians. I was also very keen to see Istanbul, a place that had fascinated me since my schooldays studying medieval history. I had been to Turkey many times, but mostly to the political capital in Ankara. There had been a NATO meeting in Istanbul, but because of the attendance by George Bush the whole city had been closed down and it was impossible to move around. At the conference, I made a speech about Turkish accession to the EU and was thanked by Abdullah Gul, the Turkish Foreign Minister for Britain's positive role in what was a tortuous process for both sides. After an enjoyable morning of sight-seeing, I met Prime Minister Erdogan; he looked very tired after a day of fasting in the middle of Ramadan. We spent over an hour going through issues of concern to both governments, ending with my commercial pitch on behalf of Vodafone, which was attempting to acquire part of the Turkish mobile telephone network. He indicated that their bid would be well-received, which delighted the British Ambassador, Peter Westmacott, who had obviously been working for many months to secure this outcome.

I was also able to continue my European interests in those east European countries that had joined the EU since I had left the job as Europe Minister. I got to know Jiri Paroubek, the Czech Prime Minister, who was trying to remould the Czech Labour Party along Blairite lines. He invited me to Prague to address his parliamentary party on managing the legislative programme. I had to leave Cabinet early to get the flight and entertained my colleagues by pointing out that the Czech Labour Party only had a majority of one. Given recent defeats in the House of Commons over terrorism legislation, there was a good deal of black humour at my expense.

After addressing the Czech parliamentary Labour Party, I had dinner with the Czech Prime Minister knowing that he was due to meet the other Visigrath leaders from Poland, Hungary and Slovakia the next day. They were likely to be difficult about British plans to reduce EU spending plans for the accession states. He was apparently pleased at the New Labour line that I had used speaking to his parliamentary colleagues, essentially because he wanted to move the whole of the party in that direction before the forthcoming elections. He asked me repeatedly whether Tony Blair would be willing to visit Prague as part of his election campaign. I was reluctant to make this promise without knowing whether it was possible. Nevertheless, the moment the dinner concluded I called Jonathan Powell who was with Tony Blair and it was agreed that the offer would be made. Possibly as a result, the Czech Government proved extremely helpful in the EU budget negotiations.

Britain held the rotating EU Presidency in the second half of 2005, and faced considerable problems in persuading the new east European states to accept new EU financing plans. In return for the promise of a visit to Prague by Tony Blair, I was able to persuade the Czechs to back a British compromise proposal; that success might well have been a step too far for me personally, as subsequent events were to demonstrate.

MINISTER FOR EUROPE (AGAIN)
A Second Time

Tony Blair used his annual reshuffles as much as anything to keep control of his government, whilst at the same time sending short term messages to the media. Consciously or otherwise, it provided a degree of discipline; since everyone knew that he reshuffled extensively and often, ministers were reluctant to stray out of line. He also introduced a novel concept in that he made it clear that being shuffled out was not necessarily the end of a ministerial career as it had always tended to be previously. This meant that ex-ministers did not automatically become government critics, as had often been the case in the past. If they still harboured ambitions to return to the government, as most did, instead of turning to the dark side of constant criticism, they tried to work their way back.

I was never really persuaded that any of this meant very much to Tony Blair personally. I was convinced that Tony Blair thought that being Prime Minister was the only job that counted, which was why he never seemed really bothered about who got which ministerial jobs. Most Labour MPs, particularly those that lived out of London, had the sense that who was up or who was down, who was in or out, was often left to the Prime Minister's London-based advisors, which was why it was often said that attending Saturday night dinner parties in Islington was more significant than any number of supportive or effective parliamentary speeches.

Having wanted to remove me from the Cabinet in 2005, it was not entirely surprising a year later that Tony Blair again decided to move me out; this time back to an earlier role as Europe Minister. There was a significant element of farce about the process. The lead story on the radio first thing on the Friday morning of the reshuffle, early in May 2006, was that Jack Straw was being sacked as Foreign Secretary. I subsequently discovered that I had to be moved as Leader of the House to give Jack a softer landing than him suddenly leaving the government.

On this occasion I did actually have a conversation with Tony Blair, as he explained the vital importance of the job of Europe Minister going through in some detail what he wanted from the role. It seemed to fit with previous conversations I had had with him about upgrading the Europe job to Cabinet status. There was absolutely no explanation in what he said to me about the job that I would no longer be a Cabinet Minister. As a result my Special Advisor, Michael Dugher, began to brief out what seemed to be a very good story for a strongly pro-European government. He explained that the Europe job was to become a Cabinet position alongside the Foreign Secretary, perhaps similar to the way in which the Chief Secretary to the Treasury sits, together with the Chancellor of the Exchequer, in Cabinet. As this briefing got back to Downing Street, there were urgent calls from Ruth Turner, Tony Blair's political secretary, to explain with profuse apologies, that I was not actually going to be a Cabinet Minister. The Prime Minister had overlooked actually telling me this fundamental piece of information. I learned later that this was not an isolated example of Tony Blair's inability to give out bad news, even bad news of his own making. During another reshuffle, a minister went in to see Tony Blair and spent twenty minutes being told what a great job he had been doing and how valuable he was to the government, only to learn from Jonathan Powell as he left the Prime Minister's study that he had actually been sacked.

I was told that, although I was not strictly a Cabinet Minister, I would always be able to attend Cabinet and that I would be given much greater responsibility in the position than previous Europe Ministers, who had always been clearly junior to the Foreign Secretary. I was doubtful about this, and replied by saying that I would think about the offer. That may sound arrogant looking back, but since it seemed at the time that I was on a downward trajectory, I wondered whether it might not simply be better to return to the backbenches and avoid prolonging the agony of more demotions.

The fact that Margaret Beckett had by then been announced as the first female Foreign Secretary did not help. Although she had always been personally very friendly and supportive, I knew that she was a traditionalist when it came to running her department. She would be in charge of all aspects of the job, and ultimately she would expect me to do what she said. I knew that was likely to cause friction because she had never been an enthusiast for the EU. She had campaigned against British membership in 1975 and continued to be distinctly sceptical. It struck me as deeply ironic that a Prime Minister who claimed to be the most European in British history had appointed three Foreign Secretaries who had all previously campaigned for Britain to leave the European Union, and certainly in the case of Jack Straw and Margaret Beckett, never really embraced the European ideal. At least Robin Cook in his later years appeared to have cast off his previous views to become an enthusiast for European co-operation and integration.

There was, however, a practical problem with my indecision; I was due to be on *Any Questions* that evening in Holmfirth in West Yorkshire. That involved getting back home to Derbyshire and then being picked up by a BBC car to take me north to the venue. At least the journey gave me plenty of time to think. When I got home, Elaine was very clear that I should take the job; she couldn't understand why I was sitting on my 'absurd' dignity. Jonathan Dimbleby nailed me at the start of the programme simply asking whether I was Europe Minister or not. I recall mumbling that I was. The programme was being hosted by the Holmfirth Women's Institute and they had thoughtfully supplied a generous spread for afterwards, including several bottles of wine. My fellow guest David Davis, himself a former Europe Minister, and someone that I had always got along with, seemed well informed about what had been happening and the two of us did serious damage to the wine at the end of the programme. The next morning I had calls from Charlie Falconer and Peter Mandelson, both obviously at the behest of Downing Street, urging me to take the job. It was Elaine's more forthright view that prevailed. She thought that I should just get on with it and stop being so precious.

And getting on with it is what I did. I was fortunate that my background as a lawyer and former Euro-MP perfectly suited me to the main job in hand, which was the renegotiation of what became known as the Lisbon Treaty. The original EU plan, beginning in 2001, had been to amend the various previous EU treaties to produce a comprehensive constitution that everyone could see in a single document. Although ratified by a majority of member states, it was rejected by referenda in both France and the

Netherlands in the spring of 2005; hence the need for renegotiation. To her credit, Margaret Beckett largely left me to get on with this without any obvious interference.

We did have one major bust up when one of her special advisors decided that she had to be seen to assert herself in respect of European issues. Up until then, I had the impression that Margaret Beckett herself had been content to leave European issues largely to me. On this particular occasion in the balloted draw for Foreign Office questions, there was only one question on the EU. The special advisor allocated this to the Foreign Secretary and put me down to answer a question on Zimbabwe; way outside anything to do with my ministerial area of responsibility. At the meeting to discuss FCO questions, I made clear that I should be answering the Europe question and that I would not be answering a question about Zimbabwe. Margaret Beckett backed her special advisor and said that if I chose not to answer any questions I should not attend the question time. I sat on my very high horse and told her that since I was an MP she could hardly prevent me from attending the House of Commons. As a result I sat in place on the front bench right through Foreign Office questions not saying a word. This inevitably made the papers the next day, providing great entertainment for the parliamentary sketch writers. It also got me a ticking off from the Prime Minister; but since we both knew what he had said at the time of my appointment to the job it was hardly serious. Looking back, my behaviour now seems pedantic – but I had made my point about my understanding about the job as set out by the Prime Minister.

To be fair it was a job which in every other respect I really enjoyed, taking full advantage of the opportunities to travel throughout the geographical area of my responsibilities. I still knew people in the European Parliament so went to Brussels and Strasbourg frequently. I maintained my friendship with Jiri Paroubek, the Czech Prime Minister, speaking at his Party Congress.

My enthusiasm for the European Parliament did get me into trouble over the controversial question of rendition. The Council of Europe had produced a report critical of European countries' co-operation with the United States in transporting alleged terrorists around the world. This was followed up by a European Parliament committee that came to London to take evidence from the British Government. I actually volunteered to meet them, but found myself on the receiving end of allegations that I knew nothing about. At least part of their case was based on research about the apparently large number of privately chartered US government flights arriving at RAF bases in the UK. The committee suggested that these were 'CIA flights', which might have been carrying detainees. I made clear that the UK would never facilitate flights carrying people who were subject to human rights violations. I knew moreover from previous MOD experience that even relatively junior US generals were entitled to their own chartered aircraft when making visits overseas. It seemed to me that most of these so-called CIA flights were routine visits by a variety of US officials. At least one of the Euro-MPs was convinced that I knew more than I was letting on, and publicly accused me of evading the committee's questions. I learned to be more careful about what I volunteered for in future.

I also made a series of visits to Eastern Europe, to the countries closest geographically to Russia, and was deeply disturbed by what I found. Having visited Russia during my first stint as Europe minister in 1999, when the country was still experimenting with democracy, a further visit to Moscow in September 2006 showed just how much things had changed. The British Ambassador, Tony Brenton, who I knew well from his days in Washington, described vividly the nature of what had become a one-party Putin state where corruption was a daily aspect of everyday life. It seemed as if Russia at every level depended on the passing of brown envelopes containing cash, paid over and above the public cost required to get anything done, or as a means of supplementing state salaries. I was given the example of an anaesthetist about to treat a member of the embassy staff, who required a cash payment as the patient was waiting on the operating table. Tony Brenton was subject to appalling Russian state supported intimidation as he tried to do his job as the senior British diplomat.

The growing assertiveness of Putin's Russia was also having a significant effect on its neighbouring states. These were nominally independent since the collapse of the Soviet Union, but increasingly subject to Russian interference in their internal affairs. It seemed this was deliberately designed to keep them off balance politically. I had got to know President Saakashvili of Georgia, and although he had problems of his own making, he appeared to have been democratically elected and enjoyed popular support for his efforts to move Georgia politically closer to the West. Vladimir Putin's ambitions for Russia in contrast seemed to be about restoring its complete control over the former Soviet states. Russia seemed to be deliberately encouraging separatist movements in parts of what was internationally recognised sovereign Georgian territory. Ultimately in 2008 Russian troops invaded Georgia, largely destroying its army, before recognising two breakaway Georgian states as independent. Those states essentially became loyal satellites of Moscow.

The message from Russia to its neighbours was clear; toe our line or face internal discord that we will foster, encourage and support. I visited Yerevan, the capital of Armenia, where the Defence Minister told me that he went to Moscow every month for 'consultations'. In Chisinau, the Moldovan President told me that he could be the first President of a country with no citizens, since many Moldovans could claim Romanian passports, whilst most of the rest had been offered Russian passports by Moscow. In Kiev, capital of Ukraine, the picture was very similar; do what Moscow says or face internal problems or even, as happened much later, invasion by clandestine Russian forces.

The message internationally had a close parallel. Russia will take whatever action it deems to be in its own national interest, irrespective of what the international community might think. President Putin has calculated that there is simply not the political will in the West to challenge him.

As Defence Minister, I had often visited British bases in Cyprus. Historically more land than was strictly needed for military purposes had been retained for security reasons after Cyprus became independent in 1960. Over the years Cypriots had moved onto this land, operating businesses that thrived by supplying services to soldiers and their families on their tours of duty. Some even started farming the land with the result that the MOD was forced to administer the Common Agricultural Policy, at significant and, as far as I was concerned as Secretary of State for Defence, unnecessary expense, after Cyprus joined the EU in 2004. This struck me as being absurd, and made the retention of the actual base areas more difficult politically; there would come a time when the Cypriots would demand the return of their land which, since it was actually lived on by Cypriots, would be difficult to resist.

As a result I suggested to David Hannay, a former senior British diplomat who was very much involved in the United Nations efforts to deal with the division of the island, that the surplus land beyond the base security fences could be used as a makeweight in efforts to resolve some of the land issues left over from the fighting in 1974. Greek Cypriots in the north had been forced out in the occupation by Turkish forces. Equally, some Turkish Cypriots had been driven from their homes in the south. I argued that surplus British land could potentially be used to help reshape the boundaries between the two communities, addressing at least some of the individual grievances that had made a settlement difficult to attain. It would have the further advantage that the sovereign base areas would be much reduced in size, making them more defensible both militarily and politically.

As Europe Minister I visited Cyprus, meeting the then Foreign Minister, Giorgos Lillikas. He was an urbane and sophisticated operator who seemed genuinely willing to look for a solution to the Cyprus problem, even if that involved concessions by the Greek Cypriot side. I found myself discussing these questions with the President of Cyprus, Tassos Papadopoulos during the United Nations General Assembly. We were both Barristers of Gray's Inn and in the course of a long meeting I decided that his legal training in London had given him a real enthusiasm for pure debate, but not in fact for reaching any actual conclusion. I enjoyed the discussion as we argued about various ways of moving the issues along, but came to the conclusion that he and most Greek Cypriots much preferred talking about a range of possible solutions rather than actually doing anything about it.

I was slightly more successful, at least for a time, with efforts to improve the position of Gibraltar, as far as Spain was concerned. I was helped by the fact that an Ambassador in the Spanish Ministry of Foreign Affairs, Luis Planas, had been a friend and colleague from my days in the European Parliament. I was able to persuade him and his boss, the Foreign Minister Miguel Moratinos, that the previous Spanish policy of making life difficult for Gibraltar and Gibraltarians only served to make the people there still more determined to retain their links with Britain. They also knew that many people in southern Spain depended for their livelihoods on Gibraltar, crossing the border for work in a daily commute. Further, given the growing volume of tourism in southern Spain, they needed access to another airport. Spanish policy had previously been to isolate Gibraltar airport which was on a strip of land right next to the Spanish border. Spanish airports would not even take flights on diversion from Gibraltar if the weather around the Rock prevented a landing.

I signed the Cordoba Agreement on behalf of the British Government with Peter Caruana, Gibraltar's Chief Minister and Miguel Moratinos signing for Spain. It established a tripartite forum in which issues involving Gibraltar and Spain could be discussed. This was a significant concession by Spain, as previously the Spanish had always argued that Gibraltar was a bilateral matter between the two governments and that Gibraltar itself could not therefore be involved. A key part of the Cordoba agreement concerned allowing the airport at Gibraltar to also be used for flights to Spain. We had spent some considerable time poring over detailed maps of the airport, working out how passengers could arrive on one side and exit to Spain, whilst on the other arrive in Gibraltar.

Some of the negotiations had been conducted further up the coast in Spain in areas where tens of thousands of British citizens had made their homes. I was given a Spanish perspective of the problem. Not only did many of these British residents of Spain not speak Spanish, they tended to mix only with other Brits, and because they had often retired to Spain they put an unreasonable strain on the local medical services as they got older. It was a good lesson. I tried to imagine the reaction of the *Daily Mail* or *Daily Telegraph* should a hundred thousand or so Spanish speaking residents move to Bournemouth or Eastbourne, clogging up the waiting rooms of local doctors or hospitals with their increasing number of ailments as they inevitably got older.

Luis Planas was actually at the time the Spanish Ambassador to Morocco, and was responsible for a major conference in Rabat organised as part of the Spanish EU Presidency. Spain, along with all of the southern European Mediterranean states, faced significant problems with illegal immigrants crossing the sea by boat – as continues to be the case. The Euro-African Conference was organised to bring together the governments of the relevant countries to try and find some common ground, both to prevent the illegal crossings and look at ways in which the prosperous countries of the EU could fund programmes in Sub-Saharan Africa to prevent economic migrants setting off in the first place. It seemed a sensible starting point for what has become an intractable problem, as people understandably try to better themselves in the prosperous countries of Europe.

Europe also featured on the domestic agenda. I stood in at the last minute for Tony Blair at the annual Finmeccanica Conference held, unusually, outside Italy at the Birmingham Conference Centre in November 2006. I gave what was described by one attendee as the most European speech he had ever heard from a British Minister. It was of course exactly what the largely Italian audience had wanted to hear. It was however almost impossible to get such views across in the British press. The Press Office in the Foreign Office attempted every day to get positive messages into British newspapers but editors were mostly only interested in copy which knocked the EU. Even when there was an EU reform that benefited large numbers of British people, there would be little or no mention of its origins. Britain has benefited more than any other country from the relaxation of the rules governing airlines. As a result, millions of people are able to travel abroad on a regular basis, often for less than the cost of going to the British coast or to London. Those reforms were driven through by the European Commission, despite the views of certain EU member states trying to protect their state-owned airlines. Similarly, I had several meetings with mobile telephone operators about the higher charges they levied on European calls. They admitted that the calls were not generally any more expensive for them to connect; rather, they levied extra charges to maintain their level of profit. When the rules to allow European mobile roaming were introduced and gradually expanded by the European Commission, British newspapers welcomed this as a significant improvement for consumers, but usually failed to mention how it had come about. In both cases, domestically-owned or based companies would have been able to use their influence to prevent national governments making such changes. Only a European organisation with political and legislative power could have made these reforms.

On a much lighter note, I represented the Government at a football match between Manchester United and a Europe Xl played at Old Trafford to mark the 50th anniversary of the signing of the Treaty of Rome. Over 74,000 people attended the game which was also shown live on the BBC and in many other European nations. In the absence of tackling and the aggression associated with a competitive match, some of the very best players in Europe were able to show off their sublime footballing skills. Wayne Rooney scored two great goals. I could never have imagined at the time that in future years I would be admiring his footballing skills playing for Derby County. More importantly, despite all of the positive publicity about the game, I knew that many more events of that kind would have to be organised on a regular basis if the British public were to be persuaded about the real benefits of membership of the European Union.

If the game represented the best of European co-operation, there was another much more divisive issue that I was concerned about at the time. Galileo is a global navigation satellite system deliberately developed by the EU to rival the United States' GPS system. As a result, the British government was never very enthusiastic about its participation in this EU project, questioning whether a new and separate system was really necessary and objecting to the billions of euros in costs. The original plan had been to pay for a new satellite system through a public private partnership, but this collapsed in 2006 with the result that the burgeoning bill had to be paid for by EU member states.

I had followed the early debates on Galileo as Defence Secretary because all sophisticated modern weapons are guided to their targets using one or other of the various satellite systems. One reason for the EU being determined to develop their own arrangements involved fears that the US administration could interfere with the GPS guidance signal. In the course of the Kosovo campaign a British cruise missile aimed at a target in Serbia had unaccountably flown off course, ending up harmlessly somewhere in Bulgaria when it eventually ran out of fuel. It was suggested that this failure might have been as a result of the Americans testing their ability to manipulate the GPS system.

Britain's lack of enthusiasm for the Galileo project left much of the early detailed research and development work in French hands. It was suggested in turn that the French were also working within Galileo to similarly be able to manipulate the positional signals for their own advantage. It was not thought that they were likely to share this capability with their other European partners. This obviously caused considerable concern. At the time the problem was resolved by much stricter British supervision of the development programme.

With Britain out of the EU, it has been made quite clear that even if Britain had wanted to continue to contribute its share of the costs of Galileo, it would still be excluded from the most sensitive parts of the system, perhaps the very aspects that are crucial to the reliability of the targeting of British weapons. It has been suggested in the alternative that

Britain could develop its own satellite system. Given current infrastructure projects, whether a British government would be willing to underwrite the billions of pounds of costs involved must be open to doubt.

Yet otherwise Britain's security and its independence of action would be dependent either on the goodwill of the United States or on our former partners in the EU. It is not without significance that the Chinese government, which initially made a substantial financial contribution to Galileo, eventually withdrew to be able to develop its own satellite system. Russia also has its own separate system.

I am sure that these security concerns will be scoffed at by those who argue that one benefit of leaving the EU will be to further strengthen Britain's relationship with the United States. They will argue that Britain can continue to rely on GPS, and that it is inconceivable that the US would interfere in the targeting of weapons by its closest ally. As someone who is about as pro-American as it gets, I still have my doubts. What if Britain becomes involved in a military adventure that the White House opposes? It is a very long time since Suez, but it is still possible to conceive of a situation where Britain's colonial history involves the country in operations that the US might find distinctly uncomfortable. This then becomes analogous to the nuclear debate of the 1950s as to whether the United States would be willing to sacrifice Birmingham Alabama, if Birmingham in the United Kingdom was destroyed by nuclear weapons. Despite all of my enthusiasm for all things American, I have never been in any doubt that a US President would not be willing to lose American lives unless those US citizens were themselves very directly threatened. In a similar manner, if the UK was involved in a military action that seemed to put US lives at risk, I have no doubt that the White House would seriously consider interfering, if it could, in UK targeting. It follows that exactly the same arguments would apply with France if it had the capability to control the targeting of advanced British weapons.

This is a further example – alongside concerns about security information sharing and the development of military equipment – where Britain's security could be seriously jeopardised by the decision to leave the European Union. The only realistic solution to ensure the security of Britain and its armed forces is for the country to spend large amounts of money once again duplicating the capabilities of GPS and Galileo. I can only hope that this amount will be weighed in the balance by those that have argued that leaving the EU will somehow save money.

As a Minister, it is all too easy to become immersed in the day-to-day detail of the job, not least because of the tyranny of the diary and the unremitting red boxes at the end of every day. However much travelling I did in the Foreign Office, it was obvious that there were big political changes underway at home. Tony Blair was finally giving in to the pressure from Gordon Brown to relinquish the job of Prime Minister.

CHIEF WHIP
Nothing is Real

I should never have wanted to be Gordon Brown's Chief Whip. I should not even have thought about it, never mind actually taking the job. Yet in the run up to his becoming Prime Minister in June 2007, I had a series of meetings in the Treasury where we discussed the idea. Gordon Brown was so keen to get me to agree that he offered to restore the Chief Whip to the house at number 12 Downing Street, the traditional and historical base for the Government Whips' operation. It had been turned over to the government's media people by Tony Blair, perhaps showing what was really important to his government.

I cannot pretend that I was not flattered by this attention, and that the political drug coursing through my veins was not always driving me to accept. If politics could be made available in pill form it would be a 'Class A' drug. Once it is in the system it seems almost impossible to do without a regular fix. I have seen countless examples of the addiction; a man who was briefly an MP from 1966 to 1970 still trying to win parliamentary selections more than a decade later, ex-ministers waiting by the phone at every reshuffle, still somehow thinking that they might be recalled to office long after their sell by date has passed.

I discovered later that the idea of me being Chief Whip in the new Brown government had come from Tom Watson, one of Gordon Brown's strongest supporters amongst the younger generation of MPs. The obvious candidate was actually Nick Brown who had been Tony Blair's first Chief Whip in 1997, but who had always served Gordon Brown assiduously. Immediately after the announcement of Tony Blair's resignation, Nick Brown had efficiently and ruthlessly organised the leadership nomination process amongst Labour MPs. It resulted in overwhelming support for Gordon Brown, scaring off those like John Reid who up until then had clearly seen themselves as potential leadership material. This meant that the idea of a challenge from a second candidate and a democratic contest would be impossible. Nick Brown was however perceived by Labour MPs as being 'Gordon's man', and seen as being from a previous older generation by many of the younger intake of Labour MPs. I was seen by Tom Watson apparently as someone who got along with people from both camps. It was also no doubt to the advantage of the new Prime Minister to have someone generally thought of as a Blairite in his team.

The fundamental flaw in all of this from my point of view was that I wasn't actually in the Prime Minister's team. I had all the trappings of being the Government Chief Whip; I even had the use of an office at number 12, but I was in reality a figurehead for a political operation still carried through by my nominal deputy, Nick Brown, and the other close confidantes of Gordon Brown. Gordon Brown had a small team of people around him that had always been his ultra-loyal supporters; Nick Brown, Ed Balls, Ed Milliband and a few others. They had previously run a separate political operation based in the Treasury; quite separate and distinct from the government of Tony Blair. Once Gordon Brown became Prime Minister, these supporters in effect became an inner government, once again separate and distinct from the wider government which Gordon Brown actually lead, but far more powerful because they had direct access to, and the full confidence of the Prime Minister.

Gordon Brown's reliance on his team, rather than his government ministers, was brought home to me on more than one occasion when we would wait during a meeting in Downing Street for Ed Balls to arrive from Education, where he was Secretary of State for Children, Schools and Families, to advise on some question far removed from his departmental responsibilities. I often wondered what happened to the diary commitments in his department when he was summoned across to Downing Street, sometimes it seemed at a few minutes' notice.

There were similar issues in the Whips' Office. On more than one occasion I went into the whips' room to talk to Nick Brown, my nominal deputy, only to find him on his mobile phone talking tactics to a person that could only have been the Prime Minister. The slightly uncomfortable and embarrassed way in which he closed down the conversation was evidence enough of what was going on. There were clearly matters that the Prime

Minister wanted to discuss with Nick Brown that he did not want to discuss with the Government Chief Whip.

I had realised what was going on through the Summer of 2007, in the immediate aftermath of Gordon Brown becoming Prime Minister, as the newspapers were full of stories about whether there was going to be an early General Election. Gordon Brown was initially a popular Prime Minister and the Labour Party was at the time ahead in the opinion polls, fuelling the idea of a snap election to legitimise his position with the electorate. My only source for this was from what I read in the newspapers. The newspapers speculated that the debate went back and forth amongst his advisors throughout the summer and into the autumn.

At no stage as Chief Whip was I ever asked for my opinion as to whether there should be a General Election. This was clearly not a matter for Labour MPs generally; it was only for Gordon Brown's inner circle to discuss. The debate seemed to end in stalemate amongst his closest advisors, as they apparently kept finding reasons for pushing back the decision – the summer holidays, the date of the Party Conferences, the availability of the Queen to make a speech at the opening of Parliament, and so on. Eventually in October, one Friday morning as I was in Ashfield on constituency visits, I did get a call from the Prime Minister saying that he had decided not to hold an early General Election; it was actually the only time that he had mentioned the subject to me. By then I was greatly relieved, because if he had called an election at that stage it would have had to take place in November. The prospect of getting Labour voters out to vote after the clocks had changed, and it was properly dark, meant that in all probability we would have struggled to hold even safe seats like mine, never mind more marginal ones.

Despite this early realisation that I was not really part of the Brown machine, I decided that since I had the job, I would have to try and make myself useful to the government. I had always admired the slick Tory whips operation and believed that Labour could develop something similar but updated for the demands of the 21st Century. In previous days when many Labour MPs came from a trade union and industrial background, they accepted, and even expected, a degree of discipline in their workplace. My brief experience of working one summer at a local colliery had showed me that most of that discipline was self-imposed by men who knew that they had to take care of themselves and their workmates in what could be a very dangerous environment. For those men, being organised and perhaps even shouted at by work colleagues if they made a mistake was not that remarkable. Once the majority of Labour MPs had been to university, and with an increasing number of women in the parliamentary party, shouting at them was never going to have the desired effect. These were people used to debate and reasoned explanation. Shouting at them seemed likely to have little effect other than perhaps making them even more determined to rebel, blaming the Chief Whip in the process.

I therefore saw the Whips' Office more like the Personnel Department or HR function of a modern company. I wanted the Whips not only to know their group of MPs but also to try and understand their concerns with policy and, where possible, to make arrangements to suit their individual circumstances. That was obviously not always possible, but with a new leader of the Labour Party there was at least initially a degree of goodwill which meant that I was fortunate that the government did not lose any votes during my 15 months in the job.

I also tried to help Gordon Brown with his preparations for every Wednesday's Prime Minister's questions, which for him seemed to become a worsening weekly ordeal. I would often get to his study at 7.30 am on a Tuesday morning, initially to discuss the likely runners and riders in terms of questions for the next day. I often got the impression that he had already been there for several hours, pounding away at his computer, as he sought to work out the best way forward for him and his government. He clearly believed that every problem could be resolved if only he worked harder. I had some sympathy for that view as a scholarship boy who had discovered that the real difference between people at school and university was how hard they were prepared to work and study. Unfortunately for Gordon Brown, the media expected the Prime Minister to make governing look effortless. That was clearly not the case as he tried to overcome a wide variety of political problems by working harder and harder, inevitably making himself look more and more tired and haggard in the process.

Gordon Brown was in large part the author of his own problems in this respect. It was almost as if he was trying to take all of the big decisions right across government; not just in the final stages of a debate but actually from first principles. He undoubtedly had a formidable intellect and impressive grasp of the relevant issues, but partly as a result, he did not trust other people to come up with the right answers. Tony Blair had always seemed comfortable with himself and therefore allowed people to get on with the job, providing it did not embarrass him or his government in the media. Gordon Brown in contrast was driven by an apparent desire to get everything exactly right; believing perhaps that he was the only one able to do that. As I knew from experience, however, trying to run one department was sufficiently exhausting; trying to decide all of the big questions in a number of departments was simply impossible for one individual.

One obvious consequence of this was that the pace of government decision-making slowed down. There could be an agreement on a new announcement from the relevant department, Labour MPs could be onside, and helpful journalists could have been briefed, but until Gordon Brown was completely and absolutely satisfied, nothing moved. Labour MPs would come and complain that the previous process of regular announcements of new national policies which they could in turn use in their constituencies was breaking down, and that the government seemed sluggish and increasingly out of touch.

Decisions began to back up as it became increasingly clear that Gordon Brown lacked the key fundamental quality of a Prime Minister; he simply could not take decisions in the urgent time frame required. I had always thought that the only real function of ministers in a system where expert civil servants handle almost all of the day-to-day detail was to take the key policy decisions and then to take responsibility for defending them publicly. Junior ministers take decisions at their level, Cabinet Ministers at theirs; but when there is a major policy initiative, or an issue that has to be resolved between departments, it is for the Prime Minister to decide. Gordon Brown seemed quite unable to deal with the constant flow of decision-making that arrived on his desk in a timely manner.

Initially I found this difficult to understand, because as Chancellor of the Exchequer for ten years he always seemed to me, and most others, to be totally on top of his brief; both domestically and internationally. Moreover, when Tony Blair's government ran into difficulty, it was Gordon Brown sitting opposite Tony Blair in Cabinet who would set out the strategic thinking required; mapping out the way forward for the government politically. That was why I had believed that he was the only person who could succeed Tony Blair as Prime Minister, a view shared at the time by most other members of Cabinet.

What I didn't know then was that most of the day-to-day decisions at the Treasury were apparently farmed out to a small number of trusted advisors such as Ed Balls, leaving Gordon Brown to focus on the key big picture decisions like the Budget and the Financial Statement. He would apparently spend weeks, if not months, considering in detail all of the implications of the budget proposals, politically and economically, in order to arrive at the exact answers he was looking for. That time and that exhaustive process were simply not available to him as Prime Minister. And as a result he seemed to fall further and further behind in the decision-making cycle.

One of the great ironies of the early days of Gordon Brown's period as Prime Minister was that it was dominated by his decision as Chancellor to abolish the 10p starting rate of income tax. He had actually introduced the rate in 1999 to help the low paid, and somehow overlooked the fact that its abolition would hit precisely the very poorest people that he had previously been trying to help. Huge amounts of government time and money were then spent working out ways of ameliorating the effect of abolition, without actually being seen to be walking back on the actual decision. Labour MPs were being told by their Prime Minister that no-one would lose out. Their constituents were turning up in droves to tell them that they were losing out. It was thought that perhaps as many as 5 million people across the country were affected.

A similar controversy concerned the length of time that a terrorist suspect could be detained without charge. The Home Office, was arguing that the limit should be 42 days, considerably shorter than the 90 days previously considered in the immediate aftermath of the 7th July 2005 London bombings. This was nevertheless always going to cause problems in the Commons, with many Labour MPs likely to vote against a long extension. There were a series of meetings in the Home Office but they essentially failed to resolve the fundamental political issue of how to get the measure through Parliament. Eventually, Downing Street, at Gordon Brown's insistence, set aside an hour and a half of the Prime Minister's diary to go through the various proposals in detail. Senior officials from Downing Street and all of the relevant departments were present, together with the Home Secretary. I was there as Chief Whip. We sat and waited in the Cabinet Room for the Prime Minister. He was almost an hour late, having overrun at a previous event. I have rarely seen civil servants so angry and frustrated, as the entire time was wasted and no decision was taken.

I could not claim to have been surprised when at the first re-shuffle I was sacked as Chief Whip, and replaced even less surprisingly by Nick Brown, who had probably been doing significant parts of the job all along. I had gone from someone idealistically willing to help a new Prime Minister succeed to someone who had come to the conclusion that he could only fail. I probably allowed those views to become too widely known. I assume that those opinions had got back to Gordon Brown. I am fairly sure as a result that he simply wanted to put me back onto the backbenches. As Chief Whip, however, I had worked closely with Joe Irvin, Gordon Brown's political secretary, and he probably saved me for a time by arguing that it would look bad for the government to get rid of a Chief Whip entirely. Instead I was moved to the Department for Transport.

Train in a Station

Although nearly six years in Defence had been the most challenging of my ministerial career, the brief time in Transport was in terms of policy issues the most enjoyable. I came from a railway family, and as a child I probably spent more time than most other children that I knew travelling by train. I continued to travel both in the European Parliament and as a Defence and Foreign Office Minister. I had a real interest in the policy issues involved in how to move people around both efficiently and inexpensively. What was mostly new to me, however, were the policy issues involved in reconciling the increasing demand for more and more travel with its impact on the environment; not simply the obvious consequences for the countryside of building more and more roads, but the wider impact of global warming and climate change caused by transport-related carbon emissions.

One of my very first decisions after my appointment on 6th October 2008 was to set up a committee reporting to Andrew Adonis, one of the junior ministers in the department, to start work on a second high speed line, linking Scotland and the North of England with London. Although the journey time, particularly from Scotland was a factor, the real issue driving this decision was rail capacity. The remarkable growth in rail travel across the country meant that even relatively recent investment on new capacity such as the West Coast main line was being overtaken by train and passenger numbers. The Beeching cuts of the 1960s heralded a structural decline in Britain's railway network, with a concurrent growth in car ownership. But traffic congestion in the years up to the Covid pandemic meant that more and more people were using the trains, both for everyday commuting and when they needed to make occasional longer journeys. Demand pricing has also meant that off-peak trains, which in the days of British Rail often operated almost empty, are increasingly attractive to customers prepared to tailor their journeys around paying a more reasonable ticket price.

As a result, the overall number of rail passengers approached the peak numbers associated with the great railway boom of the late nineteenth century. Rail lines were reaching capacity, including the main line to Manchester which had benefited only relatively recently from billions of pounds worth of investment. Even with all of this extra infrastructure investment, it was predicted that the line would reach full capacity by the early 2020s, precipitating the need for a new line linking London to the north-west and beyond.

Massive infrastructure projects of this kind are inevitably criticised; on cost, disruption and environmental grounds. With a new railway running from the centre of London right through its suburbs and on into the English countryside, before making its way north and into Scotland, the not in my backyard tendency has had and continues to have a field day. The decision by the Conservative Government in 2020 to further review HS2 risks significant delay which will inevitably increase the cost, perhaps beyond the point of political affordability.

Some years after taking the decision to start off the new high speed line, I was canvassing at local election time in Long Eaton, the town where I grew up, with a Labour councillor. Long Eaton is right on the route of HS2. By then, the route had been confirmed and assumed that the track would go through part of the town on an enormous and controversial viaduct. Many people will lose their homes to compulsory purchase and the councillor had received the full brunt of their complaints. When I casually mentioned that I had effectively initiated the project, he seemed to be struck dumb for a short time. Eventually he recovered to say how brave I was to be knocking on doors that in a few years' time might not be there. We agreed that it might be in both of our best interests not to mention my previous ministerial role.

As Transport Minister, I was also concerned that Britain was falling behind other countries in respect of the provision of high speed rail capacity. France led the way, but Spain for example has Europe's most comprehensive plans to link up all parts of the country. This has a political element as well as a purely transport one. By reducing journey times from the outlying parts of Spain the Government believes that this will bring the Spanish people closer together. That argument must surely apply to relations between Scotland and the rest of Great Britain. I travelled on high speed lines between Madrid and Barcelona, as well as across Germany from Berlin to Leipzig. Again, in Germany there was a political element to the transport investment, as they used the latest high speed rail infrastructure in an effort to encourage companies, jobs and people to go to the newly-unified eastern part of the country.

The need for an extra runway at Heathrow was a similar issue. I am sure that if it was possible to go back to the immediate post-war period, knowing what we know now, Heathrow would not have been chosen as Britain's major hub airport. Yet despite all of the complaints about noise and pollution from local residents, the reality is that almost everyone now affected has come to the area knowing that they will be living close to the flight paths of Britain's biggest airport. One of the main parliamentary opponents of the expansion was Justine Greening, the MP for Putney and herself later the Secretary of State for Transport. She claimed in Parliament that her constituency would be 'devastated' by an extra runway at Heathrow. I felt like pointing out that property prices in her very affluent constituency hardly showed any great reluctance on the part of her constituents to live there. Ashfield is nowhere near an airport and property prices are a fraction of what they are under the flight-path at Heathrow.

In the course of a consultation about the planned expansion, civil servants operated an information desk near the airport, allowing concerned residents to ask for details about how they might be affected. One told me of an encounter with a well-dressed woman who said that she thought the plans to extend Heathrow were dreadful and when travelling to her holiday home in Spain she 'always flew from Gatwick'. I had a similar encounter with the actor Emma Thompson, who argued passionately and eloquently that I should not take the decision to expand Heathrow. A couple of days after the meeting, my private secretary gave me a newspaper cutting that showed that shortly after our meeting she had travelled to Los Angeles.

No-one really argued that the expansion was not needed. I came to the view that notwithstanding the well-intentioned environmental concerns which people expressed, a much more reliable guide to their views could be found by asking for their address. The airport is of course a significant local employer. When the Conservatives opportunistically opposed the plans for a new runway in their election manifesto for 2010, they did so hoping to win Labour seats in the immediate vicinity of the airport. That plan failed because those constituencies depend on the enormous number of jobs generated by the airport, and the people who work there know that, unless the airport is allowed to expand, their future employment cannot be guaranteed.

Ed Milliband, as Secretary of State for Energy and Climate Change was strongly opposed to the plans for the new runway. He believed that air travel was particularly damaging to the environment, an argument that I understood and accepted. What I didn't agree with was the suggestion that by not building a new runway there would be any greater control over the amount of carbon emitted by aircraft. Given the growing demand for air travel, all that would happen is that the new flights demanded by consumers would simply be displaced to other airports and almost certainly to hub airports not even in the United Kingdom. Amsterdam's Schiphol Airport has often advertised itself as 'London's fourth airport', or even more recently as 'London's second hub airport'. As someone often flying back home on a Friday afternoon from overseas, it was sometimes better to connect to East Midlands Airport through Amsterdam rather than risk traffic jams going north on the M1. When I was first elected to the European Parliament, there was a regular service between Heathrow and East Midlands Airport. Because of capacity constraints at Heathrow, those services were taken off and the slots used for more lucrative services to the continent. As a result, almost everyone who wants to fly out of Heathrow from the East Midlands must either make a long and awkward journey by train and underground or, more likely travel by car further adding to the congestion on the M1 and M25. That problem applies to other parts of the country as relatively short local flights into Heathrow have been replaced by more lucrative longer haul services.

I had many meetings with Ed Milliband in order to resolve the issue, but there was no realistic possible compromise. Either we agreed to build the runway or we didn't. I expected Gordon Brown to side with his protégé and strong supporter, but when Chancellor of the Exchequer he had argued the economic benefits to Britain of expanding Heathrow, and as Prime Minister he remained consistent with that view. Sadly, the Conservatives were not consistent with their previous support for airport expansion and after 2010 the plan was shelved, at least until the Conservatives in government realised that economically it had to go ahead. Labour in opposition was equally opportunist in campaigning against the expansion of the runway.

Whatever the merits or otherwise of the arguments, this is not the way to take significant decisions affecting the country's economic future. A way has to be found to take these major decisions out of party politics whilst at the same time allowing those people affected to have the opportunity of expressing their views. It is relatively straightforward to set out the principles.

It is all too easy for Transport ministers to spend all of their time promoting public transport and forget that their constituents spend most of their travelling time in their cars. I visited a control centre managing the smart motorway concept in the West Midlands. It seemed far more sensible to try and use existing motorway capacity more efficiently. It always seemed that getting people out of their cars depended on either making it so expensive to drive that people looked for cheaper alternatives, or that it became so slow and uncomfortable that people chose to leave their cars at home. Neither approach would be popular when people had already spent their hard earned income on acquiring a car, something that almost everyone aspires to. The irony is that the more investment is made on improving the road network, covering more and more of the countryside with concrete, the more people are likely to use their cars. It is only when the roads become hopelessly overcrowded that people look for alternatives to get around more quickly.

I was impressed by the concept of road pricing; in principle, charging differential amounts for using the roads according to the level of congestion. As the London congestion charge shows, the technology now exists for a comprehensive road pricing system that could be used right across the country. To work fairly and efficiently it would have to be introduced as a replacement for all taxes on motoring – Road Tax, fuel duty and any local congestion charges. Unfortunately and perhaps understandably, no-one trusts the Treasury not to use road pricing as an extra charge on motorists. It will only work rationally if people pay a clearly understood single price for actually taking their car out onto the road. If they have already paid significant upfront costs for owning and operating their car, together with various taxes, they are understandably going to want to take advantage of what they have already paid for, distorting the underlying principle of road pricing.

Road pricing and congestion charging would also allow national and local government to promote low carbon alternatives. As Transport Minister I had the chance to drive new examples of electric cars. Tesla allowed me to drive their first model, deliberately designed as a sports car to show that electric vehicles could be more exciting to drive than milk floats. It must have had a lasting impression on me, because I have owned one of their cars for several years now and can bore for Britain on the benefits of electric vehicles. I was involved in several photo opportunities sitting in or driving electric vehicles, including with the then London Mayor, Boris Johnson. The two of us also cycled one of the new London cycle superhighways. He struck me at the time as being genuinely interested in and concerned about protecting the environment; an issue of course that has been consistently championed by the European Union. Indeed environmental legislation only makes sense and can only work if it is carried through multi-nationally. It is difficult to see how European environmental initiatives will be carried through quickly, or at all, if every line of EU legislation has to be renegotiated with a Brexit-minded British Government.

Times of trouble

At some stage in early 2009, during one of my many conversations with Alistair Darling, he mentioned that he had been asked specifically by Gordon Brown to see whether I would be interested in becoming Britain's next European Commissioner in 2010. Peter Mandelson had been appointed to the position in 2005, but had resigned on his return to British politics in 2008. Baroness Ashton had been given the job on a temporary basis, until a new permanent appointment could be made at the same time that all European Commissioners were to be sworn in towards the end of 2009. I was pleased to be asked and readily agreed to the suggestion; I had spent ten years as a Euro-MP and had two stints as Europe Minister. I assumed that the Prime Minister knew this, and thought that I would be good in the job. Politicians are of course easily flattered, as I found out some months later.

On Friday 5th June I had planned to spend part of the day in the constituency in Ashfield, but first I was due to go to Derby with my Mother to visit the Derby Roundhouse, a Grade II listed building which is the oldest remaining locomotive turning shed in the world, dating back to 1839. It had been renovated by a local building company, Bowmer and Kirkland, as part of an innovative Derby College development, combining historic railway buildings with modern facilities. I had mentioned to John Kirkland, the Chairman and driving force behind the company that my Mother had worked there in the former railway offices in the late 1940s. He kindly agreed to show both of us around the new College. Just as we were about to leave home for Derby, I had a call from Gordon Brown.

He began by saying that he wanted people in the Cabinet who would be looking forward to the election in 2010. I realised immediately that he had set me up – elegantly and effectively. By getting me to acknowledge that I would like to be a European Commissioner, he had the excuse he needed to sack me, as he did there and then on the telephone. I did push back, however. Given what he had said, I suggested that he could announce that I was to be Britain's next European Commissioner. The fact that he flatly refused to do so, without any convincing reason, seemed to reveal his real intentions. Rearranging my diary for the day, I drove my Mother to Derby for the College tour and caught the next train to London.

I had little inkling that there was to be a reshuffle that day, but by the time I got to Downing Street it was in full swing. I went in by the Whitehall entrance to avoid the TV cameras. Walking through the corridors of Number 10, I felt like a dead man walking with people that I had only recently worked with avoiding eye contact; probably because they simply did not know what to say to a departing minister. I had given some thought on the train as to how I would handle myself; I could have gone off at the deep end, threatening a personal statement in the House of Commons. However, the worm of ambition was still eating away at me and I knew if there was still a chance of being the European Commissioner I had to keep my head firmly down. I therefore had a very short conversation with Gordon Brown, agreeing he would offer me a position as his personal envoy, on matters involving environmental protection. Nothing ever came of this. I was never actually asked to do anything. I happened to know from my time as Chief Whip that exactly the same offer had been made to a previous minister. I wondered whether there was a standard set of words somewhere on a Downing Street word processor for use in letters to ex-ministers. I should have kept count of how many 'personal envoys' there were floating around, not doing very much.

Although I was deeply disappointed in the manner of my dismissal as a minister, I had always recognised that, in common with most political careers, the end would come when I felt I still had something to contribute. Looking back, by getting it out of the way well before the General Election, I realise that in a curious way Gordon Brown did me a favour, giving me a freer hand to decide what to do next. If I had still been a Cabinet Minister at the time of the General Election I would have felt honour bound to stay on and fight, even though I knew that Labour was heading for a defeat and perhaps a long period in opposition. I knew that there were other senior figures in the government who felt exactly the same way.

Elaine was also convinced that it was a good thing, allowing me to do some of the things that I had missed doing during my time as a minister. One of them came up that same evening, almost as soon as I got back home to Derbyshire. I was cycling from Breaston into Long Eaton, across West Park, which sits right in the centre of the town, when I saw one of my oldest friends, John Hassall, playing cricket. Since he was fielding on the boundary I stopped for a chat to see how he was getting on. He asked what I was doing. Given the events of the day I thought that he was referring to the rest of my life. He was actually talking about that evening, since they were short of a player for the cricket team. I went home and found what was left of my cricket kit in the back of a wardrobe; abandoned there when I gave up playing regularly after the children were born. I had an excellent evening playing cricket with a great bunch of people who have ever since allowed me to play, as I have gone from being one of the younger members of the Long Eaton Veterans team to one of the oldest.

This was the end of my ministerial career. It was a personal turning point as I realised for the first time in twelve years that I was free to choose what I wanted to do, rather than to follow the dictates of a ministerial diary.

In the course of our summer holiday in Malta, I discussed with Elaine what we should do next. I still had some, admittedly slight, hopes of being the next British Commissioner, although Elaine made it clear that she would not be joining me in Brussels as she wanted to continue teaching in Derbyshire. If that didn't work out for me, I decided it was time to move on. I had been an elected politician for 25 years, and thought that it was time to try and do something different. Having already been an academic and a lawyer before politics, I had in mind that I would like a job working with or for British industry. I had spent at least some of my political career promoting British products, and while I had little or no idea whether it would be possible, I knew there was a gap in my CV that I wanted to fill.

At around the same time I also discovered that I had been put forward to become a member of a 'Group of Experts' led by the former US Secretary of State, Madeleine Albright, to produce a report on a new Strategic Concept for NATO. I became part of a group of twelve mostly former ambassadors from across the NATO member states. I seemed to be the only one with direct experience of Defence, although as a body they had very considerable and wide ranging experience. As we were appointed by the

NATO Secretary, Anders Fogh Rasmussen, he emphasised to us that we had been chosen in an individual capacity and not because of our nationality or background. Given that NATO headquarters was in Brussels, it might have been excellent preparation for life in the European Commission.

As the time came for Gordon Brown to decide on the British candidate for European Commissioner, I realised that he had probably never intended to appoint me. He was unnerved at the prospect of having to hold a by-election in Ashfield, although there was advice to the effect it could be delayed until the General Election, which had to be held only a couple of months later. In any event, as I learned from an old friend from my Brussels days, James Pond, still an official in the European Commission, the British Government was comprehensively outmanoeuvred in the allocation of Commission portfolios by the French.

Previously both British and French governments had wanted the Internal Market portfolio in the Commission because it included responsibility for financial services; the British to protect the City of London's pre-eminent role, the French to undermine it. As a result of this heavyweight clash of two big member states, the job had generally gone to a smaller country as a compromise. In the run-up to the appointment of the new 2010 Commission, the French let it be known that they thought that, given Britain's background in foreign policy, the UK should get the relatively new post of High Representative for Foreign Affairs and Security. With little personal background in foreign affairs, Gordon Brown apparently liked the sound of this, mainly perhaps because Tony Blair had let it be known that he wanted to be President of the European Council and Gordon Brown had not backed him. He therefore needed another big sounding job for Britain – not apparently understanding that generally speaking Britain had resisted too much EU involvement in foreign affairs and defence. Moreover he failed to appreciate that the final decision as to who would get the job would be in the hands not of his government but of the Socialist Group in the European Parliament. The French understood the way that the jobs were allocated and knew that there was an understanding that the decision would be in the hands of MEPs, including of course French ones.

On the day of the Socialist Group's decision, I did manage to speak to a couple of old friends from my days in the European Parliament. They made it clear that I stood no chance. The decision had in effect been taken because the Group had been campaigning to have more women in the European Commission, and that Baroness Ashton was the only female candidate. Peter Mandelson was furious. He had decided at the last minute that he would also like to go back to the Commission. He believed that in her short time as Trade Commissioner, filling in for him, Baroness Ashton had failed to stand up for free trade and Britain's best interests. He believed that she was even then currying favour to gain support from other countries. The press were similarly scathing citing her complete lack of foreign policy and defence experience.

The French, of course, were delighted. They got exactly what they wanted which was the Internal Market job for their candidate, Michel Barnier. French President, Nicolas Sarkozy announced that his appointment was a 'victory' for France. The appointment provided Barnier with the political profile and platform to later become the EU's chief negotiator on Brexit in July 2016.

I was certainly irritated by the process, but I had been in politics long enough to know that you don't always get what you want, and that political decisions on appointments are rarely taken on merit. I had benefited in the past from getting on well with Derry Irvine, who had promoted my career at every opportunity. I am sure that there were perfectly capable Labour MPs and ministers who looked at my various promotions and thought that they could have done just as well or even better, if they had had the same sort of unqualified backing.

I had pretty much got over my disappointment by Christmas, spending more time with Elaine and the children over the holiday than ministerial life had previously allowed, when almost out of the blue, on the Saturday night before Parliament was due to return after the recess, I was called by Harriet Harman. We had always got on well as work colleagues, although I couldn't say that we were close personal friends. Our contacts away from work came through our mutual friend Anne Coffey, the MP for Stockport.

During August we had visited Harriet and her partner Jack Dromey at their holiday home in Suffolk, at a time when Anne and her husband Peter had been their guests. In the course of a long country walk, Harriet, as Deputy Leader of the Labour Party, had made clear her strong dissatisfaction with Gordon Brown's leadership, arguing that as a result of his failings the party was heading for defeat at the 2010 General Election. I shared her view, but at that stage didn't really believe that anything could be done to change the situation. Although the opposition to Gordon Brown from within the parliamentary party was strong, there had never been any co-ordinated attempt to challenge him. When James Purnell had resigned as Work and Pensions Secretary in June 2009, he had called on Gordon Brown to stand down as Labour Leader, but there had been no follow through. It had been assumed that his sudden resignation was designed to promote the cause of his close friend and ally, David Milliband, but no further resignations followed. If there had been a plot to unseat Gordon Brown, it had fizzled out almost before it had started.

Now, at the very beginning of January 2010, with an election not many months away, Harriet Harman called me to suggest just such a co-ordinated Cabinet plot. She made clear that if the question of Gordon Brown's leadership was again raised she and other Cabinet Ministers would jointly go to see him to say that it was time for him to stand aside. She mentioned that she had had a series of conversations with other Cabinet colleagues, and all that would be needed was an appropriate signal from prominent backbenchers. She mentioned the name of Patricia Hewitt, who I knew was a close friend of hers since their days together in what was then called the National Council for Civil Liberties.

Harriet Harman gave me Patricia Hewitt's mobile number and I spoke to her the next day. We agreed that we needed a formal process for determining the views of Labour MPs, and agreed on a form of words that was designed to resolve the question 'once and for all'. Labour MPs should be given an opportunity in a secret ballot to say whether or not they supported Gordon Brown as Leader of the Labour Party going into the 2010 General Election. On Monday 4th January, back in the House of Commons for the final months before an election had to be called, I discussed the plan with close political friends. I was encouraged to continue on the basis that most thought that replacing Gordon Brown would enormously improve Labour's chance of forming a government after the election. I was led to believe that Jack Straw had agreed with Harriet Harman's plan, although I had no direct confirmation from him.

After a slight technological slip up, the email went out from Patricia Hewitt and me to all Labour MPs just before Prime Minister's Questions on the Wednesday morning. I was immediately approached by a number of backbench Labour MPs, saying that they wanted to speak out in support of our case. I actually discouraged them from doing so, because Harriet Harman had emphasised to me in several conversations that this had to be seen to be coming from the Cabinet. Yet very quickly Gordon Brown's most loyal supporters, Ed Balls, Yvette Cooper and Ed Milliband, were out making statements offering their full support to the Prime Minister. The time taken for Cabinet Ministers to offer the Prime Minister their backing was actually an interesting measure of the extent to which they really supported Gordon Brown. Nothing was heard from either Harriet Harman or Jack Straw until they were pictured going into Downing Street later that afternoon. They emerged to make a statement, saying that they had had a frank discussion with the Prime Minister and that in future he would consult more widely with colleagues.

I have never found out what changed for Harriet Harman between sending out the email on the Wednesday lunchtime and the meeting with Gordon Brown. She was fully aware that the email was going to be sent. Indeed she had been sent a copy of the text in advance. Perhaps she was let down by over-promising Cabinet colleagues in much the way that she let us down. The entire exercise was clearly a complete waste of time and it was poor judgement on my part to have been involved.

I believed that the Labour Party had to take action to prevent what seemed to be inevitable defeat at the forthcoming election. Gordon Brown simply did not have the personal skills needed to win an election campaign. I am sure that if Labour had changed leaders at that point to someone like Alan Johnson, Alan Milburn or Hilary Benn, the result of the 2010 election would have been different. Labour might not have won outright – but by winning just a few more seats it could have stayed in government in coalition with the Liberal Democrats.

My involvement caused real problems for me with my constituency party in Ashfield. Many of the activists who attended meetings had never been enthusiastic supporters of New Labour, and much preferred the more traditional Labour style of Gordon Brown. A no-confidence motion in me was tabled for the next constituency meeting, with some members clearly wanting my deselection. I was also aware that Gordon Brown's political office had been in touch with at least one of my strongest critics in the constituency.

This put me on the spot. I wanted to defeat the motion, and with a bit of effort probably had sufficient support to do so. At the same time I did not want those loyal to me to stick their necks out by voting against the motion, only for me to announce a few weeks later that I was leaving politics. It seemed obvious that I had to announce that I would not be contesting the next election. That made it look as if I was giving in to the constituency pressure, but it was better than asking good people to support me and then to let them down by walking away.

Having made the announcement, I then had to find a job. I had been to see various headhunters the previous autumn. They were almost all very positive about my experience and my prospects of becoming a non-executive director or company advisor. The only exception was Virginia Bottomley, who had exchanged a very successful Cabinet career for an equally successful one as a headhunter with Odgers Berndtson. Virginia warned me that former politicians were not favoured in business, and that leading companies were very reluctant to take on ex-ministers because of the bad publicity it generated. She gave the example of Michael Portillo, one of my predecessors as Secretary of State for Defence, who had joined the board of BAE Systems in 2002. It had seemed like a sensible appointment given his background, but she said that every time the company won a major contract, his name was mentioned in the newspapers. The implication was that the contract had not been won on merit but because of some inside track he could provide. He had resigned the position in 2006.

With this in mind, I also went to see a small firm who specialised in advising people on how to secure new careers. They tended to support Virginia Bottomley's view, emphasising that I would need to sell myself and draw on my experiences over the past 25 years. The message was clear: I shouldn't assume people would employ me simply because I had been a Cabinet Minister. I would have to show that my experience was relevant and helpful to the interests of the company.

At around the same time I received an email from what purported to be a US firm of headhunters saying that they were acting on behalf of a company looking for people to sit on a European Board of the business. I looked at the headhunters' website which showed a business based in San Francisco and I called and arranged an interview at offices in St James Square, an address that housed many of the headhunters that I had seen previously.

What I couldn't know at the time was that it was a set up, arranged by a team from the *Sunday Times* in conjunction with Channel Four's Dispatches programme. They had persuaded a number of people to participate on the same basis – secretly filming their interviews and then using it to demonstrate in Steve Byers' memorable phrase that MPs were 'cabs for hire'. Ironically, when asked what I thought the daily rate for working for a US company should be, I quoted a figure given to me by Steve; I actually had no idea what the amount should be. There is no doubt that I said some foolish things in the course of what I thought was an entirely private conversation. Looking back at the transcript later I had repeatedly said that I wanted a real job; that I did not want to be some sort of a lobbyist. Nevertheless, of course, the interviewer knew what she wanted out of the interview and kept steering me back towards how I could best help the fictional US company. I duly obliged by sharing the extent of my knowledge and experience, as I daresay many would do in a similar situation.

Inevitably the story was a big splash in the *Sunday Times* and again on the Monday following the *Dispatches* television broadcast. It was not a comfortable time. I decided that it was necessary to accept an invitation to go on the *Today* programme and offer a complete mea culpa. I had messed up and thought that I owed it to my family, friends and colleagues to do the honourable thing and recognise my folly.

One headhunter that I had an appointment to see on the following Wednesday called to cancel. With only a matter of weeks before I stood down as an MP and with our youngest child still at university, the prospect of being an unemployed ex-MP was not very appealing. I knew from my time as Chief Whip following the later careers of former MPs, just how difficult it was for them to get proper paid work in mid or later life. Now I had just made it even more difficult for myself.

With an election in prospect, the Conservatives were able to make political capital out of a situation in which mostly former Labour Cabinet Ministers were involved. We were referred to the Standards and Privileges Committee of the House of Commons and the Commissioner indicated that he would be considering the complaint. We were also suspended from membership of the Parliamentary Labour Party, ironically just as the story was dying down, thereby guaranteeing another 24 hours of bad publicity.

The report of the Standards Committee was published after I left Parliament.

It was based on a detailed, word by word, examination of the transcript of the interview with the *Sunday Times* journalist. No account was taken by the Committee that I thought that I was involved in a private conversation, no account was taken of the fact that the interviewer knew what she was after and I did not, and no account was taken of the fact that I was talking about what I planned to do after I had left Parliament. The parliamentary process involved in approving the report was also deeply disappointing. I was given the opportunity to address the Committee, but their views were made very clear from the attitude of one Conservative member who asked me bluntly whether I really expected them to disagree with the findings of the Commissioner. Of those committee members that actually voted for the report, only a minority had actually bothered to attend to listen to my statement. Of those that did several abstained on the final vote.

At the time, the House of Commons was still reeling from the effects of the expenses' controversy. It was a bad time to be on the wrong end of publicity about making money. Significantly after the Leveson Inquiry into the culture, practices and ethics of the British press, the Parliamentary Standards Committee completely exonerated Jack Straw and Sir Malcolm Rifkind when they also fell for a very similar set up, organised by exactly the same people.

Whilst clearly I was the author of my own misfortune, I have often wondered how the *Sunday Times* became aware that I was looking for a job. The only people that knew at the time were Elaine and the handful of headhunters that I met. They left messages on my mobile phone that could easily have been hacked into by the *Sunday Times*, part of the same News International business as the *News of the World*.

I have always regretted that my House of Commons career ended on such a sour note. Growing up in a small town in Derbyshire, the idea of being an MP was something of a fantasy, but when it actually happened I was determined to make the most of the opportunity. As a lapsed historian I was always conscious of being a small part of a democratic tradition that lasted for hundreds of years. I was and remain angry with myself for having been caught out by journalists chasing an easy headline. I should have been much more circumspect about what I said. At the same time I was disappointed that I might be judged on a few ill-advised words spoken at a private meeting rather than more than 25 years of public service in a variety of different and demanding roles.

The Speaker very kindly offered a reception for those that were leaving the House of Commons at the 2010 General Election. It was slightly strange to sit and talk to people like Alan Milburn and John Hutton that I had worked with right from our first election in 1992, knowing that we would be unlikely to see each other on such a regular basis again. At the same time I also knew that it was the right time to leave. I was in no doubt that Labour would lose the General Election with Gordon Brown as Leader, and his woeful performance in the campaign at least to some extent vindicated the failed effort to remove him. Labour had only needed a handful of extra seats to have been in a position to form a coalition with the Liberal Democrats. That would have been a much more politically coherent coalition than the one they formed with the Conservatives and might in time have led to a sensible realignment of the centre left in British politics. Britain might even have been spared the agony of the EU Referendum; there is always a never-ending supply of 'what ifs?' in politics.

An even more dramatic 'what if' went back even further. What if Tony Blair had had the political courage to move Gordon Brown out of the Treasury and remove his absolute control over government finances? I was told that, immediately before the 2001 General Election, Tony Blair had agreed with his closest advisors that assuming a good result, he would offer the Foreign Office job to Gordon Brown as part of a major overhaul of his government. Given that the election result in 2001 was almost as overwhelming a victory for Labour as it had been in 1997, Tony Blair was all-powerful and could clearly have made any change that he wanted in the composition of his government. Immediately after the election, Gordon Brown was inevitably the first person into Downing Street to see Tony Blair in his study. Tony Blair's team, the likes of Angie Hunter, Charlie Falconer, Alastair Campbell and Jonathan Powell, waited outside the study expecting to hear the roars of anger as Gordon Brown was told that he was to be moved to the Foreign Office. Instead, after a very short interview, Gordon Brown came out smiling, his continuing position as Chancellor of the Exchequer confirmed. Tony Blair had been quite unable to tell him that he wanted to move him.

If he had done so, would Gordon Brown have accepted the job? Many people thought not, that he would have gone into internal opposition, the Labour King across the Scottish border. It seems highly unlikely, however, that he could have overthrown a sitting Prime Minister – particularly one with such an overwhelming popular and political mandate. The Labour government would then have been spared the debilitating battles between the two men. Tony Blair might still have been Prime Minister in 2010, when he might again have proved successful as the electorate at the time did not seem to want a majority Tory government. Unfortunately, they wanted a government led by Gordon Brown even less. It may be stretching this particular 'what if' far too far in speculating that, if Tony Blair had stood up to Gordon Brown, the country might have been spared the austerity years of the coalition and even possibly the agonies of the EU Referendum.

There is no doubt that the Labour Party would have been spared its lurch to the left under Jeremy Corbyn. Tony Blair is perhaps the only modern leader of a political party not to have secured the succession to someone who held similar views to his own; remarkably, given his determined repositioning of Labour in the centre ground of British politics. There were any number of potential candidates to succeed Margaret Thatcher, who one by one she eliminated as not being 'one of us'. In contrast it never appeared to be part of Tony Blair's assessment of his successor that Gordon Brown had by then staked out his political ground well to the left of government policy and in territory much more acceptable to the left-leaning members of the Labour Party. In effect, that meant that most of the hard fought for changes brought about by Tony Blair's 'New Labour' revolution were quietly abandoned by Gordon Brown, hardly mentioned by his successor Ed Milliband, and vehemently rejected by Jeremy Corbyn. The only Labour leader to have won substantial majorities in three General Elections is now an object of criticism, if not derision, for many members of the Labour Party. The contrast with the legacy of Margaret Thatcher, revered and almost sanctified by the Tory Party, could not be greater.

Got Myself a Steady Job

As I left the House of Commons in April 2010 at the age of 56, I had no regular income, or at the time any particular prospects of getting one. I had previously had various plans for earning a living after Parliament, but one by one they had fallen away. I had been offered a non-executive directorship of a FTSE 100 company, but it had been taken over and that opportunity disappeared. My experience with the phoney headhunter had been scarring. It was highly unlikely that any company would employ me in any capacity. For the first time in my life, I was having difficulty sleeping, lying awake in the middle of the night worrying about how I would be able to pay the bills and support my younger daughter through university.

A close friend, Andy Taylor, who had not long left McDonald's as Chief Executive, generously suggested that we should work together offering strategic advice to business; he would bring his considerable private sector experience and I would add my knowledge of the public sector.

We were on the verge of launching our partnership when Graham Cole, the Chief Executive of AgustaWestland, approached me with a view to working with its British arm. I was obviously familiar with the helicopter company from my days in the MOD. I also knew Graham well because of his unstinting support for the Labour Party and a variety of other good causes. There can be few leading lights of British business that have used their time and money to do as much good in Britain as Graham Cole.

He commissioned me to do some research into the global helicopter market in respect of both civil and military machines. Although he kindly made out that I would be helping him, the reality was that he was giving me the chance to learn about those aspects of the business that had not crossed my desk in the MOD; in particular the civil helicopter market. I was given an office on the top floor of their international headquarters building in Farnborough and an invitation to travel to their factory at Yeovil in Somerset whenever I wanted. The company was by then wholly owned by the Italian defence and electronics conglomerate, Finmeccanica. Agusta's Italian Chief Executive, Giuseppi Orsi, was a passionate champion of its British and international activities and would pass through Farnborough from time to time. It had been his idea to put the company's international headquarters in Farnborough, showing its commitment to the UK, and emphasising its global ambitions.

In the spring of 2011, after completing the helicopter research project for Graham Cole, I was invited to visit Agusta's Italian headquarters and main production facility at Cascina Costa, close to Milan's Malpensa airport. On the way there, not knowing what to expect, I was hoping that it might be possible to extend the temporary agreement I was working under, but arriving in the main Italian Boardroom it was clear that a significant shake up of the company's senior executives was underway.

Giuseppi Orsi was to become the Chief Executive of the entire Finmecannica group. His successor was Bruno Spagnolini, previously Agusta's Chief Operating Officer, and an equally effective and astute northern Italian businessman. Between long telephone calls to Rome it seemed clear that I was being interviewed by both of them, although at the time, I had little idea of what they had in mind. After several hours of drinking espresso and waiting for them to re-appear, I was asked whether I would be willing to work for AgustaWestland, running its international business. As the day went on I had realised that something was likely to be offered but I assumed that it would be in the UK, based at Yeovil. Instead, I would be based partly at Farnborough but as well would have an Italian office in Cascina. In reality the job was based at 20,000 feet as I was responsible for all of Agusta's international activities and campaigns. I would sit on their international board and on various boards around the world, including the United States and India. I was relieved that I would not be a member of the UK board as I had made clear for obvious reasons that working on campaigns in Britain could prove counterproductive for the company.

I thoroughly enjoyed the first few years in the job. I led a multi-national team; mostly made up of Brits and Italians, although there were also Americans, Indians, South Africans and South Americans. I travelled to Italy most weeks. When I was not heading for Italy, it meant that I was travelling elsewhere in the world. I learned to deal with the complex financial figures which were always the first item at the monthly executive meetings. And I learned how to sell helicopters, although in truth it was not actually that much different from what I had been doing for most of my life. As a student I once had a job selling brushes and other household items door-to-door. That is real selling. That experience was invaluable at election times when I felt that I was selling myself or selling the Labour Party on the doorstep. I also sometimes had exactly the same response as the front door was shut firmly in my face. Selling high quality helicopters was not therefore such a different experience as it might first have appeared; although I always left the precise technical details to those much better qualified.

Having sat on the other side of the desk, involved in the detailed process of buying military equipment also gave me a clear sense of what governments were looking for in making procurement decisions. Since advanced helicopters were built to order, the price estimate was never going to be a precise guide to the final cost. What was of much greater interest to most governments when spending significant amounts of their taxpayers' hard earned income was how they could benefit from the deal. That might involve local production or set off where there was an agreement to place other work in country, a strong possibility given Finmeccanica's wide ranging activities across a number of industries. It was always essential for any foreign bid to look as local as possible. Many of my overseas visits were to in-country component suppliers or helicopter maintainers, to get them onside to promote their company and employees to their own government as part of the overall deal. Their local voice was always vital in an international competition where foreign firms were otherwise making very similar offers.

During this period, AgustaWestland won big orders in Norway and South Korea, both in the face of intense competition from US companies, strongly backed by the United States government. I went to breakfast in Seoul in the course of the Korean competition, and entirely by chance sitting across the table from me was Bill Cohen, someone I had worked with as a former US Defense Secretary, who was there as an advisor to the US bid.

'Now why am I not surprised to see you here?' were his welcoming words. I had seen him in his last week in office in the Pentagon. The Bill Cohen Group opened its doors for business on the following Monday. It advised mainly US companies on winning orders around the world, and could call on the full resources of the American administration to support its campaigns. In contrast, anyone leaving the British government, whether a politician or senior civil servant, is warned that they must have no contact with any part of the government system, even including overseas diplomatic posts. It is hardly surprising in the circumstances that Britain often loses out to other countries in foreign competitions. I have always admired the sense of purpose in the United States. I have lived there, worked there and have more relatives in the United States than in the UK. When it comes to business and securing US jobs, however, no country is more ruthless. Donald Trump's 'America first' policy in business was the public face of the way in which all US administrations have operated, whether Republican or Democrat.

In a very similar way the Italian Government always backs Italian business. Italy's economy reminded me of Britain's nationalised industries before the Thatcher revolution; the CEOs of hundreds of businesses, including Finmeccanica, were still essentially appointed by the government. It meant that company decisions were made subject to the overriding political needs of the government. For example, it was almost impossible for a partly government owned business like Finmeccanica or AgustaWestland to close down a factory in the south of Italy or in other areas of high Italian unemployment. It also meant that the Italian government comprehensively backed Italian companies, always buying their products and strongly supporting their overseas campaigns. In stark contrast, it sometimes seems that the British government prefers to buy from overseas rather than support British industry.

Giuseppi Orsi was a successful and very able Milanese businessman who had spent most of his career in the north of Italy. The headquarters of Finmeccanica was however in Rome, and since the company was 30 per cent owned by the Italian Government it was, not surprisingly, intensely political. As a businessman he appeared to pay little regard to the politics, preferring to run the company as a business and returning to his home by the Italian lakes at the weekend. As a result, without any effort on his part he made powerful enemies in Rome. Perhaps jealous of his success, they spread malicious rumours that he had used kickbacks from an Indian helicopter deal concluded in 2010 to channel money to the Italian Northern League political party. The suggestion seemed to be that he needed the Northern League's support to get the top job since it was at the time part of the government coalition.

Giuseppi Orsi and Bruno Spagnolini were both arrested by the Italian authorities in 2013, effectively decapitating the leadership of both Finmeccanica and AgustaWestland. The long, drawn out Italian court proceedings were subsequently followed slavishly by the Indian media, reporting every single negative detail, including a suggestion that bribes had been paid to Indian officials by so-called 'middle men' acting on behalf of AgustaWestland. Not surprisingly, the Indian contract was subsequently cancelled by the Indian government. What was surprising, however, is that even after the protracted legal proceedings in Italy cleared the two senior Italians of any wrongdoing, the Indian government has continued its efforts to prosecute those said to have given and received bribes. The Italian courts concluded that no bribes had been paid, rejecting evidence to that effect as unsound. Relying only on newspaper reports of the evidence, the Modi BJP government in Delhi has gone to extraordinary lengths to continue the case. This seems largely to do with the role of the opposition Congress Party, which signed off the deal in 2010 whilst in government. Indian procurements take so long, however, that previous stages of the procurement were undertaken by a previous BJP administration, a fact conveniently overlooked by Prime Minister Modi and his supporters. He appears to believe that by continuing the case he can discredit if not destroy the Congress Party. One consequence of this political vendetta was the extradition of a British citizen and long time agent of AgustaWestland, Christian Michel, from the UAE to India, where he continues to be detained in a Delhi prison without any actual charges being brought against him.

I have always enjoyed the sprawling diversity of India, and in particular admired the fact that, compared to its neighbours, it is democratic and observes the rule of law, together with many other fundamental principles of the British way of life and government. Sadly, under Prime Minister Modi, those principles seem to be taking a backseat to his determination to continue to exercise power.

After the arrests of its two leading lights, both Finmeccanica and AgustaWestland seemed to lose their way; the share price fell, and the order book contracted. The two CEOs were replaced by less capable Italian leaders who seemed much more focussed on Italy rather than the international market. Since there were any number of people in the company who could advise more effectively about the intricacies of Italian politics, after six years of weekly international travel, I decided that I was not adding much value to the business and bowed out.

I was then back again looking for things to do, although this time part-time ones, since I finally did want to make good on the much repeated and much broken promise to spend more time with my family. I had said this as I was leaving politics only to spend more time away travelling the world on behalf of AgustaWestland. The helicopter job had taken me to countries that even during my time in the Foreign Office and the MOD I had not managed to visit – Turkmenistan, Angola and Trinidad and Tobago for example. But rather like ministerial visits, I only managed to stay for a day or two before getting on the plane back – seeing mainly the airport, or a meeting room before heading home. I now wanted to take Elaine to some of those same places, but this time stay for long enough to see something of the country and its people.

I was also fortunate in finding part-time and advisory work for both a green energy company and a zoo charity. I was in the advantageous position finally of being able do only those things that interested me, which included finding new and better ways of protecting the environment and the world's animal population. Zoos are sometimes criticised for keeping wild animals in cages when they should be free to roam. That is a perfectly proper argument and no-one could condone keeping animals in unsuitable conditions purely for entertainment purposes. At the same time, given the erosion of habitats right across the world, human beings are responsible for wiping out entire species. Zoos may be the only places in which some of these animals can survive. I have learned a great deal from the remarkable people who work at Twycross Zoo. They come from a wide range of backgrounds but are committed to ensuring that the welfare of animals is their highest priority. There is obviously a choice to be made in respect of keeping wild animals in zoos; I am convinced that it is better than allowing them to become extinct.

EPILOGUE
And in the End

It has become something of a cliché to set out Enoch Powell's comment that all political careers end in failure. The full quotation is worth repeating. Writing about Joseph Chamberlain, Enoch Powell observed,
'All political lives, unless they are cut off in midstream at a happy juncture, end in failure, because that is the nature of politics and of human affairs.'

If I had managed to leave the House of Commons in May 2010 and had managed to avoid the attention of the *Sunday Times*, I might have been able to maintain that my political career had not ended in a bad way. I had been a Minister for most of my time in Parliament, and on the front bench for all but a few years. As it was, I left following a political scandal that dominated the headlines for several days. The *Daily Mail* referred to me as 'a disgraced former Minister'. It was not exactly the political epitaph that I would have chosen.

Looking back, however, I have the sense of more fundamental difficulties about my time in politics. The two constants in my career involved trying to keep the Labour Party as a sensible, moderate and practical political force and Britain as a committed and effective member of the European Union. Throughout the 1980s I had worked with many other moderates to steer the Labour Party in the pragmatic direction taken by Neil Kinnock in Opposition, and then by Tony Blair in Government. The British people are essentially moderate and reasonable; they want a pragmatic government that puts the national interest ahead of political ideology.

Yet the Labour Party was led from 2015 to 2020 by Jeremy Corbyn, who spent most of his career on the political fringes of the far left and who was a regular visitor to my office as Chief Whip, routinely defying government three line whips on ideological grounds arising out of his own particular personal philosophy. I was once asked what the Labour Cabinet would have thought in the days of Tony Blair and Gordon Brown if they had been told that in just over five years from the end of a majority Labour government, Jeremy Corbyn would be the Leader of the Labour Party. It was a good question, and one that I struggled to answer at first because in truth no-one could possibly have believed that could happen; including at the time Jeremy Corbyn himself. There would have been incredulity around the Cabinet table. Anyone who had made such a suggestion would have been laughed out of the room. And to be quite fair, Jeremy Corbyn would have joined in the laughter.

Why then did it happen? Many people on the left would certainly cite the Iraq War as a significant reason for shifting Labour members further to the left. I would have to recognise that as a factor and accept at least some of the blame given my extensive involvement. It is not however a sufficient explanation of why the Labour Party leadership lurched to the left.

Part of the answer at least is that large parts of the Labour membership had always been on the left. People who become active in political parties are unusual and are numerically only a very small percentage of the population. They join political parties because they believe passionately in a cause and are prepared to give up a great deal of their spare time to see it achieved. Every month as a Labour Member of Parliament I would attend a meeting of the Ashfield Constituency Labour Party. Those meetings had always been arranged for a Friday evening to allow the MP to give a parliamentary report and to answer questions. I often used to wonder why it was that people were willing to give up their Friday evenings with family and friends for the dubious delight of listening to me. But it was not just one Friday evening a month; these same people would be the ones knocking on doors and delivering leaflets at election times. They did so because they believed that what they were doing was helping to bring about the changes in Britain that they wanted to see achieved; whether that was through the local councils or at Westminster. Theirs was essentially an ideological view, flowing from their principled beliefs. They could not always come to terms with the reality of taking decisions, taken by the local council leadership or at government level. Those decisions are almost always constrained by financial realities or by unanticipated events that simply cannot easily be fitted into an ideological worldview.

Donald Grundy was one of the Labour members in Ashfield that I most admired. A retired teacher and a lifelong Labour Party activist, he was for many years the chair of the Ashfield party. As well as his political activities, he was also extensively involved in the life of Selston, the village where he lived. He supported a variety of village activities including helping to organise and judge regular musical events. As the Labour government continued in office, he would from time to time ask me at the Friday monthly party meeting why we were not taking the water industry back into public ownership. I always gave him the same answer. I accepted his argument that privatising a natural monopoly did not make sense and it was something that Labour would never have done. Equally it did not seem to make sense to spend tens of billions of pounds of taxpayers money on buying up second-hand public utility shares when education and health desperately needed every last penny of the funding that the government could make available. Important though those issues were to Donald, he simply would not accept my answer. However many times he asked the question and however many times I repeated my argument, he was not persuaded. Ideologically he was right; the water industry should never have been privatised. Practically, however I was right as the government could not afford to devote scarce resources to an issue that came well down our political agenda. As a result Donald went from being one of my strongest supporters to one of those who wanted me gone in 2010.

This is the real explanation as to why the Labour Party ended up with Jeremy Corbyn as its leader. In one member one vote contests, party members generally vote for the person who seems to most closely share their views of the world. It doesn't particularly matter to them that their opinions are out of step with the views of the electorate – unless in sheer frustration the party has been out of power for so long that party members decide to choose someone that they believe can win a General Election. That happened with Tony Blair in 1994 and similarly with David Cameron for the Conservatives in 2005.

The Conservative Party, which introduced one member one vote long before the Labour Party, now has exactly the same problems with ideology. Their members are much further to the right of the electorate and choose leaders like Iain Duncan Smith or Boris Johnson, leaders who most seem to reflect their own views. At least the Conservative Party gives their MPs a much bigger say in selecting the final two candidates to put before the party electorate. The process by which Jeremy Corbyn ended up on Labour Party ballot papers was simply absurd. Those MPs that put him forward without ever intending to vote for him have a lot to answer for. They delivered the Labour Party into the hands of the ideological left and ensured that Labour would lose the General Elections in 2017 and 2019. I still find it hard to understand why right across the country, large numbers of people who believed passionately that Britain should stay in the EU, voted for a Conservative Party and Conservative leader, committed to an extreme version of Brexit. The only explanation is that they were more afraid of the short term consequences of a government led by Jeremy Corbyn than the long term effects on Britain of being out of the EU.

No one seriously or publicly challenges the idea of giving party members the final say over the choice of their party leaders. However, in light of the present polarisation between the two main parties and an electoral system that makes it all but impossible for a third party to break through unless their votes are all concentrated in a particular part of the country, it is difficult to see any prospect of material change. Ditching our first past the post electoral system would be an obvious solution, as it would require party members to think much more clearly about the electoral effects of their decisions, but it is difficult to see a Conservative Party conceding this change when they do so well out of the existing constitutional arrangements.

Right wing ideology and the politics of the Conservative Party is also why David Cameron's Government decided to hold the referendum on continued EU membership in 2016. It had nothing whatsoever to do with the best interests of the country, and everything to do with those Conservative Party members who were drifting away to Nigel Farage's UKIP. Britain was forced into a totally unnecessary referendum simply to maintain the numerical membership of the Conservative Party. It seems almost absurd to set that out but it is difficult to see why otherwise the referendum was conceded. There was no great public clamour for it. The British people when asked would always prefer not to have elections or votes. I have always suspected that at least part of the problem were Tory MPs returning from their constituencies to Westminster to complain to their colleagues that yet another of their prominent party members had left for UKIP. In total across the country this would have been an insignificant number but the psychological effect on MPs of losing their activists is huge.

The perhaps unintended consequence was these local party membership defections had a disproportionate influence on the Conservative Party's national leadership.

It is all very well for a passionate European to complain about the Tory Party's turmoil over Europe, whilst overlooking the fact that the Remain case was defeated in the European Referendum. Almost seventeen and a half million British citizens decided after more than 40 years of EU membership that they would sooner not be legally tied to other European nations through the institutions of the European Union. Pro-Europeans like me simply failed to get the argument across in a way that was convincing to the majority of voters. That failure flowed from many streams of anti-European opinion. It was led by newspapers owned by foreign nationals or tax exiles who nevertheless ensured that their editors and journalists churned out anti-EU stories on a daily basis. In the course of the campaign I was regularly confronted with the 'we won the war' argument, almost always articulated by older people who, despite their years, could not have been old enough to have actually fought in the Second World War. Perhaps like me they grew up reading comics that portrayed the heroic Brits beating the aggressive Hun in order to save supine French and Belgian skins.

Those comical views were in turn reflected in much of the newspaper coverage of the EU. I spent a year as Europe Minister trying to get positive coverage for European stories. It was almost impossible despite the fact that most of the population was benefiting every day from Britain's membership. Britain received by far the largest share of overseas investment. That will not all disappear as the result of leaving the EU, but it is difficult to see why long term strategic investors in Japan will choose to take risks on Britain's go it alone future rather than investing inside the European Union with all of the advantages that being part of the Single Market brings. This will not cause a sudden reduction in the number of jobs in the British economy but it will inevitably lead to a steady decline. Sadly, we will not even see it happening as investment decisions taken in Tokyo or New York will simply not feature the UK in the list of possible candidates. Even if Britain does make an investment shortlist, we are likely to lose out to continental competition, as happened with Elon Musk's decision to build the Tesla electric car inside the EU in Germany.

Even at the personal level people were not persuaded of the benefits of EU membership. Millions of people take advantage of low-cost flights every year as they go on holiday or take weekend breaks. It is impossible to imagine that European governments, with significant stakes in their national airline carriers, would ever have allowed the kind of low-cost competition which has revolutionised the airline industry. Similarly the abolition of roaming mobile telephone charges was forced through by the European Commission to the benefit of everyone who travels to the continent with a mobile phone. I read a detailed newspaper article about this reform, praising the benefits this would bring for consumers. It was an excellent article, save for one glaring omission. Nowhere did it mention that this was the result of decisions taken in Brussels by 'unelected bureaucrats'. It will be interesting to see if 'taking back control' leads to government decisions yet again being taken in the interests of British-based companies rather than British consumers.

Nor was there any proper consideration of the impact that leaving the EU will have on dealing with the threats we face as a country. Senior police officers have made clear that an isolated standalone United Kingdom will inevitably experience damage to its intelligence gathering capabilities. Terrorist threats can have their origins anywhere in the world and can certainly arise in other parts of the EU. Terrorist attacks in France and Germany look exactly like terrorist attacks in London or Manchester. Why are we distancing ourselves from other European countries at precisely the time we need to work together to deal with these common threats to our collective security?

The use of the phrase 'European Defence' produces immediate and emotional newspaper stories which usually in some way reference the two world wars of the twentieth century. After more than seventy years of peace in western Europe, with almost a similar length of European military cooperation through NATO and following years of reconciliation, why is it apparently impossible to contemplate the idea of British soldiers serving alongside their continental European counterparts? There are actually countless examples of such practical military co-operation already. Moreover at a time when all Defence budgets are under pressure it makes complete sense for like-minded European nations to work together to share the development costs of new equipment, to avoid the unnecessary duplication of capabilities and to pool scarce resources when required. Without this common approach and in the absence of substantial year on year increases in Defence spending, there is a very real risk that Britain will fall further and further behind in its military effectiveness.

The polarisation of views between young and old, north and south, cities and towns was also reflected in the 2019 General Election result. The vote to leave the EU and a left wing Labour leader combined to ensure that the country would leave the European Union on January 31st 2020, and that the Labour Party was comprehensively defeated in many constituencies that had never previously elected a Conservative MP. The British people were and are never likely to support a left wing, ideologically-driven Labour leadership. They are unlikely either to support right wing ideology but given a choice between the hopeless incompetence of Jeremy Corbyn and the getting-things-done mantra of the Conservatives, the election result was never really in doubt.

The result of that election is that Britain will be out of the European Union for the rest of my lifetime and perhaps for all time. I am sure that before too long there will be a political movement for Britain to rejoin the EU, one that will probably attract significant popular and business support. One day – although not very soon – there might even be another referendum, the result of which might lead at some time in the future to a British government asking to rejoin the EU. That application might even win the support of the majority of EU member states. What it will not do however is persuade France and probably Belgium and Luxembourg to agree. Those countries have long institutional memories; they know that their integrationist plans and proposals for the EU have been consistently frustrated by the excellence of the arguments made by successive British governments, both Labour and Conservative. They will not make the mistake again of allowing Britain to be a significant part of the leadership of Europe.

In Robert Frost's poem 'The Road Not Taken', he describes the choice a traveller makes at a fork in the road, knowing that having made his decision he is unlikely ever to come back to the road not taken. My career sometimes feels like that. I gave up academic life for the Bar, which in turn I abandoned for the European Parliament. I gave that up for the House of Commons and that in turn for a career in business. Everyone makes those choices in their lives and it seems likely that the current and future generations will face more and more of those career moves given the pace of technological change and its effects on the security of employment.

I have never regretted those decisions, although I have often thought that I would have liked longer in each stage. I would certainly have benefited from a longer career at the Bar. If I had stayed in the European Parliament I would have seen the institutional reforms that gave it a much bigger say in the development of European legislation. I should certainly have spent longer as a backbench Member of Parliament. A more detailed grounding in business might have helped me sustain a longer commercial career.

The difficult question is 'would you do it all again?' There have certainly been times when my answer would have been an emphatic 'no'. I always worried about the effect my continual absences had on my children and on Elaine. I am sure that she would have preferred to be married to someone who was home every night and whose name was never in the newspapers. One of our friends from my days at the Nottingham Bar, David Sneath, was recently High Sheriff of Nottinghamshire. During his year in office he kindly invited us to a number of events, including the annual legal service. I was able to meet many of the people who were at the Nottingham Bar at around the same time that I had been in practise. They had continued their successful legal careers and had become QCs or Judges or Chairs of Tribunals. All command great respect in the local communities that they have served. I actually felt something of an outsider, even though I have always lived in the East Midlands and spent 26 years representing constituencies in the area.

I am sure that is no more than the reaction that everyone experiences as they move on from the activities that defined their career. There is no doubt for me that was the six years that I spent in Defence. I am still recognised occasionally in the street or on the tube even though more than fifteen years have passed since I did that job. It was a tough time and is still hard for those that lost loved ones who I am sure are on their minds every single day. I played a part in their loss and will always carry that responsibility. I understand much better now than I did at the time what my Dad meant when he said that what I was doing in the MOD was harder than what he had to do in the Second World War.

At the same time I was also part of events which showed the very highest standards of selfless human behaviour. Bombardier Brad Tinnion giving his life to save his fellow soldiers; a recently bereaved South African widow saying that her husband had died doing the job that he had always wanted; families putting aside their fears for the sake of supporting those people that have chosen to serve their country. I could not possibly have lived up to those highest of standards, but it was a privilege to have worked alongside such remarkable people for so long.

INDEX

The letters GH refer to Geoff Hoon.